About the authors

Derrick Windsor Hand joined the legal system in 1953 in the Petty Sessions branch of the NSW Department of the Attorney General and Justice at Forbes courthouse. Forbes was his hometown. He was admitted as a solicitor in 1969 and in 1973 received a commission as a magistrate. In 1984 he was appointed coroner at Westmead Coroner's Court in western Sydney.

In 1988 when the Office of State Coroner was created in NSW, he was appointed the state's first Deputy State Coroner; Kevin Waller was State Coroner. In February 1995, Derrick Hand was appointed State Coroner.

When he retired in 2000, it was after five years as State Coroner and 47 years in the court system.

Janet Fife-Yeomans is an award-winning journalist who has worked in newspapers and television in Australia and her native England. She has specialised in writing about crime and legal affairs and met Derrick Hand while she was chief court reporter with *The Sydney Morning Herald*.

She later moved to *The Australian* where she was deputy editor (business development). She is currently manager of corporate affairs for News Limited. This is her fifth book.

The Coroner

INVESTIGATING SUDDEN DEATH

Derrick Hand
AND Janet Fife-Yeomans

ABC Books

Acknowledgements

This book would not have been possible without the help of a number of people – including those who helped jog Derrick's memories from 47 years in the court system. There were also the court staff, police officers and others who were more than willing to help us with research to back up those memories with hard facts. Among them were Graham O'Rourke, Noel Drew, Dawn Stratford, Tony Astley, Mick McGann and John Laycock.

Megan and John Hand had their own stories of their father to add to the mix and a special thanks goes to them and to Tim Storer.

Published by ABC Books for the
AUSTRALIAN BROADCASTING CORPORATION
GPO Box 9994 Sydney NSW 2001

Copyright © Derrick Hand and Janet Fife-Yeomans 2004

First published March 2004
Reprinted May 2004

All rights reserved. No part of this publication may be reproduced, stored in a retrieval system or transmitted in any form or by any means, electronic, mechanical, photocopying, recording or otherwise, without the prior written permission of the Australian Broadcasting Corporation.

National Library of Australia
Cataloguing-in-Publication data
Hand, D. W. (Derrick Windsor)
The coroner.
ISBN 0 7333 1325 6.
1. Coroners – New South Wales. 2. Medical jurisprudence – New South Wales. 3. Sudden death – New South Wales. I. Fife-Yeomans, Janet.
II. Australian Broadcasting Corporation. III Title.
614.109944

Cover design by Saso Design, Sydney
Cover photographs of Stuart Diver, Anita Cobby, Michael Hutchence
    and Derrick Hand by Newspix
Text design by Andrew Cunningham, Studio Pazzo, Melbourne
Typeset in 10/14pt Scala by Kirby Jones
Colour reproduction by Colorwize, Adelaide
Printed and bound by Griffin Press, Adelaide

5 4 3 2

To Doreen,

For the many years of love

and your support of my career.

The modern coroner's work plunges him daily into
the rich variety of human experience and, at its most
sensitive moment, death.
The coroner sees us at our weakest surrounded by the
stuff of everyday life.

(The standard English text on coronial practice)

Contents

	Introduction	1
	Prologue	5
1	Bankers and Spies	7
2	Hot Summer Nights	23
3	The Deputy	47
4	Massacre in the Suburbs	75
5	Suite 2401	99
6	Silence of the Lambs	117
7	In the Line of Duty	131
8	'I've Lost It, Clive, I've Lost It'	147
9	Snakebite	162
10	True Blue	183
11	'Thank God We Got the Coroner Out Alive'	211

Introduction

HE WAS THERE in Thredbo when 18 people died after the collapse of two ski lodges; at Sydney's Strathfield Plaza when seven people were slaughtered; on Bondi Beach after Frenchman Roni Levi was shot dead by police. He sent the five men who murdered Anita Cobby to stand trial; he sent Granny Killer John Wayne Glover to face a jury after a reign of terror in which he killed six elderly women; he oversaw investigations into the disappearance and suspected death of millionaire's wife Kerry Whelan and the mysterious death off Sydney Harbour's North Head of model Caroline Byrne, whose boyfriend was controversial stockbroker Rene Rivkin's chauffeur.

There were the honeymooners and holidaymakers who died in the Seaview air crash, the baffling sea mystery of the luxury 'unsinkable' *Patanela* yacht which vanished into thin air with its crew of four, the shooting deaths of two police constables.

At the scene of some of the worst disasters that have rocked Australia and in the middle of some of the nation's most notorious murders and mysterious deaths, there has been one increasingly familiar figure: Derrick Hand, magistrate, the first Deputy State Coroner in New South Wales and then NSW State Coroner. He was the man the community turned to for the answers.

I got to know Derrick when I was working as a crime and legal reporter for *The Sydney Morning Herald* and at *The Australian*. For years I observed him from the press seats in various courtrooms. Always the solid, reliable and often stern-looking man sitting on the bench, as they call the raised platform in court where the magistrate sits.

For someone who was in such a high-profile job, there was never any glamour or glitz about him. Born and raised in country New South Wales, you could take the boy from the bush but you couldn't take the bush out of the boy, as they say. Derrick was no slick city lawyer who moved to the bench. His remarkable career began as a court clerk in his home town of Forbes where he rose through the ranks of the public service to one of the most powerful jobs in the state. Magistrates and coroners do not wear the decorative robes and wigs of judges, they dress in plain suits. The suits Derrick wore in court were never the flash type; like Derrick, they were what you might call sensible. I hesitate to call them daggy but I used to notice that his ties were always slightly old-fashioned.

If this were Hollywood, Derrick would be the closest to a real-life version of Patricia Cornwell's heroine Kay Scarpetta that Australia is likely to get. In fact, he leaves her for dead, so to speak, when it comes to forensic skills, to solving the mystery by starting from the end, letting the dead tell their story.

As I got to know him better when we worked together on this book, I realised that people want their heroes to be exactly like Derrick Hand. With Derrick, what you see is what you get. He is like everyone's suburban dad or granddad. He is a family man who has been married to his childhood sweetheart, Doreen, for 45 years. They have two children and three grandchildren. Now retired, he likes to play lawn bowls and the occasional game of golf. He and Doreen returned to Forbes where he played a big role in the local community. A week after the Bali bombing catastrophe, he was asked to become chairman of the appeal to raise money for the Forbes Bali victims — out of a party of 26 from Forbes Rugby Club, who were in Bali at the time, three were killed and 22 injured. He also continues to give talks to various groups, young and old, about the work of a coroner.

Derrick was described by those in the legal profession as methodical, reliable, fair and studiously hard working, an all-round 'top bloke'. He has that ability shared by those who work with trauma — police officers, firemen, nurses and doctors in casualty wards on a Saturday night — to

INTRODUCTION

separate himself from the emotion around him. Without that, he would never have been able to do a job that meant dealing with death every day. That is not to say he is not emotional, just that he has trained himself over the years not to let it interfere with his work.

Yet one of the main qualities he brought to the role of coroner was sympathy; he always made time for the families of the victims. Derrick will tell you himself that he still believes in 'the old ways and things like that, the old values, I suppose you would say. But I'm not gullible and I can certainly separate the wheat from the chaff'.

He is a plain speaker with a great intellectual vigour who proved not to be swayed by political or media attention. He may be quiet but nothing slips past him. He is exactly the kind of person you would want with you in a crisis.

I was impressed with how he dealt with the death of Michael Hutchence. After the rock star was found naked in his Double Bay hotel room in what his girlfriend Paula Yates and the British media preferred to think was a bizarre high-stakes game of eroticism that went wrong, Derrick said he could not believe that Paula Yates wanted him to say that Hutchence had died from an erotic incident and that she would rather have told her child that was what had happened rather than that Michael took his own life.

I also learned that Derrick has a great sense of humour – the pair of us giggled as he told me about some of the pranks they pulled behind the scenes in court. It was a way to lighten the load of the type of work they did.

He wanted to write this book to communicate to people what goes on in the court system and to give an insight into the world of a coroner. It is not all doom and gloom. Despite all that he saw in 47 years in the court system, it has not changed his perceptions. He still sees the good in people.

It takes a special kind of man to do the work of a coroner. This is Derrick Hand's story.

Janet Fife-Yeomans, 2004

Prologue

WHEN THE TELEPHONE rings in the middle of the night, it is usually bad news. When the telephone rings in the middle of the night and you are the State Coroner, it is invariably someone else's bad news.

At 12.15 a.m. on 31 July 1997, I was in bed when I picked up the phone to hear that a landslide at Thredbo had swept away two ski lodges, Carinya and Bimbadeen. It was in the middle of the ski season at one of the country's most popular ski resorts; there was no doubt a lot of people would have lost their lives.

By 7 a.m., myself, the Deputy NSW State Coroner John Abernethy and two staff from the coronial support section arrived in Thredbo. It was a scene of devastation. The site where the two lodges had been looked like a ski run. When the inspector in charge of the rescue took me into the site later, I tell you, I was scared. There were fragile layers of rubble – any movement and the whole lot would come tumbling down.

I was back there two days later as Stuart Diver, the only survivor, was pulled out of the wreckage. Eighteen people were killed.

A month before the Thredbo disaster, six policemen had been called to Bondi Beach early in the morning following a report that a man was wielding a knife. Two of the police officers shot the man, Roni Levi, dead. As soon as Bondi police station was told of the shooting, I was called in.

A few months later, in November, I was finishing breakfast and getting ready for work when my daughter rang from Melbourne. 'Dad, are you going to do Michael Hutchence?' she asked. 'He was found hanged in his hotel room.'

I said, 'Who's Michael Hutchence?'

By the time I got to work, not only did I know all about him but the calls from media all over the world had begun. Hutchence had been found in bizarre circumstances at The Ritz-Carlton in Double Bay.

It was only when I started working on this book that I realised that all these events happened in the one year. I was certainly only doing my job but at times, it did seem that the phones never stopped ringing.

Derrick Hand, 2004

CHAPTER I

Bankers and Spies

THE LATE MODEL Mercedes-Benz sedan parked on the side of a quiet back road just over the Blue Mountains west of Sydney looked out of place. It was a spot where local thieves often took stolen cars for stripping, but the Mercedes was in one piece and at 4.20 a.m. on this Sunday, 27 January 1980, its parking lights were on. Sergeant Neville Brown and his partner, Constable Leslie Cross, who were on routine patrol from nearby Lithgow police station, pulled over beside the car on The Old Forty Bends Road at South Bowenfels.

Looking through the window, they saw a middle-aged man slumped over in the front seat. Between his knees was a powerful US Army-issue .30 calibre semi-automatic rifle, the barrel pointed up to where his chin used to be. His left hand was still holding the barrel, his right hand was near the trigger area. The bullet was lodged in the roof of the car.

He was obviously dead.

The police officers called an ambulance and began their search of the car. The body was quite cold and had started to go stiff, indicating it had been dead for some time. Blood was splattered over the entire interior of the car. Sergeant Brown leaned inside and prised the rifle from the man's grip. There was one live round in the rifle's breech and one in the magazine. The sergeant looked in the man's pockets for some identification. He found a shooter's licence in the name of Frank Nugan, his passport, driver's licence, credit cards and wallet. In the back pocket of his trousers, the sergeant found a copy of the New Testament of Psalms. Inside the Bible was a meat pie wrapper and another piece of paper. On the pie wrapper was written 'Bill Colby and Congressman Bob Wilson', on the other piece of paper was written 'The Breakers, Florida Longbeach'.

Also in the man's pockets was $61 and a business card in the name of William Colby, identifying Colby as the director of the law firm Reid and Priest in Washington, USA. The back of the card read: '27/1/80 to 8/2/80 HK Mandarin Hotel. 29/2/80 to 8/3/80 Singapore Coudat Bros'.

Once the body was taken to Lithgow District Hospital, the officers continued their search of the car. On the passenger floor well, near where the body had been, they found a spent cartridge. Everything was bagged and tagged for the forensic experts to do their magic.

Frank Nugan's family – his wife and two young children – were in the United States staying with her parents. His brother, Kenneth Nugan, positively identified the body as that of Frank, 35. The fingerprints on the body matched those of Frank Nugan.

Frank Nugan was the director of a dodgy merchant bank, the Nugan Hand Bank, which had been linked with drug dealing and was later to be linked with arms deals. William Colby had been director of the CIA until 1976.

Frank Nugan and his brother Kenneth had been charged by the NSW Corporate Affairs Commission with conspiring to defraud their own company, the Nugan Group based in Griffith and Australia's largest packer and distributor of fruit and vegetables, and to defrauding certain shareholders of the group. Charges against two former policemen working for the company, both former Breaking Squad detectives, had been dropped but the Nugan brothers had been committed to stand trial. The trial was due to start in May 1980. On top of that, questions had been raised in the NSW parliament about whether the Woodward Royal Commission into drug trafficking, which was then running, should take an interest in the affairs of the Nugan brothers. It later did just that.

The local coroner asked me to take over the case. It was too big for him, he said. Lithgow is a mining town just west of the Blue Mountains. It is working class through and through, the last place for a body linked to spies, the CIA and what the conspiracy theorists believed was possibly murder.

The Old Forty Bends Road was off the main road on the Sydney side of Lithgow – if it had been on the other side and nearer Bathurst, it would have been another coroner's case, another coroner's problem.

In those days the local clerks of the court also acted as coroners – it was convenient in remote towns. The law is that certain deaths, including suspicious deaths, suicides, homicides and others must be reported to the local coroner. The police report these deaths to the clerk of the court who would decide whether it should be taken further, sometimes referring it to the local magistrate. All magistrates were also coroners. I had been promoted to what was called a grade 1 magistrate about 18 months earlier, which qualified me to have my own court and to sit in the city courts. Before that, I had seven years experience as a traffic magistrate and a relieving magistrate and as one of my early bosses had taught me, nothing was impossible.

That was his motto: 'Nothing's impossible.' He used to say, 'Derrick, people might not like what you come up with but if you do it according to the evidence, what they think doesn't really matter.' It was one of the most valuable lessons I learned.

As a coroner, you are in charge of the investigation into a suspicious death. It's not like sitting as a magistrate where the first you hear of the evidence is when it is presented to you by both sides in court. The police investigate a death and report to the coroner as their inquiries continue and the coroner decides what needs to be further investigated. So before I opened the inquest into the death of Frank Nugan, I knew quite a bit about him as a result of the police inquiries. On top of that, the newspapers had been full of the Frank Nugan case and were ripe with the talk that he had links with the world of counter-intelligence and spies.

Frank Nugan was a lawyer and had been a speculator in the mining boom of the late 1960s before moving his money into property. He was what we would call today an entrepreneur with possibly all the negative connotations of the word. The merchant bank, Nugan Hand Bank, had been established four years earlier by Nugan and his partner Michael Hand, a former US Green Beret and Vietnam Veteran who, rumour had it, was an employee of the CIA.

The Nugan Hand Bank prospered greatly in its short lifetime, with offices in Hong Kong, Bangkok, Chiang Mai, Panama, Argentina, Singapore, Saudi Arabia, West Germany and its headquarters in the British West Indies, from where it could run tax minimisation schemes and sidestep currency regulations. Listed among its customers were a lot of powerful people, Australians included, as well as some who were prominent for all the wrong reasons, like drug trafficking.

On the personal side, Nugan was said to be a happily married man. Why was he found dead on a lonely back road at least a two-hour drive from his usual haunts and in an area where he had no known friends or associates? That's what I had to determine. It is also a coroner's job to determine the identity of the dead person. With Kenneth Nugan's positive identification of the body as that of his brother and the fingerprints matching those of Frank Nugan, I had no doubt that was exactly who it was, despite what would happen later.

As a magistrate covering four courts, I travelled with my own clerk at the time, Mark Groom, a black belt in karate and a brown belt in jujitsu. Not only did we get on well but I always felt perfectly safe with him! Before the inquest started, we were amused at a few coincidences to do with the names of people involved in the case. As the only person I know whose name 'Derek' is spelled like an oil derrick, I get quite a few comments on my own name. My middle name is Windsor because my mother was a royalist and I was named after the Duke of Windsor who had just abdicated the throne to be with Wallis Simpson. However, I have no idea where the spelling of Derrick came from. It was a long time before parents found it trendy to spell the names of their children in strange ways and the only Derrick I have heard of was the surname of someone who got a VC during the war. I was lucky my surname was simple to spell because all my life, people have spelled my Christian name wrong.

On the Friday before I opened the inquest, the bank, which had the full name of Nugan Hand Needham, had been put into liquidation by Justice Needham in the NSW Supreme Court in Sydney. Not only was Frank Nugan's business partner in the bank, and its co-founder, called Michael Hand but one of the cards found on Nugan was about a tax minimisation scheme ruled on by Justice Hand of the US Supreme Court. Of course none of them was any relation to each other, or to me, but that didn't stop the jokes behind the scenes among the court staff.

Now I think I have a fairly laid-back attitude generally and did not get anxious about whatever court case I was hearing. One of the newspaper reporters had written after one case that I was sitting on the bench relaxed and conducted the court without too much fuss. I smoked a pipe in those days. At home I have a caricature drawn by one of the court clerks at Newcastle. It was sent to me for a joke. It shows me sitting in my office with my feet up on the desk smoking a pipe. That was me.

But I was also known as a facts man. If a defendant before me appeared to be guilty, if everything told you he was guilty, but there was not enough evidence, then the charge had to be dismissed. You could never assume anything. However high profile the case, everyone was due the same kind of justice. I always decided the cases by the facts and that was how I would look at the death of Frank Nugan, rumours and innuendo aside.

When I opened the inquest in April 1980, the old courtroom at Lithgow was packed. The controversy surrounding the case had brought out the media pack. The reporters were all waiting for Michael Hand to give evidence, waiting to hear about any CIA involvement, hints of murder or to have their conspiracy theories confirmed.

Michael Hand was a tall, well-built American. He was articulate and I remember that, unlike what you would expect of a businessman or banker, he didn't wear a suit to court. Instead, he wore a sports jacket. I took it as a sign that he was relaxed – or wanted to appear so.

It was his story that since his business partner's death, he had discovered that Nugan had misappropriated millions of dollars of the bank's money. Some of it had gone to Nugan's private companies, millions more to Nugan personally. He had used the money to buy his house in the expensive Sydney harbourside suburb of Vaucluse. In addition, Nugan had made loans of up to $3 million to individuals and groups. Michael Hand estimated the bank had a deficit of $4 million and the company was insolvent. He claimed many of the records kept by Nugan were missing and it was impossible to say how long the fraud had gone on or to retrieve the money.

As I listened to him, I thought it suspicious that all this money could go missing without Nugan's business partner or anyone else knowing about it. It did cross my mind that he was talking a load of codswallop. However, he was the only one left who knew about what had been happening in the company.

So did Nugan have reason to kill himself? His troubles were certainly piling up. Despite this, Michael Hand discounted suicide. He said he did not believe the prospect of his fraud being discovered and exposed would have caused his business partner to kill himself. Nugan, he said, was a fighter who revelled in the open combat of business. There was evidence

Nugan had run the bank like a one-man band, a king with his kingdom. He was a hard businessman, said to have been as tough as nails. He had been a heavy drinker, capable of downing a bottle of Scotch by himself during working hours. He was also supremely ambitious and planning an enormous expansion with a goal to have 30 banks around the world. He had become religious, but in the Bible found with him in the car, he had written, among other notes: 'Visualise 100,000 customers world wide, prayerize, actualize.' It was apparently one of his favourite sayings and made his religious 'conversion' appear self-serving.

What were we to make of all that and did it have anything to do with Nugan's death? Frank Nugan, as you would expect of an international banker, travelled widely. He had been out of Australia, in the United States, from 9 January that year and had returned just two days before his death. Police believed that the dates on the back of William Colby's business card that was found in Nugan's pocket could well have been projected movements to Hong Kong and other places. Colby's firm was a legal adviser to the Nugan Hand Bank.

There was no doubt that Frank Nugan had bought the rifle himself. A shop assistant in a Sydney gun shop identified Nugan as the man who had bought the rifle from him on 8 January, the day before he had left for the United States. The shop assistant had special reason to remember the sale. It was the quickest sale he had ever made. Nugan walked in, asked for a short-range semi-automatic rifle and bought the only one of that type they had in the shop. Ten minutes later he was walking out with the rifle, an axe and a box of .30 calibre ammunition. He had been issued with his shooter's licence the day before, on 7 January, at Bondi police station.

Ken Nugan said his brother had been extremely upset when he had been committed to stand trial but that when he saw him in the afternoon two days before his death, Frank Nugan had seemed to be in good spirits.

As we usually did when in country towns, my staff and I were staying at one of the motels and after a day in court, we would go to the local club and have a few beers. We never talked about the case we were dealing with when we were having a drink. Sometimes the solicitors would join us because they were away from home too. If the solicitors for one side came along, the other side usually joined us as well. If I wanted to talk to any of them about the case, then I would do it in chambers at the appropriate time, not over a beer.

After a few beers, I would go back to the motel and watch TV. Being a magistrate on the road was no passport to high living! It was OK for two or three days but then it became lonely and I could never wait to get home to Doreen and our two children, John and Megan.

༺༻

Doreen and I met in Forbes where we both grew up as country kids. My father, Les, mother Clarice and my brother and sister lived for a time in Yarrabandai, a place so small you could hardly call it a village. It had about six houses in all. When war broke out, my father enlisted and my mother, brother and sister and I moved back to Forbes. The country is a great place to grow up. We were never in the house. In the school holidays I used to help my dad in the shearing sheds, picking up the wool for him. I also had a job on a bread run for a while. I'd get up at 4 a.m. and go out with the boss to pick up the bread. He was a bit of a lazy bugger and he would sit in the van and make me do all the work.

Apart from that, we were always playing sport. I played football, cricket, tennis, hockey and somehow left the Marist Brothers College in Forbes as dux of the school. Up until a couple of months before I left, I had no idea what to do. It was fairly easy to get a job in those days; you either went to a bank, joined the police, became a carpenter or a teacher. My father didn't want me to be a labourer like him and suggested I try law. He spoke to one of the local solicitors, John Meillon, who proposed that the way to go was for me to study law while employed in the Petty Sessions Branch of the NSW Attorney-General's Department – in other words, to work and study in the court system.

My father took me down to Forbes courthouse, a beautiful old building, to see the local Clerk of Petty Sessions, Gerry Locke, who got me to fill out an application form. A week after I left school at the age of 16, I was working with him.

There was a lot to learn because in those days, the Clerk of Petty Sessions in a country court seemed to hold every official position in town. He did probate, he was the registrar for the District Court, the registrar for the small debts court, the registrar of social security, the registrar of births, deaths and marriages. He was also the Commonwealth employment service officer so you would go to him to register for work, a bit like Centrelink today.

It started off as a job but I found it fascinating and decided to make it my career. I had to do public service examinations to get ahead so after 17 months I moved to Sydney. I boarded at the St Vincent de Paul Hostel at Stanmore where it didn't matter that I was by myself in the city – we were all boys from the bush staying there.

My first job in the city was at the Metropolitan Children's Court in Albion Street in a lovely old building that is still there but is no longer a court. As I moved up through the ranks, I was like a sponge, learning from my bosses. Most were hard but fair. They were draconian in the way they wanted their t's crossed and their i's dotted but if you did it their way, then it was fine. They made you do things the right way from the word go, they made you disciplined about your work. It was the best grounding I could have had in the court system and I owe them a lot.

For years I was effectively driving a desk, office-bound and dealing with tasks like issuing summons. I did not get to go into court except as a deposition clerk, the person who took down the transcript before tape recorders were used. At Forbes, I had learned to touch type as part of my training but it was arduous work taking down depositions all day. You had to really concentrate on what was being said. We had some deposition clerks who were so quick, they would include 'witness smiles' or 'witness sighs' in the depositions. That was not me.

I was doing depositions at the old Redfern court in Sydney one day. It was a private assault case and the solicitors for each side were real characters. Jack Thom was a great big man who also sat as an alderman on a local council. His opposite number was Peter Clyne, also a big man with a presence to match his size and a position as an ambassador for some Pacific island. Well, did they go at each other! It was a pretty simple case but they went at it all day and achieved little but trade insults. I had the worst time wondering which words to take down – and which ones were better to ignore.

I wanted to work my way up the ladder and complete my law studies, which I did in 1966. I couldn't be admitted as a solicitor until I had done 15 months as an articled clerk in the Justice Department so it wasn't until 1969 that I became a solicitor. I never went into private practice, although I was offered three or four jobs after I passed my law exams. I had a few brief moments when I toyed with the idea but I enjoyed the job I had too much and I thought that I could get on the bench before I was too old. All I wanted to be was a magistrate.

Doreen and I had married in 1958, after meeting at a party to which she arrived with her uncle in his beautiful old Model T Ford. We had bought a house in Baulkham Hills in Sydney and the next few years must have been hard on her and the family because as I was promoted through the tiers to become a magistrate, we moved around a lot, renting out our Sydney home.

On 27 January 1973, I finally got my commission as a magistrate. I was a grade 3, which meant I was a traffic magistrate. My first area was Parramatta, Blacktown and Penrith; those courts were among the busiest I had been involved with. One day a defendant stood up and pleaded guilty to some traffic offence but then proceeded to give me this long and convoluted explanation which was obviously just pure fantasy. I had a court full of people and a lot of work to get through that morning and off the top of my head I said to him, 'What you're telling me is a load of bull.' Immediately I realised I should not have put it so bluntly but then I looked down to the court and saw everyone nodding their heads!

We all used to smoke in those days and one of my great friends on the bench, Alan McKeown, who was the other magistrate at Blacktown, used to call me an OP smoker – OP for 'other people' because I smoked only occasionally and used to bludge cigarettes off him. There was one magistrate who would stand up in the middle of a case and walk off the bench to the door of the court. Everyone would stop what they were saying and doing but he would tell them to carry on.

'I'm listening,' he would say as he stood with one hand outside the door in the corridor. He was having a smoke.

My next promotion was to a grade 2, a relieving magistrate. I then drove a secondhand Statesman and over the next two and half years, clocked up over 100,000 miles driving around New South Wales relieving at courts when and where needed. I went to almost every court in the state. They were a penny-pinching bunch in the Justice Department then and magistrates weren't allowed to fly. We had to either drive or go by train, whichever was the cheapest. It was ridiculous. Fair dinkum, I would turn up at court at 11 a.m. dishevelled and tired from an overnight train journey to find all the solicitors and the police prosecutor waiting for me clean and fresh after having flown up the night before plus having had a good night's sleep.

I was relieving at Albury one Christmas and because there was no parking, not even for the magistrate, the police allowed me to park in one of their garages at the police station. After court finished on Christmas Eve and I drove out to head back to Sydney, all the windows opened at the police station and everyone was hanging out blowing whistles and throwing balloons at me. They had also tied a dead fish to my exhaust pipe! Well, it was Christmas.

It was a terrific experience being a country magistrate. It was the best training because unlike the city courts, you heard all kinds of cases. Even the routine stuff that fills most days as a magistrate – drink-driving, traffic matters, stealing, shoplifting, fraud, custody and civil matters – yielded surprises.

One fellow I had up before me had been seen by neighbours while breaking into a house and stealing some goods. When the police arrived, they found the burglar down the street sitting in his car, still trying to get it started. He told me, 'My car has been playing up and I knew I should have got it fixed.' Silly bugger had got in the car anyway. He was never going to make a successful criminal.

We used to have some laughs. When court was in recess, we had been known to play table tennis on the bar table.

One day an elderly lady appeared before me. She had been summonsed by the police for driving an unregistered, uninsured car. She pleaded guilty and said the police constable had been very nice to her and the reason she didn't have her car registered or insured was because the floorboard in her car was rusted out and she had to get it replaced.

'Can you excuse me for a minute?' she said and popped out of the court, returning with the rusty piece of floor from her car which had been repaired. I thought, 'Well, she's gone to all this trouble.' I didn't impose any penalty.

One Thursday when it was late night shopping, the local police received a call to say a man was riding bareback on a horse along the main street. A highway patrol officer was alerted. He was a senior constable and a bit humourless. Without realising how silly he sounded, he had drawn up in his police car alongside the man and said, 'Pull over, rider' in the same way he would have said, 'Pull over, driver.' The man on horseback took off but was caught at the other side of the park. When the man appeared before me, he pleaded guilty. The police always prepare a statement of facts about the case to help the court and if someone pleads guilty, that statement is usually simply tendered to the magistrate as it outlines the case. In this instance, instead of tendering the statement of facts, we got this humourless patrol officer into the witness box to read them out because we wanted to see how he would read the words: 'Pull over, rider.' He did it deadpan. We smothered our laughter.

There were a few solicitors who were regulars around the courts. They all knew their way around the system and they wouldn't badger you for hours about a case they knew was hopeless. Some seemed to get through the day by the seat of their pants. Most solicitors came into court with a file on their client. Abe Brindley, who appeared for many members of the well-known criminal fraternity, would come into court with his instructions written on a bus ticket. You knew it wasn't going to be a lengthy matter.

Bruce Miles, a bomber pilot during the war, always wore the same safari suit, or perhaps he had a wardrobe of cream safari suits but they always looked the same. He'd have his instructions in the margins of *The Sydney Morning Herald* or on the racing form from *The Daily Telegraph*, a newspaper which would always be sticking out of the back pocket of his pants. Despite their unorthodox approaches, their clients never seemed to suffer.

There was Phil Roach, a big tall fellow who got on well with everyone. He would represent the women who had been arrested for soliciting over the weekend. He liked to get their cases on as quickly as possible on a Monday morning because the women liked to get back out there as soon as they could to pick up some more business.

The long civil matters and cases involving the custody of children were not my cup of tea. Custody cases could be very dangerous as emotions ran high. One man screamed at me and said he was going to kill me. Another young man who was trying to appear like a nice, reasonable bloke went mad in court and had to be calmed by the police. He was not the person he wanted us to think he was.

At Lithgow, I had one fellow who stabbed himself. He was in custody at Bathurst Jail and his wife had made an application for custody of their children. Although he was serving a sentence, he wanted access to the children. He was very bitter. He was in the dock and at one stage during the hearing, his wife went too close to the dock and he lunged at her. The police made sure they were kept apart.

As I was hearing the evidence, all of a sudden this man fell to the floor in the dock. He had stabbed himself in the stomach. Obviously he had not been searched properly because he had the knife hidden down his shoe.

I was told that he had befriended a medical student in jail who had told him that if he put the knife into a certain spot in his stomach and didn't twist it, he was not going to do himself any harm. He had been right. He was taken to hospital and about three weeks later he was back in court. I didn't give him custody of his children.

By the end of some days I would end up very tired but I never wished that I was doing something else. It was through my work that Doreen and I got to meet the Queen when she once visited Bathurst.

※

Like I say, you never knew what to expect, which brings me back to Lithgow and Frank Nugan.

The inquest had generated so much publicity that even my wife's cousin, who was living in Hong Kong read about it. The papers there were full of the case because of the Nugan Hand Bank's business in Asia.

To me and to the police, everything pointed to suicide but there was still a suspicion being voiced in the media that Nugan had been murdered.

One of the lawyers requested a re-enactment of the last moments of the merchant banker's life. I had a Mercedes-Benz car similar to the one in which Nugan was found shot dead brought to the Lithgow courthouse by detectives. Using the actual rifle, the detectives demonstrated to us how they believed Nugan had shot himself and the position in which they found him. They showed how the gun was placed between his knees and how it was possible for him to have shot himself. The murderer, if there was one, would have had to have been in the car with him at the time of the shooting, an extremely dangerous place to be. There were also no signs of violence and nothing to indicate the presence of another person.

I had also called in a police ballistics expert. He said that having a rifle between the knees and the muzzle in the mouth was a 'popular' way to commit suicide. Painting a graphic picture, he said the muzzle of the rifle would have been within one-eighth of an inch from Nugan's head when he pulled the trigger.

While I was preparing my report, I spoke to Kevin Waller, who was the City Coroner in Sydney at the time, about what findings I could bring. Kevin was the most experienced magistrate at the time in coronial work; he was approachable and always willing to help. I didn't discuss the evidence with him but I wanted his advice on how certain I had to be that Nugan had committed suicide because I had to be more certain than on the balance of probabilities. If I was not satisfied it was suicide, I could find it was shooting by a person or persons unknown. Kevin told me that if I thought it was suicide, if there was evidence it was suicide then that's the official conclusion I should come to.

In May, I called everyone back to the court and handed down my findings: that the body was that of Frank Nugan and he had taken his own life by shooting. I agreed with the experts that it would have been impossible for someone to lean in to the car and pull the trigger of the rifle at such an angle. Nugan had not left a note, but in a good percentage of suicides, no notes are found. I felt he was a man who had been walking a financial tightrope and that there was more in his business dealings than was at first apparent. I could have come to a reasonable conclusion that Nugan had some connection with the CIA but that was not going to help me decide whether he had taken his own life. There was no evidence anyone else was involved.

I had no doubt that he had committed suicide.

A few weeks after the inquest, Michael Hand went missing. He fled Australia on a fake passport, reportedly wearing a false beard and moustache. He effectively disappeared.

Then one evening in February 1981, I was at home watching TV after work and heard that Frank Nugan's body was being exhumed. I couldn't believe it! I was the coroner who had dealt with the inquiry and held the inquest and I hadn't been told about what was going on with this case. It is an understatement to say so, but I was not pleased.

What had happened was that a former associate of Frank Nugan's had come back from America where he said he went to the toilet in a casino in Las Vegas and as he walked in through the toilet door, Frank Nugan had been walking out. The man's story was that he had said, 'Hello, Frank, what are you doing here?' Nugan had replied, 'Just slumming.'

Based on that, the NSW Attorney-General Frank Walker decided there was a question mark over the identity of the man who had been buried. He obtained a Supreme Court order quashing my findings in the inquest and another order to exhume the body. Walker had asked the NSW Homicide Squad for a report on whether or not Nugan was dead. Like me, they were more than satisfied that the body in grave number 110/M20 at the Northern Suburbs Cemetery at Ryde in Sydney was that of Frank Nugan. Despite the view of the police, the exhumation went ahead.

By all accounts, digging up the grave was a messy affair. The sixth of February 1981 was overcast and rainy; a southerly wind was blowing across the cemetery – rather evocative weather for the occasion. When they uncovered the plain brown chipboard coffin, they discovered the lid had caved in and there had been water seepage into the box. After 16 months underground, the body was badly decomposed and unrecognisable. It was taken to the morgue at Glebe where scientists had to rely on dental records and what was left of the thumb on the jelly-like right hand to obtain fingerprints. As long as there is some skin, they can get a print.

The media carried stories along the lines of how the second inquest would at last provide the first wide-ranging public inquiry into the Nugan Hand organisation. That was just media talk. They did not understand that was not the role of an inquest. The role is to identify the body and decide the cause of death. In some cases there are further inquiries as to how it happened but that was not the case here. The media does love a conspiracy.

Kevin Waller had moved from being the City Coroner to a magistrate at Balmain so the second inquest was given to Norman Walsh, who had taken over from Kevin as City Coroner. An examination of the body's teeth by Frank Nugan's dentist had confirmed that the body in the coffin was Frank Nugan. The body's fingerprints also matched those of Frank Nugan. I said to Norm Walsh, 'Well, did you reach the same finding as I did?' He said he had, almost word for word.

For me, the Frank Nugan case ended there. But there was still a long way for the story to go.

It turned out Michael Hand, who had taken his secrets with him when he had fled the country, had indeed been seconded to the CIA. An MP, who had been campaigning to name foreign spies operating in Australia, stood up in the Victorian parliament and announced that the CIA had decided to withdraw its Chief of Station in Canberra because of the disclosures linking it with the Nugan Hand Bank. The MP said it was well known that the bank had been totally controlled by the CIA. There was even talk that Frank Nugan had been a member of the CIA. Of course you would never be sure because both the US Government and their embassy in Canberra refused to discuss 'intelligence questions'.

The Nugan Hand Bank ended up as possibly the most investigated bank in Australian criminal history. My suspicions had been spot on and there was certainly a lot more to it than simple banking. Not only was there a NSW Corporate Affairs Commission investigation into the bank, but a police investigation and then a Royal Commission under Justice Donald Stewart, who was head of the National Crime Authority.

Frank Nugan and Michael Hand had been two men on the make. By 1970, they had been in business together in another financial company before establishing the bank. They attracted top notch investors and other – legitimate – banks gave them references. The NSW Corporate Affairs Commission concluded the bank was a fraud run by two smooth-talking corporate crooks. It made Hand and Nugan millions but the investors were not so lucky. The two men inflated their accounts, rewrote their books and used paper transfers to rob some clients in order to pay off others. It was, as people like to say, classic smoke and mirrors stuff.

There was also evidence that the two partners got involved with arms deals and their bank was used by major drug traffickers, including the Mr Asia syndicate, that got special attention from the bank. However, it seemed unlikely Hand and Nugan were involved in drug dealing themselves.

As for William Colby, the man on the card in Frank Nugan's pocket, he died in 1996, drowning in an accident while out canoeing near his holiday home in Maryland. His reputation in Australia had not followed him to America where he was remembered in a very different way. His notoriety in America came not from being secretive but quite the opposite. He was best known for exposing the secret workings of the CIA to Congress, telling them the agency had been involved in a plot to kill Fidel Castro. He said himself that he was sacked in 1975 for refusing to 'stonewall' investigations into CIA wrongdoing.

Whatever the whole truth – and people will believe what they want – the Nugan Hand Bank's notoriety lives on. Just the name 'Nugan Hand' conjures up an image of shadowy deals, the details of which a lot of people would have preferred never surfaced.

As for me, the daily drama of a courtroom carried on unabated. Not as much money or as many prominent reputations may have been at stake every day but every day people's lives were laid bare in cases that came before me in court. One of those cases was to threaten my own life and the lives of my family. Another, the murder of a young woman, was to appal Australia like no other.

Chapter 2

Hot Summer Nights

It was boundary riding in the summer of 1984 when my daughter answered a telephone call at home one night.

'Hello.' It was a man's voice on the other end of the line.

We have a friend who is always playing jokes and as the man spoke, at first Megan thought it was him.

'Oh, don't be silly,' she said. But the man kept talking. This was no friend, not even one having a sick joke.

At this point my wife, Doreen, looked across the lounge room at Megan and saw that she was shaking and visibly upset. The colour had literally drained from her face as she held the phone to her ear.

Doreen walked over to her.

'What's wrong?' she said. Silently Megan handed the receiver to her mum and the man repeated his message. It was the day my job came home.

⁂

On day one of this particular drugs case, the police had marksmen on the roof of Paddington Magistrates Court. There were more officers in and around the court, all of them armed. There was nothing unusual about the nine defendants, eight of them male, one of them female, sitting before me with their lawyers. But then what do criminals look like? If they looked like those shifty characters in Hollywood movies, straight out of central casting, chances are they wouldn't get away with their crimes. These nine people, dressed more like business people for their court appearance, were among Australia's heaviest – and as my family was to find out to its cost, most dangerous – drug dealers. They were facing charges involving what was then the country's second biggest heroin seizure, 27.02 kilograms, 19 per cent pure, discovered by customs officers during a routine search at Brisbane Airport in August 1983.

I had sat on the odd case at Paddington over the years, a day here, a week there, but I knew this time I was going to be there for a reasonably long stint from the middle of November 1983. I didn't have my own permanent court at the time so that was why I was what we called 'boundary riding'. There were three or four of us who covered Sydney, Wollongong, Newcastle and Katoomba, filling in for other magistrates or doing cases the other magistrates didn't have time for. The executive officer to the Chief Magistrate drew up the rosters and you were usually given about a week's warning of where you would be sitting but he could just as easily ring you up the day before and change it all. You could be given a case that would last a day or a case that would last a year.

I had had a couple of weeks' warning that I would be at Paddington for a while to hear a drugs case, that it would involve high security. Basically that was all I knew about it until the day I turned up. The background was for the prosecutor to tell me in court.

Another indication that it was a big case was that the Crown prosecutors had taken over the job, not the usual police sergeants who did the work of prosecutors in the local courts. It is the prosecutor's job to present the evidence for the prosecution, call the prosecution witnesses and cross-examine any called by the defence. The Crown prosecutor in this case was Brian Sully, a tall, precisely spoken and very fair prosecutor. He's now a judge on the NSW Supreme Court bench. His junior was Nicholas Cowdery, now the state's Director of Public Prosecutions. Guided by Sully, the prosecution case began to unfold.

The defendants were alleged to have been part of a heroin smuggling ring which used Australia Post to distribute its wares. The drugs were placed inside magazines rolled up in a wrapper bearing the name of a firm of Hong Kong solicitors indicating that they contained legal documents. The parcels were forwarded to fictitious people at actual addresses but only those who lived in blocks of units. This was because they didn't want the real people at the address to accidentally receive the parcel. As the rolled-up magazine wouldn't fit inside a letter box, it had to be left by the postman on the floor near the bank of post boxes. Couriers working for the drug ring would be alerted as to the destinations and timing of the parcels and waited, watching for the postie so they could simply walk over and pick the parcels up. That was how it was supposed to work. Where it went wrong was that the couriers weren't always quick enough. Some of the magazines were picked up by the real people whose homes they were addressed to – and when they opened them, instead of legal documents, packets of white powder fell out. The police were called in.

A task force was set up to track down the source and ultimate destination of the heroin. The detectives pinpointed their suspects, including Charlie Losurdo, one of the defendants in front of me. Losurdo, an Italian in his mid-30s, was one of the ringleaders. He and the others were put under surveillance and their telephones tapped. Losurdo was caught talking regularly to Hong Kong, but not, of course, about heroin. Losurdo and his contact in Hong Kong, Wau Leung Wong, known as Peter Wong, talked in code about seemingly innocent matters like diamonds and boy scouts but it was obvious that what they were referring to was the importation of heroin. Wong was not one of the defendants before me. He had not been found.

Money can buy all sorts of help and the syndicate had bribed a Telecom linesman to check on their phones and see if they were being tapped. Paid in cash, some immediately and the rest promised after the end of the operation, the man also had to check the security of premises being used to organise the smuggling. That man, who had thrown away his career of 13 years experience with Telecom, was also before me. Also sitting behind the bar table with his lawyer was a man called Tony Cameron. During that first week in Paddington court, Cameron had more on his mind than I could guess at.

Cameron had been a health supervisor with Sydney City Council who hungered for a life in the fast lane. He dressed like a million dollars, although he only earned between $400 and $500 a week at his council job. He took on extra jobs, designing night spots for some of his Kings Cross friends, running a hairdressing business and buying an industrial carpet cleaning machine to go into the cleaning business. His wife, who ran a boutique, later told a reporter that Cameron loved to be a big name. He would pick up the bill in expensive restaurants and bring people home he had never met before that night, asking his wife to make them all breakfast. Cameron also ran a piano bar which may have been a euphemism for a brothel. It was certainly a well-known pick-up spot.

Tony discovered that there was a quick way to get the big money he craved – from drugs. It was early 1983 when he helped a friend open a restaurant in a building in Edgecliff – a restaurant that became well known to police – that he apparently got involved with the heroin syndicate. He soon moved reasonably high up in the syndicate and was trusted enough to travel to Hong Kong and meet the mastermind of the operation. Like his colleagues in the syndicate, the task force also had Cameron under surveillance and his telephone tapped.

Unfortunately for the police, before their investigation was complete, two teenage thieves, by coincidence, broke into the car of one of the detectives on the task force. Among their haul, they stole documents connected to the case. In more bad luck, the thieves recognised the name of one of the suspects and alerted him to the investigation. Once the police realised the documents had been stolen, they had to move quickly to make their series of arrests.

When the defendants came before me, two of them, including the woman, were on bail. The other seven, including Cameron, had been remanded in custody. Every day after court they were taken under guard back to their cells at the Remand Centre at Long Bay Jail.

Before we got into the second week of the committal, Cameron was murdered. It was on the news on the Sunday evening:

A man due to appear in court tomorrow charged with importing heroin has been found murdered at Long Bay Jail.

I had to wait until the next morning to hear the full story. Cameron had been found unconscious shortly before 3 p.m. on the floor of the dining room on the top landing of Wing 12 in the Remand Centre. He was rushed to hospital but pronounced dead on arrival. There were two puncture marks in his neck and it was initially thought a syringe had been used to inject air into his veins. After a post-mortem and pathology tests, it was revealed he had been injected with pure heroin.

Even before the results of the tests were known, it was obvious that his death was no accident. Someone had wanted him dead, someone powerful enough to get it done in jail. On Monday morning in my chambers at Paddington courthouse, Brian Sully and Nicholas Cowdery told me what they and police believed was behind Tony Cameron's murder – there had been rumours he had been considering swapping sides and doing a deal, becoming a Crown witness. As an insider he would have been the prosecution's star witness. He had been deeply involved with the syndicate, he knew the names and faces of those who ran it and who worked for it. While the prosecution had a lot of evidence, Cameron would have been the icing on their cake. He was a key player in the heroin trade. His reward for the deal would be either immunity from prosecution or a lesser sentence. Unfortunately for him, as one detective put it, 'Obviously we weren't the only people who heard (about) it.'

We were going to need some breathing space to decide how to proceed with the case so I adjourned the hearing that day. The other six defendants on remand had already been brought into the city to face the court so they were kept in the cells beneath Central police station – under even tighter security. Some of the witnesses involved in the case were contacted and were given police protection. It appeared that whoever was behind Cameron's murder played for keeps.

⁂

Early in my career I had formulated a rule – never take work home. Doreen used to follow my cases in the papers and we used to chat about them in the evenings over dinner or while watching the TV but only superficially, never in any depth. In my job, I felt that when I was finished for the day, I had to put the cases out of my mind as much as possible otherwise I would be dwelling on them, going over and over them. I didn't want to spend all night talking about the things I did all day; my family was more important to me than that.

Doreen taught at a pre-school and she and our children used to tell everyone that I was an accountant. To a lot of people, being a magistrate was akin to being a cop and there are always people who have it in for the justice system. I tried to keep a low profile; it was like putting a protective barrier around my private life and my family.

Doreen and I briefly talked about Cameron's murder but didn't think any more of it.

The committal had to go on. On the Tuesday we were all back in court and the security was even tighter. As well as the marksmen on the roof opposite the courthouse and police all over the place, we had a metal detector on the door of the courtroom and everyone entering the court was checked. It was just as well because that Tuesday a woman was caught trying to bring a large knife into court. She was a friend of Cameron's and blamed one of the other defendants for his death. She had decided to take retribution into her own hands. Who knows what would have happened if she hadn't been stopped.

Tony Cameron had been murdered at the end of November and I sat for another three weeks as the prosecution case unfolded.

By Christmas Eve, we had gone through the evidence of 80 prosecution witnesses. I adjourned the case until the end of January. During this time the courts closed down for the annual break.

When the case resumed, the police had made a breakthrough. They had arrested another local man involved with the syndicate. The Crown prosecutor, Brian Sully, wanted to include the man in the committal, an application that was strenuously fought by the lawyers for the other eight defendants. I felt that it made sense to include him because the charges were so closely related and made that ruling on the condition that any of the 80 witnesses could be recalled for further evidence if there was anything relevant to the new defendant. The lawyers for the other defendants immediately requested an adjournment and up to the Supreme Court they went.

That Friday, I received a call from the Supreme Court telling me that their challenge had failed and my ruling had been upheld and requesting that I continue the adjournment until the Wednesday of the following week to give the latest defendant's lawyers time to consider which witnesses they may want to recall. I agreed.

That evening I was at my local bowling club having a drink with friends. I hadn't been there long when the man who was on duty at the door to sign people in came to find me. He said my daughter was on the phone. Megan, then aged 16, was hysterical. She and Doreen had just received that terrifying telephone call. Megan said a man had been on the phone asking for me.

'Tell your husband to back off,' he had told Doreen and then proceeded to tell her what would happen to my family if I didn't take notice. To this day, she hasn't told anyone, even me, exactly what that threat was. It is too upsetting for her.

I looked around the bar and saw two off-duty detectives from the local Castle Hill police station so I asked them to come home with me. I had walked to the club but they gave me a lift back.

When we arrived at my home, we found the place was locked up like Fort Knox. While Megan had been on the phone to me, Doreen had run around the house closing windows and locking doors. The detectives checked around the house to make sure it was as safe as it could be and left, saying they would put in a report at the station. Doreen and I talked about the danger of the situation and decided we didn't think the detectives were taking it seriously enough so I called a friend of mine, Bryan Kenny, who was a detective sergeant. 'Leave it to me,' he said. Thirty minutes later the police started to arrive and our lives were turned upside down.

Occasionally defendants make threats to magistrates and judges in court and usually they are passed over as being made in the heat of the moment. What made everyone take this threat seriously was not only that one defendant had already been murdered but that the threat had been made in a call to my home. I had a silent number and there was no way to find my phone number on the public record. One of the defendants was the ex-Telecom employee.

From that night, we were never alone. We were placed under 24-hour protection. A decision was made to keep the drug task force away because we didn't want anyone to be able to accuse me of bias if they were looking after my family while at the same time I had to decide if they had been telling the truth in court. So the officers were drawn from several local police stations and detective units. There was never less than two officers in the house. We weren't allowed to answer the phone or the door, the police did all that for us. Every call, every visitor, was logged. The police ate with us. We went to bed with them in the house and woke up to them. When any of us got up to go to the toilet during the night, a voice would call out, 'Who's there?'

The pre-school where Doreen taught was only 500 yards up the street but every morning an officer would drive her to work and every evening another would collect her. The police thought it would be more of a deterrent if the officers were all in uniform – but it could be off-putting. When Doreen went shopping, one of the officers went with her. As they walked beside her in the supermarket or the department store, she felt all eyes on her and the whispers, 'I know what they've got her for. She must have been shoplifting.' When she hung out the washing, they were with her. We weren't allowed to do any gardening ourselves. Luckily the neighbours were wonderful and cut our lawns. One day Doreen decided she needed some fresh air and wanted to get outside into the front garden. She thought she would trick the police by sneaking out the back door and walking down the side of the house. Just as she reached the front, one of the officers stepped out! We couldn't move anywhere without being watched.

Megan had just started Year 11 and there she was, uniformed police driving her to and from school every day. Some of her new classmates thought she was on parole. We explained what was happening to the headmistress but couldn't tell many people. It didn't go down well with her new boyfriend when he came to the house one evening to visit her, only to find the front door opened by a policeman. He never came back.

Our son John had been away on holiday from university when the telephone call came so he was spared the tight security. When he got back, the police were not as concerned for him and he was allowed to drive himself to university.

I was driven daily to Paddington courthouse, with a surveillance car riding shotgun. It was tailing us as insurance, to make doubly sure nothing happened. The surveillance car was an old Volkswagen driven by a detective looking the part in T-shirt and shorts. Almost as if it was part of the script, on the second morning, we lost sight of the tailing car and had to continue to court without his protection. We found out later that the Volkswagen had broken down.

A friend owned the nearby video shop and he said if the police went down just before he closed at 6 p.m. – yes, these were the days when shops didn't open late – he would give them some videos so they had something to watch during the night. One night, the officer on duty was sitting on our couch, with his head back on the cushions, watching one of the *Rocky* movies. Suddenly he felt something cold sticking into his neck. He thought it was a gun and his shout woke the whole house. It was our Maltese terrier Tut (short for Tutankhamen) who had jumped onto the back of the couch from the open staircase and nuzzled his cold wet nose into the back of the officer's neck.

One evening a storm was brewing as Doreen arrived home from work. When she got out of the car, one officer, Charlie, followed her to the front door. As the door opened, the officer suddenly shouted, 'Oh God, I've been shot.' He pushed Doreen over the step to safety and started to pat himself down to find where the bullet had hit, saying, 'I've been shot, I've been shot.'

Doreen turned and looked at him.

'It was thunder, Charlie, you haven't been shot,' she said.

It was the last we saw of Charlie.

There was a change of shift every night at 11 p.m. One night, as the relieving officer arrived, he spotted what looked like a bomb under one of the police cars in the driveway. He alerted his colleague and reluctantly the two of them went back to look. Crouching down carefully, they got the fright of their lives when a neighbour's cat leapt out from beneath the car.

Joking aside, neither us nor the officers could ever truly relax. We were constantly on our toes. It was a very traumatic time. One of the rare nights when a marked police car was not parked in our drive, the officer in the house with us spotted a car parked opposite with a man sitting inside. The rego number came back as belonging to the relatives of one of the defendants. It was the defendant I was most worried about, who was not Losurdo. The officer called for help and as the police car arrived, the man drove off. We never found out who was behind the threat and the telephone call. All the defendants, through their lawyers, denied any knowledge of it.

The police were tremendous. It couldn't have been easy for them but they fitted in with the family wherever they could. We became good friends with some of them. Megan had tickets for an Elton John concert and the police wouldn't let her go alone. One of the young female officers offered to go with her, not too great a hardship, I think! She did go undercover on this occasion, leaving her uniform at home. They both had a great night. Another young officer used to help Megan with her maths.

It was a big strain on all of us and it went on for four and a half months, until I committed all the defendants to stand trial.

Was I biased against them, knowing at least one of them was behind the fear they had put my family through for all that time? I had worked in the court system since 1953 and I was conditioned to be unemotional. As a matter of fact, I found there was not enough evidence to commit Charlie Losurdo for trial on the main charge against him. I felt the evidence was too circumstantial. The Director of Public Prosecutions (DPP) got what is called an ex-officio indictment against him which means a defendant goes straight to trial regardless of the decision following the committal hearing. Losurdo ended up being convicted of conspiring with others to import heroin into Australia between June 1982 and September 1983 and for conspiring to supply heroin. He was jailed for 25 years, with a non-parole period of 15 years, then a record. Peter Wong, who was later arrested, was jailed for 15 years with a minimum of ten years. The others received lesser sentences.

Years later, when Losurdo's solicitor, the always colourful Pat Costello, was before me in a case at Glebe Coroners Court, he said that Losurdo had told him, 'Tell Mr Hand he thinks kindly of him.' By then, Losurdo was out of jail and selling pizzas in Kings Cross. He knew I had given him a fair hearing.

I can't praise the police who looked after us highly enough. When John turned 21 a few months later, we invited some of them to his party. However, that whole episode is something I would never like to go through again.

Our next door neighbour owned a service station at Rozelle and a couple of years earlier he had introduced me to one of his customers, a rather dashing celebrity psychiatrist called Harry Bailey. The doctor had come around to pick up the keys for his car which had been serviced at the neighbour's garage. Dr Bailey was probably Australia's best known psychiatrist, having courted the media in his early years and later become a popular expert witness in court cases, although he had never appeared before me. We shook hands and he went off to collect his car. I thought nothing more of it.

In November 1984, he appeared before me charged with manslaughter. I was still doing my stint of boundary riding and was given the doctor's case to do at Central Local Court, a beautiful old court in Liverpool Street in the city. Bailey had been charged with the manslaughter of one of his patients, 26-year-old Miriam Podio, who had died in August 1977. The case had received a lot of publicity when over a year earlier, in 1983, magistrate Terry Forbes, sitting as a coroner, had been conducting the inquest into her death and found that on the evidence, there was a *prima facie* case established against her three doctors, Bailey and his partners John Herron and Ian Gardiner. To find a *prima facie* case, the court has to be satisfied that there is sufficient evidence for a reasonable jury properly instructed to convict the person – therefore enough evidence 'on the face of it' (*prima facie*). Once a coroner finds a *prima facie* case exists against someone, the inquest has to be terminated and it is up to the DPP to decide whether there is enough evidence to prosecute. Usually the case goes straight to a judge and jury. In this case, it was decided by the Attorney-General that there should be a committal hearing so all the medical evidence against Bailey could be aired before a magistrate. The DPP decided not to lay charges against Herron and Gardiner.

Although it was six years since Miriam Podio's death, the reason there had finally been an inquest was because of the media pressure and publicity. Miriam had died while undergoing the so-called deep sleep therapy at Chelmsford Private Hospital where Bailey, Herron and Gardiner had all practised.

At this time, Chelmsford's notoriety was in its infancy. It is now known, after a Royal Commission in 1990, that the discredited deep sleep therapy led to the deaths of 26 patients, most of whom had been suffering from depression and anxiety disorders. The idea of the therapy, according to Bailey's soft sell approach, was to give the patients a 'good rest' by putting them to sleep for a week or two. In fact these patients were put into a coma with massive doses of barbiturates. It was a highly dangerous treatment because as the body got used to the doses of barbiturates needed to keep them under, increasingly higher doses were needed.

Bailey was the first and only doctor I have had before me charged with killing a patient. Was there enough evidence to show that deep sleep therapy and negligence caused Miriam Podio's death and therefore that Bailey should be sent to trial for manslaughter? I had to decide.

The Harry Bailey that walked into my courtroom looked little like the man I had met a few years earlier. That rather dapper man had gone. In his place was this aged man, looking jowly and tired. He did, however, still sport a bit of the flair for which he had been famous, wearing a light-coloured suit and garish floral tie to court.

The problem for the Crown was that they had to show the cause of death – and there had been no post-mortem and there was no body. Miriam Podio's body had been flown back to Italy for burial soon after her death. Because she was unconscious before she died, the law said Bailey should have reported her death to the coroner, which would have led to a post-mortem and an investigation. Bailey had helped his own case by not complying with the *Coroner's Act*. He never mentioned the case to the coroner. As it was, the committal became a matter of almost pure speculation.

Bailey's defence barrister was Ian Barker QC. It was the first time I had seen Barker in action, although I had heard of him through the dingo case. Barker had become famous for prosecuting Lindy Chamberlain. I found him very impressive. Some lawyers like to hear themselves talk so much that they end up waffling on and lose their way. Barker always knew where he was going. He kept focused and to the point.

The case was complicated because the facts were not always clear. There were missing entries in the hospital records and entries inserted later in the nursing notes, the authenticity of which came under scrutiny.

Bailey claimed Miriam Podio had died from a pulmonary embolism (a blood clot leading to heart failure), depression and schizophrenia and Barker argued that at the end of the day, there was no evidence to show that the doctor had not been correct. The prosecution called a number of medical experts and each of them thought Miriam Podio had died of whatever they specialised in. Barker submitted that from the facts, as presented to the court, there were 14 causes of death to choose from, including ruptured appendix, abdominal catastrophy, toxic shock and septicaemia. The Crown had taken a wrong turn in calling too many experts who gave too many explanations.

I felt I had to dismiss the manslaughter charge. Some of the nurses from Chelmsford had given evidence and there was no doubt in my mind that it was a hospital which had been run disgracefully. Untrained nurses had been left to make decisions about administering drugs which were potentially dangerous. Records were woeful and nursing notes not up to standard. Yet at the end of the day, there was no way of being sure what had caused Miriam Podio's death and without that, the prosecution did not have a case. To commit someone for trial, you have to be sure there is enough evidence for a jury to convict them beyond a reasonable doubt. There was not enough evidence that Bailey had been criminally responsible for Miriam Podio's death.

While it was not required of me to say anything else, I felt it incumbent to say something about the lack of supervision and care shown by Bailey towards his patient. I said, 'The defendant's overall supervision of the patient has been most negligent, in my opinion having regard to the type of treatment being carried out, and his action overall in regard to the type of treatment and the subsequent signing of the death certificate and the non-report of the death in accordance with the *Coroner's Act*.'

In the light of what I know now about deep sleep treatment and Chelmsford Private Hospital, I still feel I made the right decision. If they are going to bring a prosecution for murder or manslaughter, the prosecution must have a cause of death and in this case they did not have one. It could have been natural causes which had nothing to do with the treatment. I certainly would have expected a doctor to know what was required to comply with the *Coroner's Act* and while Bailey's failure to notify the authorities about Miriam Podio's death was suspicious, it did not make him guilty of manslaughter. It was not the last I was to hear about Harry Bailey.

A few months later, the body of a middle-aged man was found dead in his car parked on a dirt track 50 kilometres north of Sydney just off the F3 freeway to Newcastle. The man was Bailey and he had drunk a cocktail of Heineken beer and Tuinal, a barbiturate. While I had dismissed the committal proceedings, he was quite rightly facing disciplinary proceedings brought by the newly created Medical Complaints Unit of the NSW Health Department. His lawyers had also told him that on top of that, he faced a lifetime of litigation from former patients and the families of the patients who had died undergoing his deep sleep therapy. Bailey was under siege from his own profession, from his patients in the courts – and also from the

Church of Scientology who had him in its sights in its war against psychiatrists.

For a lot of people, suicide is a spur of the moment decision and is part of the reason why most do not leave notes. Bailey, however, seemed to have given a lot of thought to his. In his suicide note he wrote, 'Let it be known that the Scientologists and the forces of madness have won. Doctors like [name withheld] are equally to be abhorred. They are egocentric crazies almost as bad as the Scientologists.' His death was not one of my cases as he died in another coroner's area. It was obviously a suicide so in the end there was no inquest.

⁂

While the committal against Dr Bailey had been continuing, I was asked to take over as coroner at Westmead, my first job as a full-time coroner and it was to change the course of my career.

In early 1984, Westmead Coroners Court had been opened. It was a new purpose-built building along the side of Westmead Hospital and Greg Glass had been appointed the first coroner at Westmead.

On Sunday, 2 September that year, at the Viking Tavern at Milperra in Sydney's southwest, six bikies and a 14-year-old girl died after the Bandido and Comanchero bikie gangs had declared war. The police charged 15 Comancheros and 27 Bandidos with murder but there was no magistrate's court big enough and with tough enough security to hold them all for a committal hearing. This case came under the jurisdiction of Westmead court but the committal couldn't be heard there because it wasn't suitable. The case had to be heard at Penrith courthouse. Because it was in Greg Glass's patch, he was asked to take charge and conduct the committal. Security was tight; two separate Perspex cages were built in the courtroom for each of the bikie gangs to keep them apart. It became the largest criminal committal ever heard in Australia.

The committal was expected to last for nine months so the Chief Magistrate Clarrie Briese asked me if I would go to Westmead to fill in for Greg. I jumped at the chance. It was only a 10-minute drive from home. (The bikie committal eventually took ten months and it was not until September 1985 that Greg committed 41 bikies to stand trial; one of them hanged himself in jail.)

Although I had done the Frank Nugan inquest, I had never had any particular interest in coronial work. After just a couple of months at Westmead, that all changed. It was the investigative side of the work that sucked me in. As a coroner you were involved from the beginning in a case. Sudden and suspicious deaths were reported and the coroner had a hand in which ones were investigated and how they were investigated. The police liaised with you and you directed them if you felt there was something that should be done which they were not doing. There was also the potential to make a difference because a coroner could make recommendations for change.

As the coroner, I had to sign burial orders and orders for post-mortems. All sudden deaths came within the ambit of a coroner and when police had to report sudden or suspicious deaths, they completed a form called a P79A. I had to look over every one of those forms in case there was something that caught my eye or seemed unusual. If so, I would get something done about it straightaway, perhaps ordering extra forensic tests or a specific investigation.

I have never been an avid fan of going to the morgue although there were other coroners who happily got kitted up in the uniform of white overalls and green gumboots and watched the post-mortems in most of the deaths which were reported to them. Not me. While it seems strange to some people, I have seen plenty of dead bodies but to this day I have never seen a post-mortem. I'm not queasy about death, it's just that I could never see the need for me to be present during a post-mortem examination. I figured that was why there were experts in forensic pathology. My expertise was in the law, not watching post-mortems.

I was, however, curious to see what a morgue looked like and to meet the staff at Westmead. The Westmead morgue was the first one I had visited. I walked across the staff car park between the court and the hospital and took the lift down to the basement. I pushed through the plastic flap doors that led into the morgue suite and on the left-hand side, saw the white overalls hanging up and the gumboots lined up beneath. The doors into the morgue itself were sealed and it was when I walked through them – that's when the smell hit me. It was worse than just the formaldehyde that is used to preserve the body parts like the heart, lung and brain. Morgues have their own smell and they smell like, well, a morgue.

The stainless steel fridges with the drawers for bodies were on one side and in front was a bank of stainless steel slabs on which the post-mortems took place. There was also a small lecture theatre with a stainless steel table in the centre of it, used not only for medical students but also for the unfortunate detectives who drew the short straw and were the officers from their investigation who had to watch the post-mortem. These officers verify the chain of evidence – they had to ensure that, for example, any photographs of wounds or samples of blood or stomach contents from the body being analysed were correctly labelled and processed to remove any doubt in court later where these samples had come from.

The staff at Westmead morgue were a very professional group of people and very sensitive to the families of the dead. A lot of families are not happy about their loved one being opened up for a post-mortem examination, even though as far as possible, the bodies are properly prepared again for burial. The Government Medical Officer for the Parramatta area was Dr Joe Malouf, a man then in his mid-50s, who was referred to, as 'Gentleman Joe'. He did all the post-mortems at Westmead for us with the assistance of his nephew, Graham Malouf.

To this day I have no idea why anyone would want to work in a morgue. You need a strong stomach and a sense of humour. An example of this particular type of humour was my first Christmas at Westmead. The ladies were all making something for our staff Christmas party and I asked Doreen if she could cook something for me to take. When the fellows from the morgue joined us they gave all the dishes laid out on the table their special names – there was 'myocardial infarction' and 'atheroscelerosis' and my favourite, 'pulmonary embolism'. The beer was kept cold in the fridges at the morgue. It was not being irreverent to the dead, it was a way of coping. The morgue staff had to have an outlet from their work. They needed to have some sort of relief from the type of jobs they had to do.

It was their morgue where Anita Cobby's body was taken. Ms Cobby had gone missing on her way home from work as a nurse at Sydney Hospital on Sunday, 2 February 1986. Anita had caught the train from Central Station to Blacktown but never arrived at the house where she lived with her parents, Garry and Grace Lynch.

The police rang me on the Tuesday morning to let me know that what they believed was Anita's body had been found in a paddock southwest of Blacktown. It was the coroner's job to make sure the body was brought in and properly identified but the mechanics of doing so were left up to the police. They brought Mr Lynch to Westmead Hospital and led him to the sterile room especially set up for the purpose of identifying the deceased. The room is part of the morgue and is divided in two by a glass panel. It was his daughter he saw on the table on the other side of the glass.

The weather had been stinking hot all week, up in the high 30s and it was still hot that Friday morning as I drove to work with the car radio on as usual. I am not easily roused to anger but I was furious as I listened to John Laws in disbelief. He was reading out the details of Anita Cobby's post-mortem. Goodness knows where he got it from because as a matter of course details of a post-mortem are never given out to the media. Apart from protecting the family's privacy, the report may also reveal details which the police need to use to catch whoever was responsible. It sounded to me as if Laws had a copy of the entire report. Joe Malouf had done the post-mortem and I knew there was no way Laws would have got the report from him. Someone had let us all down by leaking the details. Laws also mentioned he would be telling his listeners other details about the post-mortem on the following Monday. Not if I had anything to do with it.

Doreen told me how that morning, someone at the pre-school where she taught had told her, 'I'm disgusted at Derrick.' Doreen was surprised because the woman didn't even know me. She had been listening to the radio and she had told Doreen that she couldn't believe I would have let John Laws have a copy of the post-mortem report.

I got onto the Crown Solicitor, who is the head government solicitor, and the rest of the report was never read out by John Laws or by anyone. Laws claimed he had been acting in the public interest – while it was probably interesting to the public that is not the definition of it being in the 'public interest'. In my view it was just sensationalism.

The police continued their investigation, keeping me informed. Three weeks later, on 25 February, the police began making arrests for Anita

Cobby's murder and the case stopped being a coronial case and my role changed to that of a magistrate. It was a case the like of which I had never experienced before and thankfully would not see again.

Leslie Murphy, 22, and his brothers Michael, 33, and Gary, 28, and Michael Murdoch, 18, and John Travers, 18, were all charged with murder. The morning after their arrests, they were all making their first court appearance. They were appearing before me at Westmead. Strict security had been arranged, both to ensure the men didn't escape and also for their own protection. The murder of Anita Cobby had aroused public fury. Outside the court an angry crowd had gathered. Hospital staff had hung nooses from the light standards in the road that led to the court. There were shouts of 'hang them'. A dummy dressed in overalls had been hung from a noose on one of the hospital buildings and a handwritten sign read, 'Give Anita's killers a free operation (without anaesthetic)'. While she hadn't worked at Westmead, Anita Cobby was a nurse, someone who saved people's lives, and to the hospital staff she was one of their own.

As I walked through the door onto the bench that morning, there was more than the customary soft shuffle of chairs as everyone stood up for the magistrate. I looked down from the height of the bench and could see why – the courtroom was packed. There were no public benches as such at Westmead; the court had been furnished with plastic chairs. Every single seat was taken and the sound of all those chairs being pushed back was like rolling thunder.

To my right was the narrow dock and standing in a row in it were Travers, Murdoch and Leslie Murphy. The two older Murphy brothers had been captured together at the home of a relative in the suburb of Glenfield and had appeared briefly that morning at Blacktown Magistrates Court where they had been remanded in custody to appear before me. They were still on their way from Blacktown.

Travers, Murdoch and Leslie Murphy refused to look at me. Instead, I saw them glance around the court, their demeanor cocky. They appeared to not take any notice of what was going on, as if they were saying, 'So why are we here then?'

The three men were handcuffed and surrounded by armed officers of the Tactical Response Group who had escorted their truck to court that morning. Between the defendants and the public stood a wall of about 20 police.

The hearing that morning was more of a formality. The charges were read out. In a murder case there is a presumption against bail, meaning that the defendants have to prove that they should get it. The three of them did not even apply. Two minutes after they were led in, they were taken back out of the courtroom. The three were held in the court cells while, a few minutes later, Michael and Gary Murphy arrived from Blacktown.

Like the first three, Michael and Gary Murphy were just faces to me at the time. They looked no different to the usual type of people who came before the lower courts all the time – uncaring, unkempt and defiant. I did not really have much time to observe them. Again, the hearing was a brief formality and I remanded the two older Murphy brothers in custody. I adjourned the cases to 13 March and the five men were taken away to jail in police vans to more jeers from the crowd.

While the post-mortem report was not public I had, of course, seen a copy of it and I knew what had happened to Anita Cobby. She had been raped and her throat cut across to her right ear. What she had gone through in those last few minutes did not bear thinking about. I have been asked how I coped with such cases and after 32 years in the public service, I had trained myself not to be affected. That is not to say that sometimes it was very difficult; however, as a magistrate, a coroner or a judge, you cannot let emotion get in the way of dealing with someone otherwise there is no point in having a justice system. As far as I was concerned, those five men had to be treated no different to other people who came before me.

It was immediately obvious that the courtroom at Westmead was not big enough and did not have enough security to host the committal hearing for the five men. Their lawyers agreed and it was decided that we would move the venue to Glebe Coroners Court. The defendants had each applied to have the case against them heard separately, a request I had refused. We set the date at 23 June and got ready for the hearing.

Nobody could ever describe Parramatta Road as attractive. It runs from Sydney out to the west, past car yards and through what used to be busy shopping centres that have now been bypassed; the shops' awnings carrying the names of businesses that have closed. It's always busy and always looks grimy. The courthouse is on the stretch that runs through Glebe and Glebe Coroners Court, with its dark brick exterior, looks as industrial as its neighbours. You could drive past it and not know it was a court. Inside it is just as functional in appearance with three courtrooms, all exposed brick and timber panelling. On Monday, 23 June 1986, the largest courtroom of the three, Court One, was ready for the committal. One newspaper report described it more like a university lecture room than a courtroom which is a fair description.

The public anger directed at the five men continued and again we made sure security was tight. I had consulted with police and there were officers with tracker dogs checking nearby rooftops. Everyone entering the court had to go through a metal detector. There were about 20 police, six of them members of the Tactical Response Group, at the courthouse with about ten of them in the courtroom at any one time. We set up temporary gates at the rear of the building and had more police stationed there because of the number of photographers and TV crews straining for a shot of the defendants arriving and leaving the court in armoured trucks.

Sergeant Allan Ezzy, my prosecutor at Westmead, had moved with me to Glebe for the committal. He had been in the case from the beginning and knew it well. Allan was a very quiet, easygoing man who later became mayor of Holroyd, a council next to Parramatta in Sydney. We had discussed the sequence in which he would be calling the witnesses. It was usual for the officer in charge of the investigation to be called first. It was down to Detective Sergeant Ian Kennedy to outline the case. What happened to Anita Cobby when she stepped off the train at Blacktown and disappeared into the shadows on the walk home that hot summer's night is now well known throughout Australia, but when the details were revealed for the first time, it was to a silent courtroom.

Detective Kennedy had been sent to a cow field known as Boiler Paddock off Reen Road, Blacktown, after being told a woman's body had been found. He saw the naked body of a young woman lying face down. Her throat had been cut and she had marks on her back and inside her thighs. Her head was lying on her right arm, her legs were apart and her eyes were open. There was blood beneath her head and beneath her body.

'It was apparent that cows had interfered with the body by the amount of fresh manure in the immediate vicinity. Blood smears on her back I believe were made by cows licking the dried blood,' Sergeant Kennedy said in the sometimes stilted way that police speak in court.

Travers, Murdoch and the three Murphy brothers had come to court from their prison cells dressed in jeans, sandshoes and casual shirts. Just the same as when they first appeared before me at Westmead, they were smirking and smiling at each other, even winking. They looked around the courtroom as if they didn't have a care in the world and that whatever was happening had nothing to do with them. They showed no respect for anyone, including themselves.

There were howls of protest from their lawyers when Sergeant Ezzy sought to tender pictures of Ms Cobby's body which had been taken by the police photographer. The lawyers had all the usual arguments: the photographs were too explicit, too prejudicial to their clients, too emotive to be shown later to a jury. They were probably all those things but they were also factual and relevant. I allowed them in as evidence. The details of Joe Malouf's post-mortem report, the one that John Laws had tried to read out on the radio to his million or so listeners, emerged as the doctor gave his evidence in the witness box. Before he began, I noticed that Ms Cobby's mother, Grace Lynch, was led from the court having been warned by one of the police that it would be better if she didn't listen. Garry Lynch stayed in his seat. Malouf referred to the photographs as he gave his evidence.

Anita Cobby had died from loss of blood after her head had been almost severed from her neck. In Malouf's estimation, she had been alive when her throat had been cut and she would have taken about two minutes to die. There were three major cuts and three minor cuts. One of them had completely destroyed all tissues, muscles, nerves, arteries and veins. There were cuts on her legs consistent with being dragged through the barbed wire fence into the paddock. She had been raped and her anus was cut. She had numerous bruises on her body and head including one around her right eye that was probably caused by a 'blow of considerable force' with either a foot or a fist. When she tried to defend herself by lifting her left hand to her throat, her hand had been sliced so hard that two of her fingers had been opened to the bone.

It does not take having children of your own to really feel for someone who has lost a son or a daughter; however, you cannot know what it is like unless you have experienced it yourself. Every day I watched Anita Cobby's mother and father in court. They handled themselves with dignity and pride throughout, displaying an inner strength that most of us do not know we possess until we need it. They had such strength of character that they went on to become leading members of the Homicide Victims Support Group which was set up at Glebe under one of the grief counsellors, Martha Jabour.

The police case continued to unfold in court. The first of the five men picked up by police had been John Travers, Michael Murdoch and Les Murphy. They had been charged with the theft of the car police believed had been used in the abduction of Anita Cobby – all of them had denied having anything to do with her abduction or murder. Murdoch and Murphy had been given police bail but Travers had been kept locked up at Blacktown police station because police wanted to talk to him about a number of sexual assaults in the area. It was then the homicide detectives got their breakthrough – Travers asked for a family friend to be contacted. He wanted her to know that he was OK and he wanted her to bring him some cigarettes. When a detective rang her, she burst into tears and said she had been thinking about calling the police herself. She agreed to meet with a detective and told him how she believed Travers was capable of committing a murder like that of Anita Cobby. She told police that he had told her he had been involved in a vicious homosexual rape and the rape of a girl, both interstate, and in each attack he had used a knife.

The woman was placed into Witness Protection for her safety and I had agreed with the prosecution that she not be identified. In court, I ruled that she be called Miss X. The pseudonym had not been chosen because it sounded dramatic, it was just plain and simple. It was also a bit silly to give her a false name because everyone seemed to know who she was, including the five defendants she was being protected from, and the media. However, she had to be given as much anonymity as we could manage.

On the Wednesday of the second week of the committal hearing, it was her turn to give evidence to a packed court. She was a former heroin addict who was then on the methadone program and she looked more than slightly nervous as she appeared in the witness box. She told her story.

Miss X said she had agreed to help police before she visited Travers at the police station. At the station, Travers was in the ground floor cell block where she spoke to him through a small grille. He had told her the police were trying to pin a murder on him. At one stage during their 25 minute talk, she had taken one of his hands and put it up against her face as tears rolled down her cheeks. She told us that Travers had also been crying. 'I asked if he had done it. He replied yes,' she told the court.

You could have heard a pin drop in that courtroom.

Miss X said she had asked Travers if there was anything she could do to help him and he told her to go back to his house and get the knife with the brown wooden handle out of the kitchen drawer because that was the one he had used to kill Anita Cobby. He told her they had burned Ms Cobby's clothes in an incinerator in the back garden and got rid of the ashes at the tip.

She had agreed to be wired with a tape recorder and went back down to the cells to talk to Travers. Once again, Travers discussed the murder with her and she asked him if he had sex with Anita Cobby. On the tape he said yes, they all had.

As she gave her evidence in court, the five men in the dock mouthed obscenities at her. When she stepped down from the witness box having completed her evidence, it was time for me to call an adjournment. She was led out of the witness box and as the defendants all stood to leave the dock, Travers lunged at her, growling, 'You bitch, you fuckin' bitch, I'll get you.' A couple of police officers had seen what was going to happen and moved in front of her. She was quickly surrounded by other officers.

During the court hearing, there were times I would look at the three Murphy brothers sitting there with their friends in the dock and wonder how people came to such violence. However, I couldn't allow myself to start imagining what had turned them into a family who could do this or how you would feel if it was your three sons. In this case, as in all the others that came before me, I was only concerned with the evidence that I had heard – and the evidence was overwhelming.

On 1 July 1986, I committed Travers, Murdoch and Michael and Leslie Murphy to stand trial for kidnapping, sexual assault, robbery and murder. I would have dealt with Gary Murphy at the same time but his lawyer had asked for an adjournment. The lawyer couldn't get to court that afternoon to make his submissions because he had to go to Sydney Airport to meet a family member who was flying in from overseas. I put off the decision on Gary Murphy until the next morning.

When the lawyer did make his submissions on behalf of Gary Murphy, I must admit that I did think his arguments were a bit far fetched but I couldn't blame him for doing his best for his client. The lawyer conceded that Gary Murphy had taken part in the abduction and robbery of Ms Cobby but he said his client was not involved in her death or sexual assault. He said that on that night, Gary had heard his brother Michael tell John Travers to 'go and do your thing' and it was only with hindsight that he realised 'do your thing' meant to kill her.

Fair enough, that's the sort of points defence lawyers are supposed to make. The lawyer then tried to argue that the detectives had not complied with the Miranda warning when they spoke to Gary Murphy. The lawyer was from America or Canada and I did wonder what country he thought he was in that morning – the Miranda warning is given in the US courts but not in Australia. The wording of it doesn't differ all that much from Australian law; however, it is the timing of the warning that is crucial. Police have to warn the suspect the moment they decide to charge them. It means they can talk to them and ask them questions before they have to warn them. Then they have to say, 'You are not obliged to say anything unless you wish to do so. Anything you say will be taken down and may later be used in evidence. Do you understand that?' (The wording has changed slightly since 1986 but it is basically the same.)

In America, police have to caution the suspect at the moment they arrest them. Anyone who watches the American cop shows will be able to conjure up the scene – the officer usually has the person on the ground, cuffing them behind their back and telling them, 'You are under arrest ... I have to warn you that ...'

I found that the Australian police had complied with the law in this country and said it was obvious that Gary Murphy knew Travers was going to kill Anita Cobby and was well aware of the meaning of 'do your thing'. He had done nothing to prevent Travers carrying that out. I also committed him to stand trial.

That afternoon I felt no satisfaction that those five men were to stand trial. What I felt was the sense of accomplishment that you get when you finish an involved matter. There was the relief that it was all over.

I moved back to Westmead where the case had a sequel before me later that month. I committed for trial two women charged with being accessories after the fact of Anita Cobby's murder and harbouring Michael Murphy.

If the sadness that can become people's lives ever got to you, you couldn't be a magistrate or a coroner. Take Charla Henry.

CHAPTER 3

The Deputy

THE PRINCES HIGHWAY that runs south out of Sydney is the main thoroughfare to Wollongong, meandering on down the south coast around to Melbourne. In Room 11 of the Waterfront Motel on the highway at Sylvania, one of the last suburbs out of Sydney before you reach the open road, ambulance officers answering a triple-o emergency call found a young girl lying in the bed, naked but for a sheet. It was the early hours of the morning, about 3 a.m., the loneliest time of the night I always think, when even the places the night people go are closed, the streets are deserted and most people are asleep. The girl's friend, a 19-year-old prostitute called Toni, was bent over her. She had been desperately doing mouth to mouth resuscitation for 30 minutes trying to rouse her but the girl lay cold, her hands and face turning purple. The paramedics took over the resuscitation when they arrived but they couldn't save her. Charla Henry died on 30 May 1991 from massive amounts of alcohol and drugs in her little body. The official cause was alcohol toxicity and acute narcotism. She was 12 years old.

When I was on the Parents and Citizens Committee at Megan's high school, there was a move afoot for kids once they hit 12 to be able to block the school from telling their parents about certain things that had occurred to them at school. That included trouble they got into and help they had, such as counselling. I spoke up vigorously against it. Twelve year olds, no matter how old they might dress or how sophisticated they may pretend to be, are just babies. Charla Henry was someone's baby. How had she died such a sad death so alone in the world?

Her death was reported to me in May 1991 as a coroner's death and I had to sign the form to order a post-mortem to be carried out. The form went to the pathologist and he had the authority to have whatever tests he felt necessary performed. With her body on the stainless steel slab, her liver, her stomach and its contents, a blood sample, bile and the parts of her skin where there were puncture marks were all removed and sent for chemical analysis. Another blood sample was taken and tested for alcohol. Tests were performed on her brain tissue. Swabs and smears were taken from her mouth, rectum and vagina. This was not how a little girl should end up.

The tests came back to say she had been poisoned by alcohol and drugs. The detectives came to talk to me about their investigation and told me the information they had. There was the woman who had been trying to save her life, who said she had no fixed address, a motel room that had been booked at 4 p.m. on 29 May by a man by the name of 'Evans' and in the motel room, a pizza delivery docket with a mobile phone number written on it. The owner of the phone said he had sold the phone to an 'unknown person'.

Charla's 14-year-old sister told the police that Charla had been hanging around with a man called Peter who went by the nickname of 'Taxi'. The sister said that she had asked Taxi if he knew how old Charla was, and he had said, 'Yeah, 12.'

Toni said she and Charla had been out with this Peter since 7.30 p.m. on Tuesday, 28 May on what eventually turned into the 36-hour drink and drugs binge that killed Charla. Police had tracked the group back and discovered they had spent the night before Charla's death at a Redfern motel. The front office manager at the hotel was able to give police the registration number of a car; it was registered to a company the nominee of which was the man called Peter. Police traced the green Holden Camira station sedan to a street in Sydenham where neighbours said it had been parked since 30 May and belonged to no one local. The car was towed to Miranda police station to be photographed and fingerprinted. Inside the car was Charla's schoolbag. Peter had also been using the mobile phone with the number on the pizza delivery docket.

The police weren't in a position to charge this Peter with anything so while there were no charges pending, it remained a coronial matter. The detectives asked me to hold an inquest while their investigations were stalled.

Who was Charla Henry? She was a striking girl with long dark curly hair whose mother was a Maori. The mother and her three daughters lived in a terrace house in inner-city Enmore. Charla's mother told police she had first met Toni when Charla had brought her home about a week before Charla was found dead. Toni had stayed there a few days but Charla's mother said she had not wanted Toni in her house and had asked her to leave. She last saw her daughter when Charla left the house on the evening of 28 May.

Charla went to Marrickville High School where she seemed to be popular with her classmates, telling them she wanted to be a dancer and a model. Teachers had been concerned about her welfare for some months before she died.

A couple of weeks after Charla's death, two 16-year-old girls were reported missing to Marrickville police station. Marrickville is the closest station to Enmore. Police tracked the girls to a Cairns motel where they were staying with Peter. The girls said they were there of their own free will. Peter had made no sexual advances to them and had paid for everything since they left Sydney, including clothes and two bags of marijuana. They said Peter had told them about a 12-year-old girl who had died; they said they had also met Toni.

The police set about tracking down Toni to re-interview her. They found her on the Gold Coast. She told them she had been too afraid to tell them the truth of what had happened when they had first spoken to her the day of Charla's death. Now, she said, she would tell them the real story.

Toni had been living in Marrickville and had bumped into Charla on 16 May in the local McDonalds when it was busy and she had sat down next to her. The girls arranged to meet the next day at a local park. They spoke a few times over the phone and met up again on 24 May. Toni spent the next four days at Charla's house and on 28 May 'just after *Sale of the Century* was over' the two of them went out.

They met Peter and a friend of his outside Marrickville McDonalds. The four of them went to Players nightclub in Bondi Junction where they had dinner in the restaurant of the club and then went upstairs to the disco with a few friends of Peter's, including a short fat man who, Toni said, drove a gold Porsche and was 'filthy rich'.

Peter was buying and the girls were drinking. Charla was drinking Kamikazis, a cocktail of tequila, Sambucca and Galliano. Toni said the barman told her that $200 had been spent on those cocktails, and at $15 each that meant Charla must have had about 13. She was drinking until 3 a.m.

The group moved on to the Tabu nightclub in Kings Cross, where Toni said she had stayed in the car while the other three went inside to 'score some cocaine'. The four of them decided to find a motel where they could spend a few hours and ended up in Room 36 at the San Pedro Motel in Redfern. The two men went to get more cocaine.

They returned to find Carla on the bed dozing and Toni watching cartoons on TV. From his pocket, Peter pulled out a little plastic sachet and tipped the powder out on the desk next to the TV. The powder was yellow, not white, and Toni said she told them it wasn't cocaine. Peter's friend rolled up a $100 note and snorted it anyway. Peter encouraged Charla to have some.

'Don't have any, it is a funny colour,' said Toni.

'Shut up and mind your own business,' she was told by Peter.

Charla had three lines of the powder. It wasn't cocaine, it was morphine.

Toni took a shower and when she got out, Charla was lying on the single bed looking very sick. She handed Peter a towel and he turned the 12-year-old girl on her side where she spewed out green vomit. Her eyes were rolling back in her head. Toni wanted to take her to a doctor but Peter said she would be OK. He borrowed Toni's glasses, closed the arms and stuck the frame into Charla's mouth to clear her air passages.

'She's still breathing, she'll be alright,' he said. Twenty minutes later he was on his mobile, asking a friend to, 'Bring me a fit and some salt.' By a fit, he had meant a needle and syringe. When the friend dropped them off, Peter put some salt and water on a plastic spoon and mixed it up. He filtered the salt and water through a cigarette filter into the syringe. Charla was still lying on the bed, her eyes half open and breathing slowly. Peter injected the contents of the syringe into a vein on the inside of one of her arms. She showed no reaction at all.

They stayed at the motel until around lunchtime with Charla still not moving on the bed. They never called a doctor. When they left, Peter put Charla over his shoulder and carried her to the car park where they had called a friend to meet them.

Toni said they drove to the house of the man who owned the mobile phone – and who had obviously lied to police about selling it to an 'unknown person'. He gave Peter some money. Peter and Toni drove with the dying Charla to the Waterfront Motel at Sylvania.

With an unconscious 12-year-old girl lying in the bed, they ordered a pizza, drinks and garlic bread. Toni watched a movie on TV. When she next checked her new friend, Charla was cold, green phlegm coming from her mouth. Peter assured her that Charla would be OK. She and Peter fell asleep.

At 2 or 3 a.m., Toni was woken by Charla making a noise. She walked over to her and felt her pulse. It was very faint. She woke Peter and he felt Charla's pulse.

'I have to go,' he said. 'Do not tell them I was here. You have never seen me.' With that he walked out of the room and Toni dialled triple-o.

Could Charla have been saved if her new 'friends' had sought medical help once they saw that she was ill? I felt that she could have been. At the close of the inquest, I referred the case to the NSW Director of Public Prosecutions, finding there was a *prima facie* case against Peter for criminally causing her death – only I couldn't name him. Sometimes the law is an ass. When you find a *prima facie* case during an inquest, the law prevents you from naming the person involved, even though everyone involved knows who it is.

What happened to Charla Henry and the way she was allowed to live and die was disgraceful. Of course kids want to grow up too quickly but it is a sad indictment on family life and society that a lot of kids just don't have a childhood. Charla's mother told me that her daughter had run away twice before and she couldn't control her when Charla wanted to stay out late at night, and I accepted that. I think that a lack of discipline is a major problem. I'm not talking about a cane or a strap, but discipline means setting limits and Charla Henry had no limits. That's what really killed her.

THE CORONER

Three years before I investigated Charla's death in June 1991, I had become the first Deputy State Coroner for New South Wales.

The work of the coroner had gone through a revolution in 1988 when the NSW government had created a State Coroner system which pulled together the until then largely uncoordinated coronial system. The NSW Attorney-General John Dowd, who is now a NSW Supreme Court judge, decided it was time to follow Victoria's lead, where they had appointed Hal Hallenstein to the position of the country's first State Coroner. Kevin Waller was the obvious choice to take on the job in New South Wales. He had been Sydney's youngest City Coroner at the age of 38 and had spent 18 years in that job. He had also written the definitive book on coronial procedure and law, *Coronial Law and Practice in New South Wales*.

I liked and admired Kevin, we had always got on marvellously well and I decided to apply to be his deputy. At the time I was enjoying being the coroner at Westmead, it was a job in which I felt I could make a difference. On Monday, 21 August 1988, the government appointed Kevin as the first NSW State Coroner and I was appointed the first NSW Deputy State Coroner.

On that day the two of us moved permanently to Glebe Coroners Court on Parramatta Road. The city morgue was downstairs and the smell of formaldehyde and bodies would permeate through the air-conditioning system into the main courtroom. Death would become our home ground.

Neither of us are morbid or gruesome although, unlike me, Kevin would watch some autopsies. He found it interesting to see the human anatomy exposed. I could do without it. Both of us had long experience as coroners and we both felt that we could provide answers. We were certainly given the power to do so.

A new set of legislation meant it was routine that all sudden, violent or mysterious deaths were reported directly to the Office of the State Coroner as were deaths in prison or in police custody, deaths under anaesthetic and in a mental hospital. Basically the only type of death which was not notified to us was one where a person had seen a doctor within three months prior to death and the doctor was prepared to issue a death certificate stating it was a natural cause death and there was nothing suspicious about it. The coroner was in charge of investigating all the others and had the final say in how the police investigation was done. We could even overrule the police commissioner if we felt investigations were inadequate. We reported only to the Attorney-General.

We also had to give permission for organ transplants to take place, because most donors die due to accidents. It meant we got calls at any time of the day or night but that was all part of the job.

Kevin and I felt the weight of history on our shoulders. The office of coroner is one of the oldest known in law, established in England over 1100 years ago. It spread with the British Empire. The word 'coroner' comes from the French 'corune', meaning 'crown' and the first coroners were appointed by the King. Their thirteenth century statute said, 'The coroner should go to the place where any person is slain or suddenly dead ... and should enquire into the manner of killing and all circumstances that occasioned the party's death.' That sounds pretty much like the work we were still doing hundreds of years later.

The government gave us extra staff at Glebe. We had one grief counsellor but as things developed, the system became more professional and the numbers increased to three. They were employed by the Health Department and could call on others to help if and as they needed them – which they were going to later in 1988. There were times when after a case, or even during a case, I would suggest that the grief counsellors speak to family members. When we moved to Glebe some building work was given the go ahead to give us more space but, like renovating your house, it always takes longer than you plan. It is only since I retired that all of the building work has finished and they have achieved what they set out to do. Kevin and I were in neighbouring offices with the library between us. Our doors opened onto the corridor directly behind the courtrooms. On the other side of the corridor were the doors up onto the bench in the courts. Each office had a glass wall which looked into the internal courtyard; but as it happened the only way you could set the offices up was with the desk in front of the window and the view at your back! You could smoke inside buildings in those days; I used to smoke about ten a day, not too many I thought back then.

If Kevin and I wanted to get to the courtyard for a bit of fresh air, our route took us along the corridor and round the corner past the laboratories of the forensic scientists in their white coats under the charge of Godfrey

Oettle, Gus to his friends. Gus had been head of the Division of Forensic Medicine since 1960. He had retired before Kevin and I were given our new posts but try keeping Gus and a body apart! He loved his work, even after more than 11,000 autopsies. He was still acting in charge of the forensic section and when he later retired properly, we still used him to do a lot of contract work. When we needed post-mortems done at country hospitals, we would ring Gus. He was once at Deniliquin where he had completed an autopsy and we rang him about a suspicious death at White Cliffs. With no hesitation, he jumped in his car and off he went. It didn't matter to him that he had to drive from one end of the state to the other.

Not only did I have the utmost respect for Gus, he was highly respected all over the world. He had been nominated by the federal government to join an Australian team to examine the remains of bodies dumped in the mass war graves in the Ukraine. He was a man you would rather have on your side than against you, as was John Hilton.

John replaced Gus. He moved across the country from Perth where he had been the chief forensic pathologist to take over as head of the newly-formed Office of the NSW Institute of Forensic Medicine two years after the Office of State Coroner was formed. John Hilton presented as your archetypal dour Scotsman with a broad brogue but beneath the exterior, he was a great bloke and I liked working with him a lot.

It is incredible what forensic scientists can uncover but I dealt with them in the same way I dealt with pathologists; I was happy to leave them well alone with their work. They were the experts. I did not want to watch them dealing with body parts. It was enough for me that they would tell me what they had found. They generally only looked at matters referred to them by the coroner's office, including still births. What I would have liked was to have had one big combined body of forensic experts covering all the coroners' and police work including ballistics work in the state. It would streamline the work. They already had such an organisation in Victoria with the Victorian Institute of Forensic Medicine. It was often talked about in New South Wales but it still remains a dream.

Kevin was easy to work with. He was unflappable, knowledgeable and down to earth. He used to bring his own sandwiches to court every day in his briefcase. I wasn't a big eater of lunch and if I needed it, I would go out to the small but excellent homely canteen just inside the entrance to the court which was run by the Catholic Women's Association. It was run for years by Phyllis. Doreen and I still exchange cards with Phyllis every Christmas.

Kevin was always willing to offer advice if you sought it. In some ways we are alike, both family men who had come up through the old petty sessions system. At the start, Kevin and I discussed how we were going to approach this new job. His attitude was that he was there until he retired and he wasn't going to hold back if there was something that needed to be said to benefit the community. He was just going to go ahead and say it, which he certainly did. I agreed wholeheartedly with his way of doing things and it was a tradition I carried on when I became the State Coroner myself, but that is a story for a few years later.

We liked to learn how other coroners worked. Visiting coroners looked us up when they were in Australia and when we were overseas we often did the same, swapping war stories. What we did have in common with coroners the world over was a lack of funds; we could always do with more. I was in Dallas, Texas visiting my son John not long after being appointed Deputy State Coroner and called into Parklands Hospital. The medical examiner – as they call coroners there – had just received a body. A man had woken up to find someone climbing through his bedroom window at 3 a.m. and shot him dead. It turned out to be his son who had forgotten his key. I asked the medical examiner what would happen to him and he said that the father had suffered enough. In Australia he would have been charged.

Like many people, I used to watch Jack Klugman as Quincy, the TV coroner. Unlike most law and order series, I found it wasn't too sensational and bore some semblance to reality. The character was based on the man who was probably the most famous coroner in the world, Professor Tom Noguchi. As medical examiner with the County of Los Angeles for over 20 years since 1961, he became known as 'coroner to the stars'. It was Noguchi who pronounced that Marilyn Monroe had probably committed suicide when her body landed in his morgue a year after he took up the post. He found that actor William Holden had so much alcohol in his system that his blood would not clot when he cut himself in a drunken fall. He investigated the death of Natalie Wood after she fell into the ocean from a boat off Catalina Island and found the actress had been too drunk to swim.

When he was in Australia for the twelfth triennial conference of the International Association of Forensic Sciences he contacted our office in

Sydney and came to see us. He and I had a great old talk. Although his 'war stories' had a cast of characters more famous than mine, at the end of the day our jobs were not that different.

It was Kevin's decision which cases he took on and which ones I did, and we certainly didn't quibble if he heard the more prominent cases. As State Coroner, if it was a high-profile or notorious case, he accepted the responsibility to investigate it. Because there hadn't been an office like this before, we could mould it how we saw fit. At the end of 12 months in the job, four disasters would test us and demonstrate just how steep our learning curve was.

At 4.50 a.m. on Sunday, 17 September 1989, the fire alarm outside the Down Under Hostel in Kings Cross began to ring. Inside were 51 guests, mostly young backpackers, sleeping in dormitories. There was no internal alarm and no one on duty during the night. The fire, which began in the foyer, quickly spread up the staircase and through the building, helped by the fact that every fire door had been jammed open. Six of the backpackers were killed, choked by carbon monoxide and thick black smoke.

The building was already well known to Kevin. It had a sordid, seedy history. It had previously been the Kingsdore Motel which was really a brothel and Kevin had conducted the committal of two men who had beaten a 17-year-old to death after he ripped them off in a heroin deal. The young man had been tortured on the rack in the bondage room at the brothel. He was found with a whisky bottle tied to his penis.

It used to be that a coroner was required to go and view every body where it had been found before it could be moved. We didn't need to go to those lengths but we did feel that we should go to the scene of public disasters where there were multiple deaths. It gave us a better perspective when inquiring into what went wrong. This was the first such scene Kevin had attended while I stayed back at the office assisting in whatever way I could.

When he got back from the scene, I went into his office and we discussed what was to be done. Kevin and I had soon slipped into an easy relationship where we would sit down and talk about our cases, working on the assumption that two heads are better than one.

In this case there was a lot of work to do and because most of the hostel guests were from overseas, and many wanted to return quickly after such an experience, we had to act quickly.

While Kevin was busy working with the police and the coronial staff to get the inquest started as soon as possible, I witnessed one of the most bizarre episodes in my career ...

On the Monday, the day after the Down Under fire, I began the committal hearing into three charges of murder and one of attempted murder against a man called Tim Anderson. Two Sydney council workers and a police officer had died when a bomb planted in a garbage bin exploded outside Sydney's Hilton Hotel at 12.40 a.m. on 13 February 1978, while the Commonwealth Heads of Government Meeting (CHOGM) was being held there.

By the time Tim Anderson appeared before me, he had been through one committal, two District Court trials, appeals to the Court of Criminal Appeal and the High Court, an inquest by another coroner into the Hilton deaths and an inquiry under Section 475 of the *Crimes Act* (such an inquiry was presided over by a judge and was the end of the road for an appeal). Anderson and two others had been pardoned on conspiracy to murder charges and had been given ex-gratia payments of $100,000 each. He had spent seven years in jail – none of it over the Hilton bombing deaths. All those hearings (apart from the inquest) involved the so-called Yagoona conspiracy, the conspiracy to bomb the home of Robert Cameron, the leader of the National Alliance Party and a former Nazi Party member. Of course, Anderson was so well known and the Hilton bombing was so notorious that this committal was always going to be a media circus.

The prosecution case was that Anderson had masterminded the bombing while he was a leading Australian member of the Ananda Marga sect. The intention was to deliver a sharp message to the Indian Prime Minister, Moraji Desai, who was staying at the Hilton as part of CHOGM. It was claimed the Sydney branch of the Ananda Marga, run out of a boarding house in Newtown, wanted to force Desai to release their leader, Baba, from an Indian jail.

Although the bombing had happened over ten years earlier, the case had been reopened after Raymond Denning, then one of Australia's most notorious criminals, told police that Anderson had allegedly confessed to him while they were both in jail (Anderson for the Yagoona conspiracy). He claimed that he and Anderson had some conversations over the 'big white telephone', a means of communication by which prisoners emptied their toilets and talked through the pipes, and Anderson told him he had been involved in the bombing. The confession was enough to dig out the long-lost file and begin a re-investigation of the Hilton bombing and a task force was set up.

Before arresting Anderson in May 1989, homicide detectives with the task force had been in to check out some details with Kevin as the deaths had been the subject of an inquest several years earlier. They also wanted to show him a copy of Denning's statement and appraise him of the evidence which they then had. Kevin had told them that he believed that *prima facie*, they had evidence of motive, opportunity and a confession. It was all they needed to charge Anderson. It was the flimsiest of evidence but if you believed Denning, then Anderson had a case to answer. The officer in charge of the task force, the wily Aarne Tees, later recalled an old police maxim: 'One old detective used to say, "When you haven't got much, pull them in. The brief will only get better".'

This case, that proved true when the day after Anderson was charged, a man living in Brisbane called Evan Pederick stepped forward and said that he had been the one to plant the bomb on behalf of the Ananda Marga and on the specific orders of Tim Anderson.

Earlier, in July 1989, I had committed Pederick to stand trial charged with conspiracy to murder and three counts of murder. Unlike Anderson, he didn't contest the committal and require evidence to be called so it was what we call a paper committal when the police brief of evidence is tendered without objection. That was not the case with Anderson.

It was against this background that I was hearing the committal proceedings against Anderson. Soon it was the turn of Denning, one of the star witnesses, to take his turn in the witness box. Denning had already said he was frightened of recriminations and was reluctant to give evidence. He certainly had made himself a lot of enemies over the years. He was a lifelong criminal who had been a prison right's agitator during his time in nine maximum-security prisons. He had taunted police during three well-publicised escapes, the last of which had ended over a year earlier when he was captured with another 'most-wanted' man, Russell 'Mad Dog' Cox.

The police had been searching all bags and screening everyone entering the court while Denning was in the witness box. One fellow had turned up with a white plastic supermarket bag containing a large raw bone with scraps of meat and blood still clinging to it. He told the police it was 'to give to my dog for his dinner'. They let him take it into court. We were in the middle of hearing Denning's evidence when suddenly this fellow jumped up from the public benches and rushed towards the bar table. He pulled out the bone and threw it down, shouting at Denning, 'Here's your dinner, you dog.' The man was quickly surrounded by police who hustled him out of the courtroom, along with his bone. The story quickly became a legend in Sydney's jails. The crims loved it. Denning had been one of their heroes but now he had committed the ultimate sin in their world and become a prison informer, a 'dog' in crim-speak.

I could have had the man up for contempt of court for his antics but it was more trouble than it was worth. It did give Denning a fright, though. As the police removed the man from court, Denning said he wanted to get out of there. It was getting late in the afternoon so I adjourned the court until the next morning to allow everything to calm down. Denning was most reluctant to come back unless he could be assured that nothing like that would happen again. Security was stepped up to make sure it didn't.

On the Thursday of that week – day four of the Hilton committal – in another court Kevin started the inquest into the Down Under Hostel fire. It was a huge task. In the one day he heard 31 witnesses, beginning early in the morning and ending late in the day. It has been said that the main requirement for the job of coroner is sympathy and this is definitely correct. Dealing with the dead is the easy part of the job; it is helping the bereaved that is the hardest part. It is the most draining but, in many ways, one of the most satisfying areas of the job. The main thing the families are looking for is that the matter has been thoroughly investigated and I would say that 99.9 per cent of the time, a family leaves the inquest feeling satisfied. I always felt it important to speak directly to them in the courtroom, to make sure they understand what is happening.

In the case of the Down Under Hostel fire, there were families who, in one night, had their worlds ripped apart and if anything could make it worse, it had happened away from their homes, at the opposite side of the world in a place which was alien to them. The grief counsellors did a tremendous job working with these families by listening to them and helping them deal with what had happened as best they could.

After hearing from the witnesses to the fire, Kevin adjourned the inquest to allow the investigations to continue. When he later handed down his findings, he did not mince his words. He criticised the management, the owners, Sydney City Council and South Sydney Council for doing nothing about the shortcomings of the hostel. A postscript to Kevin's inquiry into the fire was that in August 1990, a pyromaniac called Gregory Brown was arrested for starting a fire in Sydney's Matthew Talbot Hostel, admitting he lit the fire at the Down Under Hostel. Brown, who was from Adelaide, had been fascinated by fire from an early age and, as he put it, got off on the destruction and the power of fires. He was convicted of manslaughter and not murder because of diminished responsibility caused by brain damage blamed on alcohol and was jailed for eight years.

I committed Tim Anderson to stand trial at the NSW Supreme Court. My involvement was over but a year later, there was a blaze of publicity when he was convicted. He subsequently appealed and his convictions were overturned by the NSW Court of Criminal Appeal. Pederick served time in jail and I have heard he is now living in Perth where he is studying to become a priest.

Denning was released from jail and went into Witness Protection but it wasn't long before he was back at Glebe – this time in a body bag. No amount of protection could save him from himself. He died from a heroin overdose and was found lying in bed next to his girlfriend. The overdose was probably self-inflicted but while there was no evidence he had been given a 'hot shot' there are still those who believe he had been killed by one of the many enemies he had made over the years.

A month after the Down Under Hostel fire, another major tragedy shook the state. Around 4 a.m. on 20 October 1989 on the Pacific Highway, 23 kilometres north of Grafton, while 45 passengers slept on their bus travelling north, a semi-trailer driving south from Brisbane slewed across the road and smashed into the bus. The driver of the semi-trailer was killed as were 19 passengers. Five of those killed were members of the same family. It was the worst road accident in Australia's history.

Neither Kevin nor I went to the scene, a decision he later regretted as he was being asked advice on questions like where bodies should be taken without knowing first-hand what was happening. We decided the bodies, including that of the driver of the semi-trailer, should all be brought back to Glebe morgue.

It was discovered that the truck driver had an incredible amount of the drug ephedrine in his blood – 80 times in excess of the normal therapeutic level. Ephedrine works like amphetamines, causing insomnia, and it has become known as the 'truck driver's friend' because it keeps them awake on the long distances they have to travel. It also causes hallucinations so it can cause the drivers to see phantom vehicles coming towards them. Added to that, this truck driver had a terrible driving record with 27 driving offences over the previous seven years, including numerous speeding tickets and unsafe tyres. His trailer was unregistered, uninsured and had three bald tyres at the time of the crash. When all of that was known, there was really no question as to the cause of the crash.

Back then, Doreen and I always spent Christmas in Forbes at Doreen's mother's place on the farm a couple of miles outside town. The kids, John and Megan, usually joined us. That year was no different and we were getting ready to go at the end of the week before Christmas when there was another bus crash and it was even worse than the Grafton crash. Kevin and I couldn't believe it.

It was around that same time in the morning, 3.30 a.m., on 22 December 1989, and again on the Pacific Highway. This time it was 15 kilometres north of Kempsey at Clybucca where two coaches smashed into each other. This time Kevin flew to the scene in a plane chartered by the state government. The buses, one from McCafferty's, the other a Trans City Tours bus, were full and 35 people were killed. It was a record number of fatalities, far outstripping the previous one at Grafton. Imagine, those people all going somewhere to see loved ones for Christmas, just as we were about to do, and then in a split second their lives and those of their families were turned upside down.

I stayed in the office to accept the bodies, which were again all brought back to Glebe morgue for post-mortem examination. We found that only refrigerated trucks were big enough to transport the number of bodies. There was a lot to organise and much communication between what was happening at Clybucca and the office. The telephones were busy with calls from the police, relatives of the deceased and from the media. Down in the morgue, the bodies were kept refrigerated in body bags while police contacted the relatives and arranged for them to come to Sydney for formal identification. Once they had been identified, I signed the forms to permit post-mortems to be carried out. We had about six pathologists at Glebe and the morgue was well equipped enough to allow all of them to work at the same time. We had most of the bodies identified and examined by 25 December. It was a very bleak Christmas that year.

Ephedrine was also involved in the Kempsey bus crash but did not appear to be a contributing factor. Investigations showed that the McCafferty bus had failed to negotiate a slight left-hand bend in the road, instead going straight ahead into the path of the Trans City Tours coach. The McCafferty driver had not put on his brakes and his headlights were still on high beam, leading Kevin to the conclusion that he must have fallen asleep at the wheel. Analysis showed he had taken a moderate amount of ephedrine shortly before the crash indicating he had probably been feeling tired.

In both the Grafton and the Kempsey crashes, Kevin was able to go one step further – what would have prevented the crash? Part of the job of a coroner is to consider the issues raised by such tragedies and to make recommendations directed at reducing similar disasters. Kevin recommended that ephedrine be added to the list of drugs banned under the *Motor Traffic Act*, making it an offence to drive under the influence of ephedrine. He also recommended that the NSW and federal governments get together to plan and build a dual highway between Newcastle and Brisbane to avoid head-on smashes. Kevin said that despite the amount of traffic using the Pacific Highway and its importance as a major route, it was too narrow, had too many bends and was unforgiving to any driver who

THE DEPUTY

made a mistake. The fact that it had been the site of the two worst traffic accidents in the country's history was testimony to how urgently the roadwork was needed.

The governments weren't listening. The press officer for one minister labelled Kevin, off the record, a 'bumbling fool'. What ignorance, how rude and how wrong. It was one of Kevin's biggest regrets that when he retired in 1992, his recommendation to upgrade the Pacific Highway had still not been acted on.

That Christmas, Doreen and I managed to get up to Forbes where we stayed on when Megan drove back to Sydney. On 28 December at about 11 a.m. Megan called us. 'There's been an earthquake at Newcastle, Dad.'

It was just six days after the Kempsey bus crash. An earthquake? I got on the phone to Kevin who had been sitting in his office at Glebe when his chair had taken off across the room as the earth shook as far south as Sydney. I told him I was coming straight back. Doreen and I packed quickly and jumped in the car. During the five-hour drive we had the radio on to keep up to date with what was happening.

The earthquake, which measured 5.6 on the Richter scale, had happened at 10.27 a.m. At the Newcastle Workers' Club, one of the walls had fallen onto the concrete slab that made up the floor, which had in turn collapsed under the impact. Five bodies were found among the rubble. Three people were killed in the suburb of Beaumont where shop awnings had crashed down and walls had collapsed. Patients had been evacuated from the Royal Newcastle Hospital onto the lawn overlooking the ocean. Some of the other of the city's major buildings had been badly damaged. Doctors were warning people in the area to take it easy on the roads because they just didn't have the facilities to look after any more cases if there was an emergency. If any other major accidents had happened, I really don't know how we would have coped.

The day after the earthquake, Kevin and I drove up to Newcastle with Chris Surplice from the Coronial Investigation Unit and Lynelle Osburn-Gard, who was one of the unit's grief counsellors. We arrived to find the whole city centre blocked off for safety. There was an eerie feel; it was like a ghost town. As well as the danger posed by the unstable buildings, there was a fear of an aftershock of almost equal severity to that of the original quake. The NSW Premier Nick Greiner was also there so we joined his entourage before being briefed separately.

A lot of the structural damage to buildings was not immediately obvious, apart from the site where the Workers' Club had stood. It was a scene of devastation. It was like looking at a scene in a movie. We were only allowed onto one part of the site, where the car park had been, because the site was still unsafe. There were still a lot of rescue people around and what struck me was the bravery of the rescue workers who were willing to go back in again and again to the ruin of the club to see if anyone else could be saved.

You would never think of an earthquake being strong enough to cause damage in Australia, never mind in a city. Two more bodies had been found at the club and another two were found later in the basement. A total of 13 people died and 162 people were injured seriously enough to need hospitalisation. Meanwhile, three of the wings of the Royal Newcastle Hospital, the historic North and York wings and Wheeler House, had been condemned until a structural report could be done and the empty beds from them stood on the hospital lawns. Patients had been moved back six to a ward instead of the usual four into those wards declared safe. Some patients had been transferred to outlying public and private hospitals at Cessnock, Maitland and Wallsend.

We visited the morgue at the Royal Newcastle Hospital to talk to the forensic pathologist there and discuss how we were going to get the bodies back to Glebe for examination.

What we learned from all this was that we really did not know how we would react until something happened. We could do all the planning in the world – and then something totally unexpected would happen, for example when we had to get the refrigerated trucks to move the bodies from the Kempsey bus crash to Glebe.

As a result of the series of disasters, Kevin set up the NSW Disaster Victims Identification Committee. The State Coroner is always the chairman and the members include pathologists, morgue workers, the police and funeral directors. The committee set protocols for dealing with disasters and the identification of victims, tightening up the whole system and making sure that at every stage, everyone knew what to do. Under the protocol, the bodies would go to a central point and not be identified at the scene. There is a lot of sense to this and it was reinforced by the Port Arthur massacre in Tasmania when they allowed the bodies to be identified at the scene and one of them was wrongly identified.

With six people dead in the Down Under Hostel fire, 20 people dead in the Grafton accident, 36 people at Kempsey and then 13 in the Newcastle earthquake, never had the burden of any coroner been greater and the community was looking to our office for the answers. Kevin had an unprecedented task; it seemed he no sooner opened the inquest into one disaster when there was another one to deal with. The country had seen nothing like it. It did not pass us by that the disasters had only started to happen after Kevin was appointed State Coroner. Was he jinxed? We used to joke with him to lighten things up that once he retired the disasters would stop. They didn't. While it did seem that in 1989 and 1990 we were overwhelmed by tragedy after tragedy, Kevin and I worked methodically through the cases.

A coroner could try to make a difference in advising authorities to prevent head-on crashes on the Pacific Highway, but an earthquake? Kevin wondered how the emergency services in countries like Iran and the Philippines coped when hundreds and thousands of people died after massive earth tremors. We could only learn from our experiences at Newcastle on how to cope better should there be another earthquake. The Newcastle inquest was the first in Australia into deaths caused by an earthquake.

What emerged were squabbles between rescue services and concerns that rescue workers were told by the police to leave the site of the Workers' Club for no good reason, leaving people trapped inside. Kevin found that the senior police officer at the scene had been right to move people out because he had been given three crucial pieces of information; of the fear of a severe aftershock; that a structural engineer said the building was unsafe; and that the concrete blocks that had collapsed in the building were moving. Some firemen were also critical of the decision late on 28 December to demolish the dangerous northwest wall of the club which it was feared might collapse on rescue workers. Kevin specifically asked Dr Jo DuFlou, one of the forensic pathologists at Glebe, whether from an examination of the autopsy reports it was possible to ascertain whether anyone would still have been alive when the wall was demolished. Dr DuFlou believed that the injuries of the victims were so severe that all those who died in the club would have been deceased either instantly or within minutes.

One of the main recommendations Kevin made was that a proper chronology be kept by police in the future at all disaster scenes because in the confusion the rescue workers at Newcastle had lost all sense of time. This has become recognised practice and enables investigators to look back and ascertain if things could have been done better or quicker.

Around this time, downstairs in the Glebe morgue, the pathologists were uncovering an increasingly puzzling mystery. By the end of November 1989, it had become the home for the bodies of three elderly women. All were from Sydney's north shore, all had suffered terrible head injuries. On 2 November, Margaret Pahud, 85, had been hit on the head several times with a hammer as she had walked down a private walkway to her home unit in Lane Cove; the next afternoon, Olive Cleveland, 81, was found dead in the grounds of the Wesley Gardens Retirement Village in Belrose where her head had been smashed repeatedly onto the concrete and she had been strangled with her pantyhose; on 23 November, Muriel Falconer, 92, was found murdered in her Mosman home, again hit over the head with a hammer and her pantyhose were also tied around her neck. Earlier in 1989, two more elderly women in the area had died from head injuries: Gwendoline Mitchelhill, 82, had been attacked with a hammer on 1 March as she walked into the entry foyer of her home in Military Road, Mosman; and two months later, on 9 May, Lady Winifred Ashton, 84, was also attacked in the entry foyer of her unit block on Raglan Street, Mosman. Her head had been repeatedly slammed onto the concrete floor and her pantyhose tied around her neck.

It was obvious these murders were not isolated homicides. A serial killer was out there and had been getting away with it for at least nine months. The media had labelled the offender the 'Granny Killer' and with the murder of Muriel Falconer, hysteria had gripped the north shore. The State government posted a reward of $250,000 for information leading to the apprehension of the killer. Inquests into the deaths of each of the women had been opened and adjourned because there was little a coroner could do while the feverish police investigation continued.

On Sunday night, 6 May 1990, Kevin rang me at home to say there was a rail crash. Two days earlier, on the afternoon of Friday, 4 May, Kevin had handed down his findings in the Down Under Hostel fire and in a few hours, on the morning of Monday, 7 May, he was due to open the inquest into the deaths of five young children trapped in the cabin of the leisure cruiser *N'Gluka* when it sank off Port Stephens. The inquest was being held in a Newcastle courtroom still shored up with wooden planks – a legacy of the earthquake. In two weeks he was due to hold the inquest into the Kempsey bus crash. To say he was busy was an understatement. He asked me to do the inquiry into the crash of the 3801.

The 5.20 p.m. train from Newcastle to Sydney had ploughed into the back of the historic 3801 steam train which was returning to Sydney packed with families after visiting the annual Morpeth jazz festival. It was on a stretch of track difficult to access just outside a tunnel near the small town of Cowan, five kilometres south of Brooklyn Bridge. It was dark and hundreds of people were trapped. I drove to Kevin's house in Sydney's north where a highway patrol car was waiting to take us up to the scene. We parked on the Pacific Highway and walked about three kilometres through the dark along a dirt track.

The scene that greeted us was eerie. Powerful spotlights lit the rugged valley at the foot of the notoriously steep Cowan Bank where the leading carriage of the silver double-decker commuter train had come off the tracks and now lay on its side. In the wooden carriages of Australia's most famous steam train, seats had been ripped from their mountings by the impact. It was as if the trains had been picked up by some giant hand and tossed back down. Stairs were buckled and doors blocked. Passengers had to climb to safety out of windows. The driver of the inter-urban train had been killed on impact as had a 16-year-old passenger who had been standing behind the driver's compartment. Four people had been killed in the rear carriage of the 3801, including the retired vice-chancellor of Sydney University, his wife and daughter. We could see that all the bodies were still in the trains awaiting the arrival of the scientific officers.

Luckily, the State Rail Authority (SRA) had recently upgraded a narrow track specifically to allow access to this stretch of line, although it was still pretty rough, and the passengers had all been moved away by the time we got to the scene. The 93 injured passengers had been taken to seven hospitals and the police had begun to interview the others. Those who were able to make their own way out had been led out in groups where they were taken by bus and taxi back to their homes.

There was a lot of speculation as to what had caused the crash. The 3801 had been stopped when it was hit by the inter-urban train. We could see that the emergency handbrake in the third carriage of the 3801 had been turned on and there was a thought it may have been done by train buffs who loved the sound of a steam engine struggling to make it uphill and had wanted to make the climb more difficult. It was pointed out to me that there was a lot of sand and grit on the track, placed there to give the 3801 more grip to climb the hill and tests were being conducted on the signalling system to see if the sand had prevented the signals working properly.

The speedometer of the inter-urban train was broken; it had the words 'not working' handwritten across it and the pointer was on zero on the dial.

We were at the crash site for about five hours and by the time we left at 2 a.m., I felt we had found out as much as we could at the scene. We spoke to police and rail inspectors and rescue workers.

Despite all the speculation, there were two questions that needed to be answered – why had the 3801 stopped and why had the driver of the inter-urban train not known this? A key witness was an off-duty train driver, Geoffrey McLeod, who had been travelling in the cabin of the inter-urban train with his workmate Gordon Hill. We got working on what we needed to know and I had John Gibson assisting me on this one. John was an ex-police prosecutor who was what we called a case manager on the coroner's staff. The job of case managers was to make sure the brief was prepared properly to put before the coroner and then to appear before the coroner when the case came on for hearing to assist the court. John was a very thorough operator. There were a number of experts from the State Rail Authority who we could speak to but I felt we needed an independent opinion so I commissioned an outside expert.

A lot of people were waiting for the outcome of the inquest into what happened to the 3801, an elegant and much-loved train. Built in 1943, it had set the record of two hours and one minute from Sydney to Newcastle in 1964 and in the bicentennial year, after being rescued from the Rail Transport Museum and with $500,000 spent on restorations, it became the only steam train to cross Australia from east to west a second time. The future of the train enthusiasts' beloved steam trains rested on the results of the inquest. The NSW Government had banned all steam train trips in the wake of the 3801 crash.

John Gibson kept me up to date with how the investigation was going in piecing together the moments leading up to the crash. We talked about how we would conduct the inquest. Did we need to call all the experts? Did we need to hear from all the passengers who had given statements to police? We got together all the statements that had been taken and made sure that everyone interested had a full copy of them. The interested parties included the lawyers for the victims, the SRA and the Government Insurance Office of NSW who were the public liability insurers of the 3801. I asked their opinions as to what witnesses should be called. It was always my contention that there was nothing to gain in calling ten witnesses to say the same thing. It was a waste of time and money. If there was a variance in witness statements, only then would we call the people to talk about it. In this way, we decided not to call all the passengers on the two trains but I would simply accept their statements as tendered to the court. As usual, I would have some of the more important statements read out in court while others would simply be handed up at the inquest. I allowed the media access to everything which was tendered to the court. They were public documents and the public got to know what was happening through the media. We were always as open as possible.

When I opened the inquest at Glebe on Monday, 3 September 1990, one of the first people I took evidence from was the off-duty driver who had been in the cabin of the inter-urban train, Geoffrey McLeod. He said the train, with four carriages, had been waiting at the other side of the Cowan tunnel for ten to 15 minutes at a red signal. The lights had kept fluctuating from red to green. The driver, Gordon Hill, had called Hawkesbury River station and asked what was ahead. He was told the steam train was to be 'refuged' at Cowan so he could pass it. Eventually the lights on the signal stayed permanently on green and the inter-urban moved through the tunnel.

It was doing about 50 kilometres an hour as it pulled out of the other side of the tunnel when he and Mr Hill saw the red marker signal on the back of the steam train. Mr Hill dropped what was called the 'dead man's lever', slamming on the brakes, and shouted at his colleague to get out of the cabin. As he leapt, Mr McLeod said he looked back and saw Mr Hill trying to get out of the cab. Moments later he heard the sound of the crash.

The driver of the 3801, Stewart Eyb, was able to tell us what was happening on the other side of the tunnel. He said the 3801 had slowed from 60 kilometres an hour as it entered the tunnel. It had gone into a violent wheel spin which was arrested when Mr Eyb put sand on the tracks to gain some traction. About one train length outside the tunnel, he opened the valve to full throttle but the train had come to a standstill by the time it reached the gradient. Mr Eyb put more sand on the rails. After two attempts at moving the train, Mr Eyb asked two volunteer crew members to check if anyone had interfered with the brakes.

Part of Mr Eyb's job as driver was to give a running commentary to the passengers and there was a tape of those last few moments. We played it in court. You could hear the sounds of the train slowing down and then Mr Eyb asking if 'some lout' might have put on a handbrake in one of the carriages.

As Mr Eyb tried to move the train a third time, Keith Audet, another volunteer, saw the inter-urban train coming through the tunnel. In his statement, which I had read out to the court, he said he thought at first it had been sent to push the 3801. He started to run to tell Mr Eyb the train was getting close. Then he pressed himself to the side of the track and waited for the collision. There was nothing else he could do.

There was evidence that there had been several occasions in the past when trains had been 'lost' to the signalling system because of sanding. I had a model of the crash scene brought into court and it proved invaluable. One of the SRA's electrical engineers was able to demonstrate on the model how the efforts to get the 3801 moving again could have broken the signal. As the steam train rolled backwards, all its wheels could have been on the sand-covered track. This would have indicated to the signalling system that the train had moved on and automatically changed the red light which was holding up the inter-urban to green.

I agreed with my expert that the chain of events which led to the crash were a one-off; the crash was caused by a 'million to one chance'. Sand on the rail had caused the signal fault but the 3801 had never before had problems climbing the steep Cowan Bank. It was possible that the handbrake in the number three carriage had been partially applied. Once the chain of events was set into motion, could anyone have stopped it? I thought not. The drivers, guards and volunteers had all acted reasonably and when I handed down my findings, I cleared them all of any blame.

The SRA's own Board of Inquiry had already come up with a number of recommendations and some were already in operation. One of the main ones was that a rail cleaning device had been installed on 40 trains and more were to follow. The use of sand was to be restricted. I felt the signalling system at Cowan Bank should be updated as soon as possible.

I was being urged by train enthusiasts to recommend that the 3801 be allowed to travel the rails again and I said I had no objection to that whatsoever. In April 1991, the 3801 was rolling again.

The rest of our work at Glebe did not stop for these disasters. Kevin and I were the only two coroners at Glebe but we kept going.

During this time I had to deal with the inquest into the zookeeper who was killed by a Sumatran tiger at Taronga Zoo as she was trying to take photographs of her cubs. Victoria Scrivener, 33, had moved what she believed to be the only adult tiger into another area before she entered the tigers' enclosure. Without warning, she was attacked from behind by another tiger. Two other keepers put their own lives at risk to try and save their colleague, with one of them trying to pull Miss Scrivener away from the tiger. It was a tragic accident; Miss Scrivener did a job that was inherently dangerous. I felt that unfortunately, as quite often happened with even the most experienced people, she had for a short period of time become a little complacent or careless.

There was the man who stabbed his flatmate 76 times because he thought the flatmate had hired a hitman and was plotting to kill him. He also said he thought the TV set in his flat was talking to him and after hearing voices in a taxi, he had jumped from it while it was still moving. I committed him to stand trial.

And there was Amanda Cunningham, a 16-year-old who had run away from home four years earlier after a family row. She had been made a ward of state and had drifted between various girls' homes and refuges before moving onto the streets of Kings Cross where she made her living as a prostitute. Her death was reported to me in July 1990 after her body had been found by the side of Croydon Road in the suburb of Hurstville with an amount of MDA in her body which our forensic scientists determined was more than twice the toxic level. In her bile there was 39 milligrams per kilogram. The toxic level is 18 milligrams. MDA is commonly known as ecstasy. At the time, it was just coming to public notice as a so-called 'party drug' and had its defenders who said it was a safe drug, a drug you couldn't overdose on. There is no such thing as a safe drug. Traces of semen were also found in Amanda's mouth.

So how had Amanda died in Hurstville, so far from her usual haunts, and had she taken the drug herself or had something more sinister happened? The only way to piece together the last days and hours of her life was through talking to fellow street kids and street workers. My heart went out to her mother when I learned that Amanda had called her three days before her death. Her seventeenth birthday was the following week and Amanda wanted to get together with her mum for a Chinese meal to mark the occasion. She never made it.

The night before her death, Amanda had been seen working at 'the Wall', the area in Darlinghurst around the corner from the NSW Supreme Court building at Taylor Square which was well known for prostitution. On the day she died, she was seen around Kings Cross. One woman said she had seen the girl in a pinball parlour, a dirty white rat lying around her neck. The rat was apparently an early birthday present. The last sighting of Amanda was at around 9.15 p.m. as she staggered into the Kings Cross railway station, apparently affected by drugs. Amanda was found dead one hour and 15 minutes later. It was sad but it seemed that living the way she did, the odds were that something tragic was going to happen to her. She had been experimenting with drugs and was working as a prostitute. I felt it was quite probable that a man she had met, perhaps a customer, with whom she had oral sex, had given her the drug but I had no evidence of this. I found that she died from an ecstasy overdose but it was impossible to determine whether she had taken the drug herself or had been forced to take it. There had already been five documented deaths caused by ecstasy overdoses and as I have said before, you try to make a difference in your work as a coroner. The message I wanted to get out there through the media was it was a myth that you could not die from ecstasy.

※

The deaths were mounting up. A pensioner, George Woodcock, who did not seem to have an enemy in the world, was nearly decapitated by five swings of a razor-sharp machete in his home in a Hunter Valley mining village. Underworld figure Roy Thurgar, who had been a close friend of so-called Sydney identity Tom Domican, was shot in the head as he waited to collect his wife outside their laundrette in Randwick. An 18-year-old male prostitute was dropped off dead at St Vincent's Hospital in Darlinghurst by a middle-aged man in a gold Mercedes-Benz. The man, called Bill, was never seen again. A 64-year-old woman died after a man in a white panel van grabbed her bag as she walked through the city. She held onto the bag and was dragged along the road, dying of head injuries. We never found the man in the van; another crook had got away scot-free.

There was the strange case of the 75-year-old man who was found dead on the shore at Pittwater on Sydney's northern beaches behind the popular Newport Arms Hotel. In the last year of his life he had been introduced to a local couple and had changed his will four times that year leaving his entire $165,000 to the couple. The man's family told me they thought he had been conned. He had lunched with the couple the day he died. I found the man had drowned but as there was no evidence that anyone played a part in his death, I could not say if it was accidental or otherwise.

※

How could you not know that your 15-year-old daughter was pregnant? In a case that came before me that year, the girl's parents said that although they had noticed their daughter had obviously been gaining weight, they had no idea she was pregnant because she wore baggy clothes. The girl herself said she had not known she was pregnant. She had gone into labour at about midnight, went into the bathroom and sat on the toilet. The ambulance officers, answering a triple-o call, believed they were going to a miscarriage. Imagine their response when they found a newborn baby girl lying in the toilet. The investigating officer, Detective Gary Logan, told me that he felt the mother and father had seemed indifferent but he did feel they were genuinely shocked by the birth. The couple was described as 'humble people, seemingly not well educated, far from worldly or sophisticated'. Detective Logan said the father had appeared to be more worried about whether he was going to work that day and the mother's priority was where she was going to put the cat. The prosecution case was that the mother, father and daughter had failed to exercise a duty of care by not removing the baby from the toilet after the birth and not seeking immediate medical attention. I committed them to stand trial for manslaughter.

I thought I was at the stage where nothing amazed me, I thought I had heard it all. I hadn't.

CHAPTER 4

Massacre in the Suburbs

ON A WINTER'S Saturday afternoon I was doing what I usually did, watching the rugby league on the TV, when Kevin rang. He was on his way to Strathfield Plaza shopping centre.

'I'll meet you there,' I told him and jumped in the car. Strathfield is a sedate, tree-lined, reasonably wealthy suburb where the three-storey shopping complex is usually full of families, young people and mums pushing prams. Megan went to school at Strathfield and the Plaza was a regular haunt for her and her friends in their last couple of years at school where they would meet for coffee and hang out.

On this winter's afternoon, despite the chill wind blowing along the street, there were hundreds of people just standing around outside the centre. Yet there wasn't much noise. They would turn their heads to speak quietly to each other and then turn back to stare blankly at the complex's automatic sliding glass doors where a sign hung, 'Closed – No entry except tenants.'

Behind these doors it looked as if everyone was moving in slow motion. It was strangely, eerily quiet. Kevin was already there, as was the pathologist Jo DuFlou.

Behind the rows of plants that marked off the Coffee Pot coffee lounge, just about 100 metres from the doors, was a scene the likes of which I never want to witness again. People ask what was my most harrowing experience. This was it. Six bodies lay where they had fallen.

Fifteen-year-old Bo Armstrong, who had been sitting with a friend in the coffee lounge while they waited for other friends, now lay with an enormous machete-like Bowie knife still embedded in her back. Patricia Rowe, 36, had been shot but she had successfully managed to put a table between her two sons, aged 15 and nine, and the gunman. Her mother, Joyce Nixon, 61, lay dead nearby. Rachelle Milburn, 17, had been having a coffee with her friend Belinda Dickinson, 20, and Belinda's mum, Carol Dickinson, 47. Rachelle had also been shot dead. Mrs Dickinson, who had been shot in the chest as she tried to save her daughter's life by pushing her out of the way, died later in hospital. One of the owners of the coffee shop, George Mavris, 51, had been killed as he walked out from the kitchen to see what all the noise was. It was a horrible sight, unbelievable. It was very hard to accept what I was seeing.

Past the Coffee Pot and near the stairs towards the southern end of the Plaza, lay Robertson Van Hook Voon, 53, also shot dead. The next two levels of the shopping complex were for parking. We went up to the second level where a police generator bathed the area in light. There was no mystery as to who the gunman was – he lay there in front of us on the concrete behind one of the parked cars, face down in a pool of his own blood. The massacre ended ten minutes after it started when Wade Frankum, 33, had held his SKK semi-automatic military assault rifle under his chin and shot himself dead. Between 3.35 p.m. and 3.45 p.m. on Saturday, 17 August 1991, seven people, including Frankum, had died, the lives of their families turned upside down. The bodies were waiting for the crime scene officers to finish their work, marking out the area and recording it on video. The eighth victim, Mrs Dickinson, died later. Seven others were being treated in hospital for gunshot wounds. I rang Doreen to cancel dinner. It was going to be a long night.

Kevin and I couldn't hurry at the scene, we needed to be clear about what had happened so we watched and listened. After three hours, Kevin went out into the street to make a statement to the media. He said the scene in the coffee shop was dreadful, although there were hardly words to describe what we had seen. 'These were obviously innocent people who had been having a cup of coffee when they were killed,' he said. 'We know who the perpetrator was and we know where he lives but not much else at this stage, I'm afraid. He was a Caucasian male aged 33 with no criminal history.'

After we had finished at the shopping centre, Kevin and I went to see where Frankum lived. His home unit was not far away in Beronga Street, North Strathfield, a couple of minutes by train to Strathfield station. He lived in a two-storey block of four units which had been built by his father 20 years earlier. Frankum lived there with his sister, Gaynor, and her boyfriend. It was dark by this time and the police were already there waiting for us. It was a rather messy flat and Frankum had an extensive library of various books ranging from the autobiographies of Gordon Liddy and Oliver North, to *Crime and Punishment* by Fyodor Dostoyevsky and other works on military subjects. But there was one book on his bed that caused us the most consternation. It was *American Psycho* by Bret Easton Ellis which had been on restricted sale in Australia, to people over the age of 18, for four months by that time. The book had passages of sexual violence and sadism, including a woman being cut in half with a chainsaw and another woman having a live rat placed in her vagina.

Who was Wade Frankum and what would have made him, or anyone, do this? At the flat, Kevin and I discussed getting a psychological profile of him. It was something Kevin had thought about when he considered how New South Wales should deal with a mass murder such as those at Hoddle Street and Queen Street in Melbourne in 1987.

⁂

Three years earlier I had a weird case at Wentworth, down on the Victorian border just north of Mildura in New South Wales and I had called in Rod Milton to help. Rod is a forensic psychiatrist, the best in Australia, often used by the police. A tall man, he wears glasses and is fairly softly spoken, taking his time between words when he talks. I liked working with him because he is very practical and calls a spade a spade. There's none of this airy-fairy language with Rod; you can understand what he is talking about. He had been profiling criminals since 1982, beginning with hostage situations when the life of the hostage depended on how the police negotiated with the offender. The case at Wentworth involved a young man whose body was found chained to bricks in the river. There were all sorts of stories about him being involved in drug deals and his parents felt he might have been murdered by the Mafia, although there was no evidence of this. Nor was there a suicide note. The young man had apparently thought of himself as a bit of a Houdini. I had asked Rod for his opinion on whether his death was consistent with suicide, a terrible accident or murder.

Rod looked through his personal documents and found drawings he had done which showed he was feeling desperate. The young man's parents had separated, his father had remarried and the young man had felt rather lost. It was Rod's opinion that he had killed himself but that his family was full of guilt because they had not been able to stop him. They were normal feelings for any family in such a position and that was why it was easier for them to believe he had been murdered. At the inquest held at Wentworth, Rod gave evidence that he felt the family had done their very best by the young man, comments which eased their pain. I found Rod's role and sensitive approach very helpful. I recorded a verdict of suicide. I mentioned Rod's skills to Kevin and a detective was sent to track down Rod to get his help on the Strathfield massacre.

The Strathfield case had really rattled me as there seemed to be no clear explanation at this stage as to why Frankum did this. We all have our ways of dealing with things. Just because you don't cry doesn't mean you do not feel sadness. When I get upset, I withdraw into myself and become very quiet. It was fairly late when I got home that night and I didn't say a word.

⁂

The next day, the predictable debate about gun laws began. The NSW Police Minister Ted Pickering was alone in his vocal opposition to any new restrictions on semi-automatic weapons, such as those used by Frankum. Importing these types of guns was already banned by the federal government and by the Monday, Pickering's boss, NSW Premier Nick Greiner had placed an immediate ban on the sale of the military-style guns. It became illegal for gun owners to resell any stocks they had of Chinese and Russian automatic and semi-automatic weapons.

On the Monday morning, Kevin and discussed whether such a law would have prevented the Strathfield massacre. I have always thought that there are a lot of people who should not be allowed to have guns. I can't think why the ordinary person in a city or town would need one while I can see why there are some people, like farmers in certain situations, who should be allowed to have a gun. The problem is that there are people who are going to obtain guns illegally whatever the law says and all you can do is make it as difficult as possible. The issue of gun control is certainly not simple. Then there are people like Wade Frankum who was in such a state of mind that he may well have killed a number of people without a gun. He did start the killing with a knife. The inquest into the Strathfield massacre was held in mid-November 1991, a very emotional time for the families of Wade Frankum's victims so Kevin called only selected witnesses. He had the evidence of the scene presented by way of videotapes showing witnesses who had been interviewed at the scene describing what had happened. From the profile done by Rod Milton and the police investigation under the command of Detective Inspector Bob Godden, who was a mountain of a man as sharp as a tack, and aided by the coroner's officer Senior Sergeant John White, the court was able to piece together the events that led to the massacre.

Frankum had an unremarkable upbringing. He was reasonably bright and was never out of work. He ended up working as a taxi driver. He had no criminal record and apart from seeking counselling for depression, had no history of psychiatric illness. His father had died of emphysema in 1986 and his mother committed suicide by gassing herself in her car in the garage at their North Strathfield home in April 1990. Frankum felt guilty about his mother's death and lied to his sister, telling her that their mother had died from natural causes. He inherited over $30,000 on his mother's death and spent the bulk of it on prostitutes, having just over $50 in his bank account before he died.

Frankum obtained his shooter's licence in September 1990 and bought the semi-automatic military rifle in January 1991. In the four months before his killing spree, he bought the Bowie knife and some handcuffs. There was evidence the gun had never been fired before 17 August in Strathfield shopping centre. Frankum was 171 centimetres tall with a crew cut and on the day he set out with his Bowie knife and his gun, he wore jeans, a denim jacket and a grey beanie. He also carried his shooter's licence with him for some strange reason.

He left the flat around 1 p.m. and bought a train ticket at North Strathfield station. He told the stationmaster, Clive Young, whom he knew,

'You'd better go home, Clive.' Frankum let one train go by for Strathfield and got on the next one. He sat in the Coffee Pot coffee lounge for about an hour, drinking four cups of coffee, before he picked up his knife and attacked Bo Armstrong.

Rod Milton concluded that it would have been impossible to predict what Frankum had done. Over 80 per cent of homicides in New South Wales each year are committed by offenders with no previous conviction for a violence offence. In Frankum's case, Rod determined that he was motivated by anger at his own failures, guilt over his mother's suicide, conflict over trivial disputes with family and neighbours and loneliness because he had no more money to continue to assuage his loneliness with prostitutes. The experts said that psychological testing before handing out gun licences would have done no good in Frankum's case; he would have passed. Dr Milton surmised that those with vulnerable personalities could be affected by the constant exposure to violence in the media, and to violent pornography such as the book *American Psycho*.

Kevin's findings were very interesting. He said that with Australia's habit of following American trends, he was afraid that the availability of guns and violent pornography meant there would probably be more Strathfield-style mass murders. On the same day he handed down his findings, the conference of the country's premiers being held in Adelaide moved to toughen gun laws. It is sad how it seems to take a tragedy to spur politicians on to action. There were already 150,000 SKK rifles, similar to the one Frankum used, in Australia.

Would tighter gun laws have also prevented the murder of Australia's leading heart transplant surgeon, Victor Chang, a month earlier? It was a killing that shocked the Australian public. At 7.45 a.m. on Thursday, 4 July 1991, Dr Chang died instantly after he was shot in the head at point blank range by two young Asian men after a struggle in a quiet lane off the busy Military Road in Mosman. His killing landed on my desk.

As head of the national cardiac program, Dr Chang had performed more than 260 heart operations at Sydney's St Vincent's Hospital. He was a former Australian of the Year and holder of an Order of Australia.

Unfortunately for his killers, one of them, Chiew Seng Liew, 48, left his wallet at the scene.

Kevin conducted the committal hearing of Liew. It emerged that Chang's death was a $3 million extortion attempt that went wrong, set up by Liew, fellow Malaysian national Phillip Lim, 36, and Lim's former brother-in-law Stanley Ng, 37. The plan had been to find a very rich businessman from whom to extort money and Dr Chang was one of three potential targets simply chosen out of a magazine. The other two potential victims were both Chinese businessmen. The photographs had been selected by Phillip Lim who had told Liew and Ng that if they couldn't find one of the businessmen, they were to simply find the next on the list. The police breakthrough came when Ng turned Crown witness and was given indemnity from prosecution.

Ten days before Dr Chang's murder, Liew, Lim and Ng staked out the doctor's home and his workplace at St Vincent's with the aim of identifying his Mercedes saloon and his work route. They planned to stage an accident with Chang and force him to go to a bank and withdraw money which they would use to finance a massage parlour or gambling house. It was Ng's role to cause the accident but a week before the murder, he had pulled out when an attempt to carry out the plan came unstuck because Ng saw another person in the car with Chang, possibly his son.

So on the morning of 4 July, Liew and Lim forced Chang's car off the road. They demanded $3 million and Chang refused to pay. The doctor took out his wallet and tried to buy his freedom with a few dollars. When he called out in the street for passersby to call the police, Liew put a gun to the surgeon's head and pulled the trigger. He shot Dr Chang again after he had fallen to the ground. Liew later told a friend, 'I have killed a doctor ... Chang. He loves his money more than his life. He wasn't afraid of death. I don't know why, he had so much money, he wasn't afraid of death.'

Kevin committed Liew to stand trial but the man who was alleged to have set up the plan and provided the guns, Lim, was missing. The NSW police alerted Malaysia and Interpol to search for Lim. In November 1991, they hit paydirt. Lim was found by police at a house in Kuala Lumpur, extradited from Malaysia and brought before me at Glebe for his committal proceedings. Lim said he had got frightened and ran to his car while Chiew Seng Liew pulled out a gun. I committed Lim to stand trial. He was eventually convicted and jailed for a minimum of 18 years. Liew was jailed for a minimum of 20 years.

After the Strathfield massacre, Dr Chang's daughter, Vanessa, wrote an open letter to the NSW Premier Nick Greiner in which she said that while she knew that criminals could not be stopped, surely society could limit their easy access to lethal weapons. She was correct, of course, both in her plea for stricter rules on the sale and ownership of guns, and to say that criminals cannot be stopped. How could anyone have predicted that Wade Frankum would have picked up any weapon and used it in the way he had? Some people go off at the drop of a hat yet show no signs that they have such a predilection while others may have a profile that shows they may do something violent but never do.

One case that does stick in my mind when I think about gun laws was the murder of a member of the extremist right-wing National Action at the organisation's headquarters in Tempe in 1991. The victim, Wayne 'Bovver' Smith, 25, who stood 185 centimetres tall, weighed 108 kilograms and would drink three or four stubbies of beer for breakfast, was shot eight times as he wore a singlet bearing the message 'No to the new gun control laws'.

The evidence was that Smith was so aggressive and abrasive with a tendency towards unprovoked violence that his fellow National Action members had voted to expel him from the organisation, but no one had the courage to tell him.

Unfortunately for the man accused of his murder, ASIO not only had the telephone at the National Action headquarters tapped, they had installed several listening devices in the building. Everything that happened was recorded. The tapes revealed Smith's last gasps and the murderer telling him, 'Hurry up and die.' They also recorded him talking to the corpse as he put a knife in his hand so he could later claim Smith had attacked him first saying, 'Hey, Smith, you're dead. Dead, dead, dead.' I decided not to have the tapes played in open court – the transcripts were graphic enough. While Smith was a giant, his killer was just 163 centimetres tall and weighed 49 kilograms.

※

If criminals looked like criminals then it is likely very few of them would ever get the opportunity to commit a crime. In the same way, murderers rarely look like you expect them to, except with the benefit of hindsight.

MASSACRE IN THE SUBURBS

Take John Wayne Glover, the Granny Killer. In March 1991, police had caught Glover, a pastry salesman, after he killed his sixth victim, Joan Sinclair, 60, and then tried to commit suicide in the bathroom of her house in Pindari Avenue, Beauty Point.

Who would have thought that the podgy, florid-faced, 57-year-old family man with white greasy hair who sat before me in the dock could have caused such terror, murdering six elderly women and attacking and indecently assaulting a number of others? Anyone who looked less like a monster would have been difficult to find. Even the cluey Rod Milton, one of the few Australian forensic scientists to have visited the FBI's behavioural science unit, got it wrong up to a point.

The police had called in Rod back in June 1989, after the murders of Gwendoline Mitchellhill and Lady Winifred Ashton to profile the killer for them. The basis of profiling is looking at the evidence and trying to work out the sort of person it points to. When Rod came to read the emotion of the crime scenes, what had struck him was the massive violence involved, the speed of the attack and the orderliness of the scenes. He felt the offender may be in the armed services where it was not uncommon to find people with an interest in violence. The orderliness would have come from their training. He looked for common denominators between the attacks. They happened in broad daylight, in the late afternoon, after school was out. This, according to the evidence, pointed to a young person because risk taking was adolescent behaviour. The killer was probably not a woman because of the strength and ferocity of the attacks, and was probably someone who had a hatred of women. Rod felt that whoever it was, it was certain he would strike again. Police canvassed the schools and the military and naval bases around Mosman. Rod's theory about the age of the likely offender was backed up by research done by the FBI.

In late November 1989, with the bodies of three more elderly women in the morgue, police had called in Rod again to take another look at the evidence. I saw his profile and he did preface his summary by noting that his conclusions were at best educated guesses and that the offender could be outside his profile. However, he was still thinking along the lines of the young male offender, possibly a serviceman, who lived with his family in the Mosman area. He felt the killings showed misplaced anger, that is, hatred against one person taken out against someone else. As the victims were elderly women, Rod felt the man hated a woman in his family – his wife, his grandmother, mother, his mother-in-law. Rod also predicted correctly that this man would attack someone he knew.

While Rod Milton had been wrong about the age of the offender, he had been correct about his motivations of hating a particular woman. Two months before he was arrested for the murders, John Glover had been questioned by police about the indecent assault of an 82-year-old woman in the palliative care ward of Greenwich Hospital. He had tried to commit suicide and wrote a garbled suicide note to his family, scrawled on his superannuation form. It included the words, 'No more grannies ... Essie started it all.' Essie Rolls was Glover's mother-in-law who died four weeks before the first murder.

Glover was a migrant from England who had changed his name from John Walter to John Wayne Glover when he reached Australia at the age of 25. He arrived with several convictions for petty theft, did a stint in the National Service and got a job driving the Melbourne trams. He continued his part-time career as a petty thief but also collected two convictions for assault, both on women. He thought himself a bit of a ladies' man but settled down when he met Gay Rolls.

A year after they married, Glover and his wife moved to Sydney from Melbourne. They found house prices beyond their reach and moved in with Gay's wealthy parents, Essie and John Rolls, at their impressive Mosman house. Glover tried to reinvent himself as a gentleman but that never impressed Essie. Well known in the neighbourhood for her domineering behaviour, with one neighbour describing her as a nasty version of Dame Edna Everage, glasses and all, Essie Rolls saved her worst for Glover. She was sure her daughter had married beneath herself. Glover could do nothing right in Essie's eyes and she never missed an excuse to tell him so. Eighteen years later Gay and John Glover were still living in the same house as her parents, 18 years of his mother-in-law's nagging and bullying.

Since his arrest in March 1990, Glover's court appearances had been well attended by the media. The faces of the regular court reporters for the various newspapers, radio and television stations had become familiar to me over the years. I was acutely aware that in this case, identification evidence of Glover may be crucial; not all of Glover's victims were dead. His charges included attacking and indecently assaulting elderly women. I made a point of ordering that no photographs be taken of him in the precincts of the court, just in case the photographers had been able to sneak a look at Glover being driven in and out of the building. For a few of the preliminary hearings, Glover remained in the cells and was not brought into the crowded courtroom as he feared for his safety. I also ordered that the address where he had lived with his wife and two daughters not be published to protect the family's privacy; they had nothing to do with his crimes. Since his arrest, he had been kept in the psychiatric section of Long Bay Jail where he was undergoing counselling.

On Monday, 8 October 1990, in a packed Glebe courtroom, I began to hear the evidence police had against Glover. Procedure required that I formally close the inquests into each of the women's deaths, which I did before hearing the outline of the prosecution case.

Glover was up on 13 charges – six of murder, one of attempted murder, a wounding, an assault and robbery and four counts of indecent assault. In all, there were 13 victims and what struck me was their names – old-fashioned names like Gwendoline, Olive, Euphemia. It brought home what frail old ladies they were, ladies who should have been able to live out their lives in peace and safety.

The seriousness of the charges dictated that the Director of Public Prosecutions (DPP) take over the case from the beginning and as DPP prosecutor Wendy Robinson stood up in court to outline the case, it was the first time the public had heard how the police had caught their man.

The North Shore Murders task force had been alerted to Glover as a suspect after the 82-year-old Greenwich patient complained about the indecent assault on her. A nurse who had seen Glover lurking in the hospital corridors recognised him as the Four 'N Twenty pie salesman. Police were also aware of the suicide note he left. They had a strong suspicion but no evidence to connect him to the murders so they placed him under surveillance. They followed him as he drove around the north shore suburb of Wollstonecraft, peering into apartment blocks and watching elderly women.

On 19 March, they followed him to the home of Joan Sinclair. Glover knew Mrs Sinclair (again, as Rod Milton had predicted, he attacked someone he knew). He had telephoned the 60-year-old woman that morning and made arrangements to meet her that day. From his garden shed, he collected his claw hammer which he placed in his briefcase before driving to a local bottle shop and buying a bottle of Scotch. He then drove to Mrs Sinclair's house in Beauty Point where she let him in.

A short time later, as she was showing him a leak in the ceiling, he took the hammer from his briefcase, approached her from behind and struck her a number of times on the head. He pulled her clothes over her head and removed her panties. Then he took a pair of pantyhose from a drawer in her bedroom and tied them tightly around her neck. The post-mortem examination revealed she died either from strangulation or her head injuries.

As the police waited outside, Glover ran a bath, stripped naked and lay down in the tub, drinking the Scotch and swallowing prescription drugs.

After eight hours of surveillance, the police became suspicious and finally went into the house where they pulled Glover from the bathtub, saving his life and making sure he would stand trial for murder. When they spoke to Glover the next day, he confirmed that it was his mother-in-law who had started his killing spree.

Glover decided to consent to a paper committal, so he did not require witnesses to be called for his lawyer to cross-examine. In effect, it meant the police brief of evidence was handed to me and none of it was read out in court. However, I made the statements available to the media because they were on the public record. There was Glover's record of interview, taken while he was recovering at the Royal North Shore Hospital.

> Police: 'Why do you pick on elderly women?'
> Glover: 'You probably noticed the photos in the paper, they all have an uncanny resemblance to my mother-in-law.'
> Police: 'Do you have some sort of problem with her? Did she create problems with the family?'

Glover: 'Oh yeah. In my first suicide I wrote a note mentioning Essie. She began it all. Essie. I just wished she would hurry up and die. Even my wife said that.

'I have done the deed, I should not be worried about my safety. I should be strung up ... My problem was as soon as it's over, I just jumped in the car and carried on as normal. Invariably I'd go down to the club.'

Glover told police that he did not have sexual motives but his relationship with Mrs Sinclair had involved 'a bit of hanky panky'. When asked why he had approached Doris Cox, whom he attempted to murder on 18 October 1989, Glover had said, 'I don't know. You just seem to see these old ladies and it seems to trigger something. I've just got to be violent to them.' He said he could not control his 'dark, evil side'.

Of course, these statements were only what the police alleged Glover had told them but there was other evidence, including identification evidence. The exhibits which were included with the brief were two pieces of carpet taken by police from Muriel Falconer's house. On the carpet were bloodstains in the shape of a shoe which the prosecution alleged matched prints taken from a pair of brown brogues belonging to Glover.

I was satisfied a jury would find sufficient evidence to convict Glover on all 13 charges. As I was required before I committed him to stand trial, I asked Glover if there was anything he wanted to say. This pleasant-faced, seemingly innocuous family man stood up behind his solicitor and said, 'Well, your worship, I wish to say that I reserve my defence.'

When I got home to Doreen that night, I said to her that I couldn't get over it. John Glover looked like a grandfatherly type of person. I told Dor that I would have invited him home for lunch – had I not known what he had done. It was no wonder that women trusted him.

In November that year, I saw that Glover was convicted by a jury of the murders and given six life sentences. I always thought the evidence against him was overwhelming and I was not surprised the jury rejected the only defence he could have raised in the circumstances, that of diminished responsibility. Two psychiatrists gave evidence at his trial to say that he was either a sexual deviant suffering from paraphilia with the sub feature of sexual sadism, or a mixed neurosis with compulsive and disassociative features. Called by the prosecution, Rod Milton disagreed with these opinions. By this time he had met and interviewed Glover in jail, listening to him for hours. At one stage, Glover had told the psychiatrist that when he was committing the assaults and murders, he felt 'the other' John Glover emerge. 'It's hard to describe because I've got this duality, it starts to appear then. Normally John Glover, the happy working person, the life and soul of the party, wouldn't hurt a fly; then his alter-ego comes out, wants to hurt people.'

Rod Milton was not taken in by him. He thought the 'bad' John Glover was an elaborate charade designed to deflect guilt. Dr Milton's report said Glover had no recognisable mental or emotional illness and therefore had no defence of either insanity or diminished responsibility. His motivation for the killings had been sexual. Rod stated:

> A more likely explanation is that the series of killings occurred because of longstanding sexual and emotional conflict regarding Mr Glover's feelings for women older than himself. It is likely that killing gave him both pleasure and relief, and it is also likely that fantasy over the murders continues to supply him with gratification. For obvious reasons Mr Glover is not prepared to admit this but says the murders were committed by a hidden part of himself and that he obtained no pleasure or satisfaction from them.

While Kevin was busy overseeing the inquiry into the Strathfield massacre, he also had the deaths of 12 boarders at the Palm Grove Hostel in Dungog to look into. The hostel was really an old weatherboard bungalow in an isolated spot about ten kilometres north of Dungog, a peaceful little place about three hours' drive north from Sydney. The hostel's 40 residents mostly suffered from alcohol-related brain damage. On the night of 1 August 1991, the night staff had left around 9 p.m. and two hours later fire broke out in the television lounge, racing through the timber building. It emerged that there had never been any fire drills at the hostel because the owner, who did not live on the premises, believed the residents would not have understood evacuation procedures. The smoke alarms were not working because the batteries were flat. However, the residents had been happy, well cared for and well fed by all accounts.

The problem for the police officers investigating the cause of the fire and for Kevin by the time he came to hold the inquest was that many of the residents could not remember statements they made to police the day after the blaze, others could not recall the names of their former room-mates and some barely even remembered the fire. The ferocity of the blaze had made it impossible to determine the cause other than it started in the television room. Most of the residents smoked and there were two wood-fired stoves and an open fire in the hostel.

∞∞∞

That November we never seemed to stop. I went up to Kurri Kurri to conduct the inquest into the strange death of the Hunter Valley pensioner, George Woodcock. Kurri Kurri was as close as I could get to Weston, the mining town where Mr Woodcock had lived.

Unlike those penny-pinching days when I was a relieving magistrate, as Deputy State Coroner I had an expense account verging on the reasonable. When we were hearing a case outside Sydney, we no longer had to get the train through the night and arrive that morning looking like something the cat dragged in. Fair dinkum, now we could even fly and arrive the night before so we had a good night's rest. Kurri Kurri was an easy drive north of Sydney so I drove up there on the morning of the inquest with a couple of my staff. I felt it was important to get out to where the deaths had occurred to hold the inquests. It not only made it easier for witnesses and the family to get to court – not everyone had the means to travel to Sydney – but it gave me a feel for a case.

Weston is one of those places where everyone knew everyone else's business and strangers stuck out a mile. When Mr Woodcock was found dead in his pyjamas, propped up in his bed in the blood splattered bedroom of his cottage, you could have been forgiven for thinking that finding the killer in such a close-knit community would not be difficult, but Weston was not going to give up names that easily. I had no doubt that someone in Weston knew who had killed Mr Woodcock – and that a lot of the witnesses called to the inquest had not told the truth.

Two locals, both young men, had been watching the movie *First Blood* together on the day of Mr Woodcock's murder. They said a conversation between them about robbing the pensioner had been 'just silly talk'. A witness said he had seen one of those young men eating the heart of a rabbit while it was still pulsing. Another witness said he had seen the same man tie a bird up, douse it with petrol, set it alight and watch the bird die. The young man said both incidents had innocent explanations: the bird was already dead and he burned it to kill the lice and the rabbit heart he ate came from a rabbit which had been shot and skinned and was not still pulsing.

Another witness said he had heard the young man say one night in the local hotel that, 'I'd like to kill someone just to see what it was like'. Yet another told how the young man would swat moths and eat them and would go on pig hunting trips where dogs cornered the pigs and then the men went in and killed them with knives. The young man's explanation for that was that he was just a good bushman and all good bushmen acted like that. That was another reason I liked to get out of Sydney for court cases – I simply enjoyed being back in the country.

We stayed at the local motel and that night had a meal and a couple of drinks at the local club to digest the events of the day. Talk about bizarre!

Detective Sergeant Alex Pollock, of Cessnock police, had been investigating the murder and he had told me that there was no hard evidence to link anyone to the crime. The motive was also a puzzle. Mr Woodcock had only $60 to his name so it could not have been robbery. The attack had been vicious, five swings of a machete. Who could possibly kill the harmless pensioner in such a horrific manner? Whoever it was is still walking around out there because I was unable to answer the question. The next day I had to deliver an open verdict and I felt particularly bad for his family. I had been unable to provide them with the answers and for them there would be no closure. 'I wish I could tell you who killed Mr Woodcock but I can't. There was not sufficient evidence,' I told his family as I wound up the inquest.

Once you stop treating everyone as important before the law, then there is no justice. Roy Thurgar was about as far from George Woodcock as you could get. Mr Woodcock had no known enemies, Roy Thurgar had more than a few, but his death was just as thoroughly investigated.

MASSACRE IN THE SUBURBS

Thurgar had survived a long time in his line of work and was 49 when he was shot dead on 20 May 1991 outside Randwick Self Service laundrette in Alison Road, Randwick. One of the newspapers quoted his wife Marjorie describing him as a gentle giant. He was certainly a giant of a man, tall with wide shoulders that demonstrated the muscle of his trade – he had been a professional boxer, a standover man and doorman, among other things. During his criminal career, he was once charged with shooting with intent to murder another criminal, Patrick McNally. Thurgar was acquitted. McNally was later bashed to death in Elizabeth Bay but no person was arrested for the offence. I would differ with the description of him as gentle. At least it was comforting that he was gentle with his wife.

Thurgar was shot as he sat in his 120Y Datsun station wagon waiting for his wife to finish work. He had been out of jail since December 1990 after serving a four-year sentence for possessing an unlicensed pistol. He and his wife had taken over the laundrette in March because Roy needed a job and he had been working 12 hours a day to make a go of it ever since, according to Mrs Thurgar.

The police had arrested two men for his murder and they came before me in November 1991 for a committal hearing. The prosecution case was that Thurgar was killed because of his role in a plot to rip off 100 kilograms of hashish being moved from Brisbane to Sydney. The story was that the two men before me, Dallas Harlum, 48, and Garry Nye, 39, had agreed to obtain the 'golf ball hashish', a form of cannabis resin, from Brisbane. Harlum had recruited another man, Danny Shakespeare, to collect and deliver it. Shakespeare contacted Thurgar, who he had known for several years – and they decided to steal the drugs. When Harlum and Nye found out, they executed Thurgar. Eight days later, Shakespeare was arrested at Port Kembla on 41 warrants relating to dishonesty and fraud and immediately started talking about Thurgar's murder. Shakespeare became a Crown witness with immunity from prosecution. Or so the prosecution case went.

Thurgar's wife, Marjorie, had her own theories. Just months before he was killed, Thurgar had made written complaints to the NSW Independent Commission Against Corruption (ICAC), the Internal Police Security Unit and the National Crime Authority (NCA) about the behaviour of two senior NSW detectives who he said had fabricated evidence against him. Mrs

Thurgar believed the only people she could think of who might have wanted to harm her husband were the police officers she said had been involved in 'loading' her husband up.

On the face of it, the prosecution certainly had a case against Harlum and Nye based on the word of Danny Shakespeare. The defence had given Shakespeare a good verbal going over in the witness box, strongly challenging his evidence, but I felt it was always going to be a matter for the jury whether or not they believed Shakespeare. I committed Harlum and Nye to stand trial.

When they went to trial, it took the jury just 20 minutes to reach its verdict and acquit both men; the jurors were obviously not impressed with Shakespeare. At the time of writing, Nye had been awarded $1.3m in damages, including $750,000 in exemplary damages, after suing the state, the DPP and four police officers, claiming malicious prosecution, wrongful arrest and false imprisonment. He was dying of mesothelioma

When I think about it, I have been involved with the cases of a few successful criminals who have gone to meet their maker. A few years earlier I had done the inquest of Danny Chubb, who could be connected to Thurgar through six degrees of separation. They were both involved in different ways in the gang wars of the mid-1980s over Sydney's drug trade.

Chubb used to give his occupation as seaman but he was known to police as a safebreaker and prolific punter, a regular at the Harold Park Trots on a Friday night and at the greyhound races. He also owned a number of racehorses. He was a mammoth punter at south coast racecourses where, because of the magnitude of his bets, most bookmakers found it prudent to put a limit on him. He drove a brand new Jaguar sedan, owned a house, land and boat and was rumoured to have several million dollars in overseas bank accounts. In November 1984, he had separated from his wife and was living with his mum in High Street, Millers Point near The Rocks in Sydney.

At about 10.30 a.m. on 8 November 1984, Chubb, 43, took a telephone call. While he was on the phone, an acquaintance, Bruce McCauley arrived to collect some wine. McCauley was well known to the federal police, having been a target during a protracted inquiry involving drug importation into Australia. McCauley was at the time suspected of being the 'financial adviser' for the drug deals and was later jailed for heroin smuggling.

Chubb told McCauley he had to go out for a short while. He drove his Jag to the nearby Captain Cook Hotel in Kent Street, Millers Point where he met the infamous Arthur Stanley 'Neddy' Smith and his sidekick Graham 'Abo' Henry. When he left them, Chubb bought some fish and chips and drove home. The shotgun blast got him as he stepped out of his car, blowing away half his face. He was also shot in the chest. He died immediately. The fish and chips were found unopened beside the car. McCauley was in the house, and made a quick getaway himself because he feared he might be the next target.

While the cause of death was simple to determine, who had pulled the trigger was going to be much harder. After his murder, the police discovered Chubb was heavily involved with heroin and hashish smuggling, using his drug dealings to finance his racing investments. In his line of work his enemies were many. The police discovered Chubb was owed about $400,000 by another drug-dealer-cum-punter, Mick Sayers. Sayers had lied about his alibi at the time of Chubb's murder but Chubb's death was to the detriment of Sayers' business. Chubb had been supplying Sayers and with him dead, the source of Sayers' supply was cut off. On the face of it, it was unlikely that Sayers had been behind the shooting. Sayers later said he had been on his way to visit Chubb and had witnessed the killing.

In the words of the TV Demtel salesman, there was more. Greg Glass, who was then the City Coroner, conducted the first inquest into Chubb's death and it threw up a veritable who's who of Australia's underworld. Speculation was rife that it was the feared assassin Christopher Dale Flannery who had pulled the trigger. Flannery was a Melbourne criminal who had moved up to Sydney and had set up as a gun-for-hire. Several months after Chubb's death, Flannery, Smith and Sayers got together for a meeting over the payment of protection money to Flannery.

Then, in January 1985, an attempt was made to shoot Flannery dead outside his house in Turella Street, Arncliffe. A month later, Sayers was shot dead outside his house in Hewlett Street, Bronte. In May 1985, Flannery famously disappeared after leaving the apartment in the plush Connaught building overlooking Sydney's Hyde Park where he had moved with his wife. He was probably murdered.

Enter Roy Thurgar. Over the next three years, Thurgar's mate, Tom Domican, was charged with the murder of Sayers, the murder of Flannery and the attempted murder of Flannery. He was eventually cleared of all three charges with most of the evidence against him coming from unreliable prison informers. (Actually, showing what a small world it is in such circles, a director of the Nugan Hand Bank once issued a summons claiming Domican owed him more than $5300. Domican said he had repaid the money and the summons was later dismissed.)

So who killed Chubb? Greg Glass recorded an open finding, saying there was insufficient evidence to charge anyone with the murder.

Not long after I had become Deputy State Coroner in 1988, the NSW Supreme Court quashed Greg's finding and ordered a new inquest after an application by the NSW Attorney-General. There was evidence from federal police telephone taps which had mentioned Chubb. The telephone taps had been known about at the time of the first inquest but never presented to the coroner. The second inquest was to be mine.

The taped telephone conversations had occurred while the federal police were conducting Operation Lavender into drug smuggling. The conversation I was concerned with occurred on 2 May 1985 between Dr Nick Paltos and a solicitor, Ross Karp. When I listened to the conversation tape in court, it was obvious they were discussing Chubb.

Paltos was what you might call a character. Harry Secombe had famously credited the doctor with saving his life after Paltos told the 127 kilogram entertainer that he would die if he did not lose weight. On his advice, Secombe dropped 35 kilograms. In the 1980s, Paltos also looked after the health of a host of Sydney criminals, listing Chubb, crime boss George Freeman and drug lord Robert Trimbole among his patients.

The background that led to police setting up Operation Lavender was that in mid-1983, Chubb had approached Paltos because he had heard the doctor was heavily in debt from his gambling. According to Paltos, Chubb wanted a Greek-speaking person to liaise with a Greek contact over the importation of five tonnes of hashish through Darwin. Paltos in turn arranged for two other people, including Karp, to be involved.

About two months after the conversation with Chubb, Paltos said he had travelled to Greece and negotiated with people who were associated with Chubb. Upon his return, his job was to maintain contact with a Greek man while Chubb travelled to Darwin to make arrangements for the arrival of the ship transporting the hashish. But the ship ran out of fuel and Chubb made arrangements for its illegal load to be transferred to a trawler and transported to Sydney. Two tonnes of the hashish, which was poor quality, were recovered by the federal police after the arrests of Paltos, Karp and the third man. All three were subsequently convicted and jailed for conspiracy to import hashish. Paltos received the toughest sentence, 20 years, and was released after just under nine years. Karp received 14 years with nine years non-parole.

In the taped telephone conversation, Karp was recorded saying, 'Right, but let's say, for instance, let's work it completely backwards and say, alright, say they start looking at Danny and Danny was still, right, and we didn't know it.' The conversation continued.

> Paltos: 'Oh, it was my shot that Danny's dead you know.'
> Karp: 'Yeah, that's right.'
> Paltos: Yeah really, Ross, he would have brought us all undone.'
> Karp: 'Oh look at the way he used to talk on the phone.'
> Paltos: 'Yeah.'
> Karp: 'We'd visit him, they'd be looking at his joint watching the cars coming and going, you'd come undone from things that aren't really, you know, anything vital, um, look how we come under notice with Terry and Denise ...'

When Paltos was interviewed by police in January 1986 at Long Bay Jail Remand Centre, he told police he couldn't recall the conversation. He said that on the day Chubb was murdered he had been at home when he received a telephone call from Mrs Chubb who, he said, appeared to be under the misapprehension her son had committed suicide. I felt it was possible to interpret from the taped conversation that Paltos had either killed Chubb himself or had someone do it because Chubb had a loose tongue that could have brought them all undone. On the other hand, he could have been trying to impress Karp. There was also the point that it was Chubb who had masterminded their drug operation. It didn't really bring me much closer to being able to recommend someone be charged with Chubb's murder. One of the theories was that his killing was connected with the distribution of heroin after its arrival in Australia, a business Neddy Smith was involved in and that therefore Smith and his associates were strong suspects. Smith denied any involvement.

As with the case of George Woodcock, I had to record an open finding on the Chubb case. No one has yet been charged with Chubb's murder. Smith is serving two life sentences for the murder of brothel keeper Harvey Jones and for stabbing to death Ronald Flavell, a truck driver who flashed his lights at Smith in traffic.

A few days after the inquest into Mr Woodcock's murder, I had a sad case back at Glebe. There were two brothers, Sam and Con Efthimiades, who had been helped by their parents to set up a plumbing business but the two of them were as different as chalk and cheese and could not stop fighting. The evidence I heard was that Sam, 23, had a collection of knives, swords, bows and arrows. He often spoke of going off to live in the Queensland bush. Con, 21, was the religious one, who enjoyed getting together with other Christian evangelicals.

Their parents, Atina and Theo Efthimiades, witnessed their last fight. Mrs Efthimiades told me in a statement that she was lying in bed in their Marrickville home in the early hours of 21 April 1991, listening to the brothers arguing in the lounge room. Con was calling Sam 'the devil' and Sam labelled Con a 'religious freak'. Con called on their father to step in.

Mr Efthimiades said he saw Sam go to the front balcony and return with a 60-centimetre knife and stab his brother. Mr Efthimiades ran to get someone to call an ambulance and when he got back, Sam had stabbed himself. Both brothers died. It was a terrible tragedy for their parents. Sam had suffered from a manic illness for which he had been hospitalised four times. I felt for the family.

'It does not matter how much we try to do our best for our children, some things can go wrong,' I told Mr and Mrs Efthimiades.

I heard another terrible case. The inquest into an elderly couple who died of carbon monoxide poisoning after the man used homemade connections to convert an old gas heater. Giuseppe Curcuruto, 76, was an active man who was always fixing things and had a garage full of tools, his son, Leo, told me in court.

In July 1991, he dug out an old heater which had been gathering dust in his garage for 21 years. The heater had been made to run off town gas but since it had last been used, the area where the Curcurutos lived had been switched to natural gas and old appliances either converted to run off the new gas supply or condemned as dangerous. Mr Curcuruto had cleaned up the heater and attached it to the gas main using two metres of hose from a washing machine and some garden hose fittings. He and his wife died in their sleep from asphyxiation. At least the couple would not have suffered any pain in their manner of death, I was able to reassure their family.

Leo Curcuruto told me that his father had thought that town gas appliances simply burned with a stronger flame when used with natural gas and would have known nothing about the dangers of carbon monoxide being emitted. In Mr Curcuruto's garage were two other town gas appliances which the pensioner had connected to the natural gas supply. The gas company had circulated brochures to everyone in their area since the switch to natural gas two years earlier, warning of the dangers of using appliances without safety labels.

This was one of those cases in which I thought I should issue a warning, to try and stop this happening again. I felt the gas company had done everything it could to try and warn people not to fiddle with these sorts of things without properly qualified people being present and I warned the public not to try and do so.

Christmas was coming round and it had become traditional to have Christmas lunch in the main courtroom. The bar table became the dinner table and all the staff, including the police, scientists and those who worked in the morgue, were invited. The ladies organised it all. The dishes weren't given the sort of names they had been at Westmead but the occasion was no less sedate. There were some very funny people working at Glebe and that year it was our usual hilarious Christmas lunch. We laughed about one of the school visits. One of the investigators, Sean Godkin, and one of the prosecutors had been conducting a lecture for a large group of year ten children. All had been going well. Sean had fielded the usual array of questions kids at that age asked such as, 'Have you ever seen a dead body?' All of a sudden one of the kids put up his hand and asked an extremely complicated legal question based on the *Coroners Act*. It was a question that may have stumped even me initially. What Sean didn't know was that I had put the schoolboy up to it. I wrote down the question and gave the piece of paper to one of the prosecutors, Tony Astley, to hand it to the schoolboy. Sean had been slightly flustered before offering to research the question for the youngster and forwarding it to his school. Sean saw the humour of it when we told him how we had set him up.

It was also Kevin's last Christmas as State Coroner. His three-year appointment was up and he was ready to retire – he had certainly had an eventful few years and served the people of New South Wales well. Before he announced his retirement, he spoke to me about becoming State Coroner and I decided to apply for the job.

CHAPTER 5

Suite 2401

THE WEATHER HAD been perfect for night sailing. There was a 15–18 knot breeze and the sky was clear when the *Patanela* contacted Sydney Radio to say she was heading for Sydney Heads. She was low on fuel and advised the radio officer of the plan to tack out to sea before sailing through the Heads at first light. At 1 a.m., the 20 metre steel-hulled yacht was ten nautical miles east of Botany Bay heading north. Skipper Ken Jones was a highly experienced yachtsman, an expert navigator who also had a pilot's licence and had flown jets for Alan Bond and the Shah of Iran. He had a crew of three, including his wife Noreen. The *Patanela* was equipped with extensive safety equipment including an electronic locator beacon. On board were 28 lifejackets, two windsurfers, a black Zodiac dinghy and a 15-man life raft.

At 1.57 a.m., when the yacht radioed for an updated weather report, she would have been sailing well in easy conditions. Skipper Jones said the wind was dropping off and he didn't want to get caught out at sea with no wind to sail back into the harbour. Then he asked how far Moruya was from Sydney, saying he was unfamiliar with the coast. He was told it was about five hours' driving time. At 2.02 a.m., through the static came another call from the ship. Sydney Radio only picked up the words, 'Three hundred kilometres south is it ... south ...'

THE CORONER

That was 8 November 1988. The yacht never made it to Sydney. The *Patanela* vanished into thin air along with its crew. It wasn't quite Australia's *Marie Celeste* but its mystery was almost as gripping. All that has been found of the yacht was a barnacle-encrusted lifebuoy drifting off Terrigal on the NSW central coast in March 1989, six months after it sank. Under the *Coroners Act*, if there is no body, you have to have an inquest. What made this investigation stretch longer than most was with no bodies and no boat, there were many loose ends to try to tie up.

That is why it took until 24 February 1992 before I got down to seeing if anyone could help with the puzzle of what happened to the *Patanela* and the inquest into the suspected deaths of the yacht's crew opened at Glebe.

There were all sorts of rumours, including that the yacht was hijacked by drug traffickers. The four years since the yacht's disappearance had given people plenty of time for speculation. The story, as I saw it, was much more mundane but no less tragic. The *Patanela* was 23 days into its voyage from Fremantle in Western Australia to Airlie Beach and the Whitsunday Passage in Queensland. It was scheduled to call into Sydney. There was Ken Jones, 52, his wife Noreen, 50, and two NSW men, Michael Calvin, 21, and John Blissett, 23, both experienced sailors. By all accounts the ship was robust, well maintained and sailed well. Sergeant John White was assisting me with the inquest and one of our first witnesses was the *Patanela*'s owner, Allan Nicol. Nicol had left the yacht a week before its disappearance to attend to urgent business. John asked him what he thought could have happened to the yacht. Mr Nicol replied that he could not say because he had no proof.

Mr Nicol was a businessman who owned roadhouses in Western Australia and he had that look about him of a yachtsman; he was the healthy, outdoors type. He travelled to Glebe obviously wanting to help find out what had happened but he found it hard to accept the boat had sunk because there was no evidence to see. It was surprising that not more wreckage was discovered, for example, the life raft was not tied down and would have floated to the surface. Mr Nicol said he found it difficult to understand why the skipper would need to radio that he was low on fuel and needing help to get into Sydney Harbour. He also could not understand why other ships and boats had not seen the *Patanela* on what was a clear night in one of the busiest shipping lanes in the world.

SUITE 2401

A navy submarine had been about six kilometres from the *Patanela*'s last reported position and Mr Nicol said he had spoken to one of the submariners and even they had not spotted the yacht on their radar, something the submariners told Mr Nicol they found very surprising with all their sophisticated equipment.

The federal police officer who had been leading the investigation into the yacht's disappearance, Detective Superintendent Edmund Tyrie, had investigated all the conspiracy theories. He said it was known that Calvin and Blissett were cannabis and hashish users. There had been a suggestion the two men had been overheard talking about hijacking the *Patanela* and taking off to South America but he said he felt the conversation could be passed off as bravado and fantasy of young people affected by alcohol. He had found no evidence to substantiate the men were involved in the yacht's disappearance.

I had been wondering why, when the ship never arrived in Sydney despite the yacht's last message saying it was on the way, there was no search launched. The Sydney Radio communications officer who had been the last person to speak to the *Patanela* said it was not their policy to ensure a ship carried out its stated intentions. He said skippers often changed their minds. Had the ship indicated there was an emergency, then it would have been different but there was nothing to indicate the ship had been in distress, he said. It was not until 12 days later, when the ship failed to arrive at Airlie Beach, that the alarm was raised.

The water ten nautical miles off Sydney is 75 fathoms, or 135 metres, deep, too deep for a diver using tanks. Trying to find whether the wreck of the *Patanela* was down there was, according to the navy, like finding the proverbial needle in a haystack.

How could a ship sink without trace? We were left with only educated guesses so John White and I decided to call in some experts. Maritime Rescue Coordination Centre assistant manager Graham Mapplebeck suggested the yacht may have sunk after being overpowered by a sudden strong gust of wind. Peter Dummet, a naval architect, told me that the structure of the *Patanela* was such that it would have been difficult for the yacht to founder even in 35-knot wind conditions. It would have taken a catastrophic event, not a minor bang or structural failure, to sink the steel-hulled vessel. Such a catastrophe could have happened if the yacht was struck by a much bigger ship.

'For a vessel like that to sink very quickly without giving anyone a chance to put out a mayday or fire a flare, it has to be almost cut in half,' Mr Dummet told me.

In the middle of the night, in the dark out at sea, it was a frightening scenario. For a landlubber like me, who knows nothing about the sea or sailing, it was hard to imagine. It was also a bit way out to think that could happen without anyone knowing about it, but it was the only reasonable explanation. There was no alien ship out there to spirit it up and away.

The other theory, that the *Patanela* may have been hijacked and was being used for drug running, was beyond the realms of possibility, and I said as much when I handed down my findings. There was absolutely no evidence that any member of the crew was involved in anything illegal to do with the disappearance of the yacht. Unfortunately I was unable to give the families of the crew members a definitive answer but I could certainly give them my opinion that the boat sank and that their relatives were dead. It was most likely struck by a larger vessel such as a tanker which would not have noticed the impact. The details of what really happened to the *Patanela* out there that night will probably never be known. To me, the sinking remains a mystery.

As I had been getting ready to open the *Patanela* inquest, I got a phone call from Peter Collins, then the NSW Attorney-General, asking me to go and see him the next morning. Kevin had a few more days as State Coroner before he was due to retire in the second week of February and there had been no announcement as to who would be moving into his office. When I got the phone call, I knew it was not going to be me. If it had been good news he would have told me over the phone.

Next morning in Peter Collins' office in Macquarie Street, I knew I had been right. He told me that I deserved the job; however, so did Greg Glass. I would get my opportunity later, he said. Greg Glass had been the City Coroner before the state position was created and his last position was as a magistrate at Central Local Court in the city. I had always been given the impression that I would be getting the job of State Coroner but by the time I was given the news, I had accepted the fact that it wouldn't be me. I was not real happy about it.

SUITE 2401

Peter Collins said that he would like me to stay on as deputy and I told him OK, but that I wanted another three-year appointment. I didn't want to find out 12 months later that somebody else didn't want me. He agreed and I accepted the deputy's position again. The Chief Magistrate, Ian Pike, also wanted me to stay on as deputy. As a carrot, or as an escape route, whichever way you want to look at it, he told me that if at any time I really wanted another position, then he would consider favourably any application I may make.

When I got back to Glebe, I told Kevin the news. Like me, he had realised by then that there had been something in the wind and that the job was not going to be mine. He had backed me for the job and that meant a lot to me.

We felt Kevin deserved a big farewell so the ladies in the office organised a great do at Sydney University with a sit-down dinner. Doreen came with me. Terry Griffiths, the Justice Minister, was there and he got his wives mixed up. He walked up to Doreen and said, 'Welcome, Mrs Glass.' She heard him make some remark to Greg like, 'Well, we got you there.' When Doreen came over and sat down next to me, Terry Griffiths got the shock of his life. Little things but they made us laugh.

Of course, I was disappointed about the job but it didn't affect my work. I was always able to separate my personal feelings from the way I worked. However, like with every new boss, things changed at Glebe under Greg Glass. I have always got on with him and working with him was not a strain, despite the circumstances of me being his number two. When Greg moved into Kevin's office, I let him know how Kevin and I had worked together and what the system was and he was happy to continue that way, but it was a different atmosphere. The office had been shaped by Kevin, while Greg was a different personality. Of course, everyone likes to put their stamp on things and that was reflected in the tone of the office.

※

The disappearance of the *Patanela* was not the only mystery of 1992. Why did two healthy young people suddenly die for no apparent reason? They had literally just dropped dead.

In July 1992, the body of Sonja Jarvis-Mullins was brought into the morgue at Glebe. She had been found dead in her bed the morning after her thirty-seventh birthday, the discovery made by her 12-year-old daughter. She had spent the previous evening at a quiet celebration dinner at a local Italian restaurant, drinking just a couple of glasses of wine. She hadn't complained of feeling sick before she went to bed. The most serious medical problem she suffered from was sinus and a possible viral infection. Jo DuFlou and his staff in the labs at the Institute of Forensic Medicine found no traces of poisons, bugs or diseases, no medical reason for her death. We recorded her death as 'undetermined'. That was always unsatisfactory.

In October 1992, a similar thing happened to Peter Thermos. He was 26, weighed about 80 kilograms, played tennis and, according to his parents, had never been sick in his life. His mother and sister returned to their home from shopping one evening to find him lying face down on the kitchen floor. They were unable to revive him. It appeared as if Jo DuFlou had identified the first cases in the country of adult SIDS, or SADS, Sudden Adult Death Syndrome. Jo DuFlou explained that just as SIDS was a convenient diagnosis for something we did not know the cause of in infants, so it was with SADS and adults. In up to about five per cent of all deaths we saw, the cause could not be determined. There was a pattern. Most of them were elderly people who had a variety of illnesses and ailments. However, there was a sub-group of young people where the cause of death was just not known. These people usually died in their sleep, the cause unexplainable in any other way, so we gave it a name – SADS.

Like Peter Thermos, Bradley McNamara was a fit young man. He was a police officer who at 24 had been chosen to join the elite Patrol Support Element, formerly called the Special Weapons and Operations Squad or SWOS. Eleven days into his training, Bradley was taking part in a five kilometre run at the Goulburn Police Academy when he collapsed and died of multiple organ failure from heatstroke, or muscle meltdown as it was explained to me during the inquest.

The best way to get answers is to call in the experts. In this case we called on Professor John Sutton, professor of medicine and exercise physiology at Sydney University. Professor Sutton was a runner himself and he was able to provide me with invaluable help on such an unusual case. He explained that heatstroke occurred when the body's heat-regulating mechanisms failed and the muscles literally broke down. The treatment for people with heatstroke is to give them fluids, either through the mouth or intravenously as a matter of emergency, and to cool their body with ice. When the body got to the advanced stage of the muscles breaking down there was little if anything that could be done to save the person.

I wondered if there was anything about the police officer that made him more susceptible to muscle meltdown. He did a bit of weight training and at 195 centimetres tall and weighing 111 kilograms, he was a big man and therefore would have generated more body heat than a thinner person running at the same speed. He would also have taken longer to cool down. Professor Sutton said that those facts alone would not have caused the meltdown.

Constable McNamara had been sick with the flu and taking medication including Nurofen, and it is well known medically that exercise when unwell is never a good idea. He may also have been dehydrated after driving down from Sydney that same day he did the run. Another factor was that he would have been highly motivated to do well, but that had been the same for the other trainees. Professor Sutton described a five kilometre run as a short run and not usually a distance you would even make a point of checking that runners had taken adequate fluids beforehand.

When I handed down my finding, I found that there was no warning that this could have happened to Constable McNamara. He was a young man who had gone away as part of his job. It could have happened to anyone, no matter what age or fitness. The ambulance officers, the police, the doctors and nurses had done all they could. I had to conclude that there was probably nothing that could have prevented this death but I recommended police instigate pre-course medical examinations as a matter of course for all officers undertaking physical training.

I would arrive at Glebe about 8.30 a.m. each day. Monday mornings at Glebe were usually busiest, with the bodies that had come in over the weekend waiting to be dealt with. I would pop into the main office and check with the coronial manager, Graham O'Rourke, and the other staff on the state of things and then disappear into my office with the overnight's P79As – the forms that police had to fill in for all suspicious or sudden deaths – and sign the orders for post-mortem examinations if the body had already been positively identified. One body was of a man who lived on the streets and had died at the Matthew Talbot Hostel. One of the hostel managers identified him by the name he knew him by, let's call him John Smith. On the man's body was a wallet containing cards identifying him as John Smith. The police contacted John Smith's wife and daughter, who came to the morgue for a viewing. On being shown the body, the wife said, 'I've never seen him with a beard.' Being an innovative lot at Glebe, the morgue attendants proceeded to shave the man. On seeing him again, the wife said, 'Yes, that is him.'

The funeral was held a few days later at the chapel at the Matthew Talbot Hostel with an open casket. Before the service began, the wife changed her mind. She said, 'I'm not really sure whether that *is* him.' Our office was told the news and one of the officers explained to the wife that the muscles of the face relax when death occurs, making visual identification difficult sometimes. The woman was asked to have a think about it and if she was still not satisfied that the body was her husband, then the body had to be returned to the morgue at Glebe. The wife decided she was not sure and the body came back.

On that very weekend, who should walk into the daughter's house but the 'deceased', her father. She told him, 'Dad, the police are looking for you, you must go and see them. A man has died and he had your wallet and papers and has been identified as you.' Her father said OK but instead of going to the police, he went to Queensland. His daughter tried to persuade him again to go to the police but to no avail, nor could he explain to her why this dead man had his wallet. The father then disappeared to Italy and to my knowledge has never returned to Australia or been questioned as to whom he thinks the dead man could be. To this day, neither the coroner's office nor the police know what happened. The man was never identified and was buried as a Destitute Burial, an unknown person.

It was a sad outcome for the man who died but did demonstrate why visual identification may not always be acceptable and why it often needs more, like dental charts or even in some cases DNA tests.

On Monday, 21 June 1993, one of the bodies lying in the morgue with the non-removable tag secured around his wrist was the man known as the face of AFL football, Alan Schwab. He had been found dead in Suite 2401 at the

SUITE 2401

Boulevard Hotel in Kings Cross on the Friday afternoon, naked with a false red fingernail stuck to the back of his left shoulder. The news had been full of him all weekend. I signed his P79A and the post-mortem went ahead.

The interim autopsy report landed on my desk within 48 hours while the tests on his blood and the contents of his stomach took a bit longer. When the results came through, they showed unequivocally what had killed Alan Schwab. He had a blood alcohol reading of 0.214 milligrams, over four times the legal limit for driving, and 0.13 milligrams per litre of methadone, more than enough to floor a non-user. Combined with the alcohol it was a fatal mixture. Trace amounts of codeine and quinine were also found.

In Melbourne the media went mad. To them, Sydney was Sin City and Schwab, one of Melbourne's favourite sons, had died an ignominious death in the den of iniquity that was the NSW capital. As executive commissioner of the AFL he was one of the country's leading sports administrators. He had spent just over a month in Sydney as interim chairman of the ailing Sydney Swans assessing what was needed to restructure the club. Now he had died in decidedly seedy circumstances. He had left behind a wife and three children. The last person known to have seen him alive was the prostitute who had walked out of Suite 2401 at about 11.35 p.m. the night before his body was discovered.

It was not for me to make any moral judgment about his actions and I didn't. A coroner or magistrate cannot use his personal feelings, likes or dislikes. He must remain objective. It took police two months to track down the prostitute and even longer to complete their investigation into Alan Schwab's death. It took almost two years before the inquest was held.

※

I had begun to rethink my own future. I had been deputy to Greg Glass for 18 months and I decided I would enjoy working on my own much more. Doreen's cousin lived in Port Macquarie and we had other friends there who we visited often and we had commented that we would eventually like to live there. I regularly received the circulars sent out by the Chief Magistrate advertising vacant positions and I saw the job of magistrate at Port Macquarie had come up – you could say it was the right job at the right time. I mentioned it in passing to Doreen. While we didn't speak of it again for about a week, we had both been thinking about it. One day I said to her, 'I've had enough here, let's go.' There was nothing to hold us in Sydney. Megan was living in Melbourne and John was in Dallas, Texas working as a petroleum engineer. Doreen did not mind giving up her job at the pre-school because she wanted to go as much as I did.

I remembered Ian Pike's words about looking favourably on any job application I might submit so I sent off my application and waited. I was pleased when I got the posting.

We sold our house in Sydney and had a big send-off out at Wentworthville League's Club in the city's west, organised by the police and magistrates I had worked with. We bought a house in Port Macquarie and I started work there in September 1993.

I enjoyed being back in the country courts. On a Monday we would have the list day at Kempsey and on a Wednesday it was list day at Port Macquarie. List day is for running down the list of cases before the court and taking pleas of guilty, adjourning longer cases and if there is time, hearing some not guilty pleas. Nearly every solicitor in town turns up on list days to represent their clients so it was an ideal time for me to introduce myself to them and start things off the way I expected to continue.

On those first two list days, I called the solicitors into my office to tell them how I liked things to run. There were about five or six solicitors in each town. For a start, I told them, I wasn't real keen on them wasting time by beating their heads against a brick wall when the evidence against their client was such that it was quite clear they were going to be found guilty. That was the defence side of things sorted out. It was the businesslike way Kevin and I had run things in Sydney.

As far as the prosecutors went, I told them that if I was quite satisfied early on that there was never going to be a case proved against a defendant, I would say so and that would be that. I wasn't going to sit there while either side just rambled on. It had to work both ways if the courts were to be kept on the right track and not get bogged down. They all got onto my wavelength. Within about six months, instead of being behind by six months in defended cases, we all had the time lag down to four to six weeks.

SUITE 2401

The return to the magistrates' bench brought me back to real-life cases. What struck me straightaway was the number of domestic violence cases. Things had changed a lot in the nine years since I had last sat on a local court bench. In the earlier days of my career, I would hardly have seen a domestic assault, although I have no doubt they had always happened. The increase could be put down to more women reporting such violence to the police. Drink-driving was another area that had changed and the number of repeat drink-drivers before the court surprised me. I might have imposed good behaviour bonds on some of them but I made sure they realised that if they broke the terms of the bond, the next stop was jail. Port Macquarie being the coastal town that it was, meant we also had a lot of blow-ins end up in court, out-of-towners passing through who had committed crimes on the way.

While I was confident with the way I wanted my court to run, I was initially a bit hesitant about the changes to the law and the new penalties since I had last sat as a magistrate. However, I wasn't embarrassed to pick up a book and look up the new penalties while I was on the bench. It didn't take me long to get up to speed.

Doreen and I quickly settled back in to life in a country town. I joined the local golf club and Doreen, who enjoyed making porcelain dolls, got into a doll-making group. These days you might call it a 'sea-change' although Doreen and I didn't name it as such at the time. We have always found it easy to make friends. It was an easier way of life, a lot more relaxed than in Sydney. I was enjoying it. It was a pleasant and comfortable place to live and work. I thought to myself, 'Well, I'm 57. I will stay here until I'm 60 and retire.' Then I did a Dame Nellie Melba and came back.

John Hannaford had taken over as NSW Attorney-General and he dropped in to see me at Port Macquarie a couple of times when he was in the area. On one of these visits, he said that Greg Glass was coming up to retirement and would not be reappointed as State Coroner. He asked if I would be interested in the top job. My reply was no. Doreen and I were enjoying life in Port Macquarie and we had never thought about going back to Sydney. Then I received a couple of telephone calls from a magistrate in Sydney who was also a friend, talking me into applying for the post. It started to become more appealing. Doreen and I discussed it and, well, it had been what I had wanted in the past and I realised that it was still what I really wanted although I felt I would never get the chance after being overlooked for Greg Glass and then moving to the country. So I applied.

Late one afternoon in December 1994, after I had finished in court and was in my office, John Hannaford rang and said, 'Derrick, I'm just signing your appointment as State Coroner.' Eighteen months after leaving Sydney, Doreen and I were on the move again – back there.

Greg Glass retired in February 1995 and I took over straightaway. It meant I had to pass up a holiday in Alaska to see our first grandchild. Our son John and his wife Ineca had moved to Alaska and their daughter, little Caitlin, was born in early March. Doreen took her 80-year-old mother instead of me and they had a ball.

Not much had changed at Glebe Coroners Court. Since Kevin's day, the office occupied by the State Coroner had been renovated. The wall between it and the library had been knocked down so it was no longer a pokey room, making it a better working space with more light and more room to store files and have meetings. However, the familiar faces were the same. Most of the staff were there from my first stint and we easily resumed where we had left off. John Abernethy had been appointed deputy after I left the first time and he stayed on in that role. We had known each other as magistrates but had never worked together before. As it happened, we got on pretty well. It was very easy for me to slip back into things at Glebe. I felt that I was fairly easygoing in the job. I found that if you treated other people properly they always gave you their best.

One of my first visitors was John Laycock, now a superintendent, who was then the head of task force Snowy. I always had a lot of time for John. He is a decent man and a good police officer. Snowy had been set up to investigate 13 unsolved murders, all of them a few years old and all of them suspected to have been committed by Neddy Smith, then in jail for life for the murder of the truck driver, Ronald Flavell. The investigation was triggered after a police informant, codenamed Mr Brown, had been put in a cell with Smith and their conversation secretly taped. On the tapes, Smith was heard boasting about several murders. John Laycock would come into my office, we'd have a coffee and he would keep me up to date regularly with the investigation as I made case notes of our discussions. I was involved because inquests had not been held into all of the deaths because few of the bodies had been found. The question was whether I would hold inquests without a body or whether criminal charges would be laid against Smith.

One of the bodies found had been that of Sallie-Anne Huckstepp, a prostitute and a drug addict. She had been found dead, lying in a small lake known as Busby's Pond in Centennial Park in 1986. Before I returned as State Coroner, task force Snowy had sought an order to exhume her body to check it for DNA evidence which might link it with Smith. The order had been signed by Greg Glass. As far as I could ascertain, it was the only criminal exhumation since Frank Nugan.

The other deaths included that of Brian Alexander. Alexander was a legal clerk who had fixed it several times for Smith, and other criminals, to beat charges by acting as a go-between with corrupt police. He went missing in 1981. If you have seen the ABC drama series *Blue Murder* (which is partly based on one of Smith's own books) Alexander goes out on a boat with Smith and others, laughing and drinking. He is tied to an old gas oven and thrown over the side, pleading for his life. If this is possibly what happened to him it is not a pretty scene. Based on that, his body was unlikely to be found.

In 1988, the body of another alleged Smith victim, drug dealer Gary Sandrie, had been found in the sandhills of Botany Bay when his leg and arm had popped out of the sand. In 1995, a man walking his dog found another body there, or rather his dog did. It is a fact that most bodies are found by dogs. Storm action had eroded this sandy grave and the dog found a skull sticking out of the sand. According to Mr Brown, Smith had told him that he had shot and buried would-be gangster and former brothel owner Harvey Jones there. Would the body be Jones, a man who by all accounts had idolised Smith? The problem with identification was that after a possible 12 years in the sand, all that was left of the body was a skeleton. It was buried about five feet deep but it needed to be kept intact for forensic purposes. A backhoe was brought in to take off the top layers of sand – in the process the foot of the skeleton was snared, ending up as a shoeful of bones.

When the skeleton was exposed, a spinal board was slipped beneath it to keep the body in one piece; it was slowly levered out and carefully put in a body bag. It was brought to Glebe where Paul Botterell and Chris Griffith did their magic.

You may not think there is a lot to discover from a pile of old bones but Paul Botterell, one of the forensic pathologists, did an extensive post-mortem and managed to reconstruct what had happened when the skeleton had last been a living, breathing man. On the tapes, Smith was recorded boasting he had shot Jones dead on the foreshore at Botany Bay by blowing his heart out. According to the tapes, Jones had told Smith, 'I'll die for you,' and Smith had replied, 'You're about to, you f...... mug.' Then he pulled the trigger.

Paul Botterell found evidence that the victim had been shot through his fingers as he brought them up in a defensive action when he realised what was happening to him. The bullet chipped one of his ribs and lodged in his chest cavity, which made the cause of death exactly as Smith had described on the tapes – this person was shot in the heart. Bits of lead were found on the chipped ribs. If the bones had just been dug out of the ground and jiggled together in a bag that evidence would have been lost.

We had to be sure who it was. Chris Griffith was called in. He was to teeth and skulls what Paul Botterell was to bodies. Chris Griffith is an orthodontist at Westmead Hospital, an ex-air force man who wears a bowtie. Chris and I worked together on many cases where bodies were unable to be visually identified, either they were burned beyond recognition or badly decomposed or mutilated. The teeth of the victim are checked against the dental records. The pattern of the teeth and dental work of a person are used like a fingerprint and are unique to each individual.

With the forensic evidence from Paul and Chris, the police were pretty sure it was Harvey Jones. His dental charts matched those of the body. If Smith was charged with his murder, they did not want to leave the defence any chance to muddy the waters by claiming a mistaken identification. Chris Griffiths went about reconstructing the skeleton's face. The police had a photograph of Harvey Jones smiling, standing next to Neddy Smith. They had got the picture from Smith's photo album! Chris cut Smith out of the frame and concentrated on Jones. He took a video of the skull and a video of the photograph and superimposed the photograph on the skull

SUITE 2401

using a computer. It was painstaking work that Chris has got down to a fine art over the years. He was able to identify particular points of comparison between the skull and the photograph, such as the development of the cheekbones and the distance between the eyes. Everyone's teeth are different and Chris was able to match the gaps, the length, width and shape of the teeth. There was no doubt it was Harvey Jones. Smith was charged with his murder and even his defence agreed to the identification, although Smith denied having anything to do with Jones' death. The jury didn't believe him. He was convicted of Jones murder in September 1998 and sent off for his second life sentence.

I was back at Glebe in time to finish the work I had started on the death of Alan Schwab. When I held the inquest in April 1995, Mr Schwab's three children were sitting in court at the bar table, to hear the evidence. I felt that a death in these circumstances would have been even harder for them to bear. We started with what we knew about the events leading up to the discovery of their father's body in Suite 2401.

On Thursday, 17 June he had left the Boulevard Hotel at about 11 a.m. for a long lunch at Canterbury-Bankstown Leagues Club which lasted from about 1.25 p.m. to 5.45 p.m. He drank quite a lot and returned to the hotel about 6.55 p.m. In the next two hours, he made eight telephone calls, including one to his wife Lynette. She had told police that he had seemed 'well intoxicated' on the phone. He had told her that he was going to bed to watch the cricket but he was seen by a street prostitute on the corner of Crown and William Streets, not far from the hotel, at about 9 p.m. It has been said that what Alan Schwab did that night was stupid, but he had only behaved like many lonely businessmen away from home.

He arrived back at the Boulevard Hotel some time before 11.10 p.m. when he called room service and ordered a bottle of whisky, some Coke and two serves of strawberries and cream which were delivered in parfait glasses. The hotel waiter who delivered the food and drink said he had heard a female cough from behind a closed door in the suite and saw a strip of light beneath the doorway. He looked around to find a clear space to place the silver tray he was carrying. Drafts of letters and other papers lay strewn around. Five minutes later, Alan Schwab called the waiter to ask the time. That was the last hotel staff heard from him.

The officer in charge of the investigation, Detective Sergeant Mark Murdoch, told me that several hours later, a taxi driver was hailed across the street from the hotel by a woman who said, 'It's dangerous, it's dangerous on the streets. They've killed a man tonight in the Boulevard.'

About 7.45 the next morning, a housekeeper who had gone into Suite 2401 to see if it needed cleaning, saw Mr Schwab lying in the double bed. Thinking he was asleep, she left the room and rescheduled the cleaning for 4 p.m. At 3.56 p.m. that day, housekeeping discovered he was dead. His wallet, a mobile phone and two watches were missing from the room.

The whisky bottle stood empty on a bench with other bottles of liquor. In the fridge were the two glasses of strawberries and cream. On a bedside table were two unfinished cups of white coffee. Detective Murdoch said Mr Schwab drank black coffee, not white, and hardly, if ever, ate desserts of any kind. In ashtrays scattered throughout the suite, including the bathroom, were butts from more than one brand of cigarettes. It appeared that Mr Schwab had been entertaining.

Police fingerprinted the suite. Detective Murdoch said the owners of two sets of fingerprints remained a mystery but that half the fingerprints belonged to a prostitute, Nicki. The DNA testing on the cigarette butts showed they had been smoked by two different people, but not Alan Schwab or Nicki. The owner of the false red fingernail was never traced.

It had taken police two months to track down Nicki and she was found only after a public appeal led to a tip-off about her whereabouts. She had not only shared the last hours of Alan Schwab's life, she may indeed have been the last person to see him alive. She could have been crucial to the investigation, if she had told the truth. Her three statements to police were contradictory and unreliable to say the least. In her first statement, she had said she knew Mr Schwab but had never been to the Boulevard Hotel with him. She said he had solicited her on nearby Darlinghurst Road and they had $60 sex but not at the hotel. The fingerprints in the room told a different story so police spoke to her again. This time she admitted she had been at the hotel with Mr Schwab, but not on 17 June. That night they had sex at the Club 48 brothel in Kings Cross.

Police raided her home and there they found clothes belonging to Mrs Schwab, who at times stayed with her husband in Sydney. Mrs Schwab's

SUITE 2401

last visit had been at the hotel two days before he died. Nicki told her third story to police. She said that on the evening of 17 June, she and Mr Schwab had been to the Bourbon and Beefsteak bar in Kings Cross, then to Club 48, then to another hotel and then she admitted that she had accompanied him to the Boulevard Hotel. Police discovered that Mr Schwab had used the services of prostitutes at least twice in the previous week, each time in his hotel suite.

Nicki was an ex-heroin addict who was using methadone. She told police she had a bottle containing 300ml of methadone in her bag. She said Mr Schwab had grabbed the bottle and drank it when she told him it was pure alcohol. He had farewelled her from the hotel room around 11.30 p.m., dressed only in his underpants.

What was the truth? As a crucial witness Nicki was given the opportunity to be represented by a lawyer at the inquest and to question other witnesses, such as Detective Murdoch. She arrived from her new home in Queensland, where she lived with her two children, on the first day of the inquest but could not afford a lawyer. I granted her leave to ask questions herself. She sat at the bar table, spiky hair, several earrings in each ear, distressed and crying. When it came to the day she was supposed to go into the witness box and answer questions, Nicki didn't turn up. Police had organised accommodation for her at a nearby youth hostel but she didn't stay there.

Nikki had already indicated that she would refuse to answer any questions that may have incriminated her in a crime, as was her legal right. Was there anything to be gained from postponing the inquest to allow police to track her down again? I had already come to the conclusion that calling further witnesses was not going to take the matter any further. While it is a matter for the coroner to decide which witnesses were to be called, the wishes of the next of kin have to be taken into consideration. I asked Mr Schwab's children, through their QC, for their view. They agreed with me and did not want to prolong the hearing.

It left the mystery as to who else was in Suite 2401 that night and also the question as to how Mr Schwab came to take methadone. There was no evidence to suggest that he would have voluntarily taken it and I was unable to say, on the balance of probabilities, that he knew that was what he was taking. There was also the possibility that someone had spiked his drink with methadone. I felt Nicki's story that he had grabbed the bottle of methadone from her and drank it was extremely suspect, and said so when I handed down my findings. Other parts of her evidence were completely incorrect and there could be no reliance placed on her whatsoever or on anything she said, except that she had been in Suite 2401 that night. I found that Mr Schwab died from the combined effects of alcohol and methadone. My main concern, as always, was to ensure that his family was satisfied his death had been properly investigated, but without knowing how he had come to have methadone in his body, I had to deliver an open verdict.

In a transcript to this sad tale, two days after Mr Schwab died, after 26 consecutive losses, the Sydney Swans finally won a game by 40 points. A few months after his death, his missing wallet was found in the kitchen of Suite 2401. He had hidden it so that he would not be robbed.

CHAPTER 6

Silence of the Lambs

I WAS DRIVING TO work listening to the radio on 3 June 1994, when I heard a name I remembered only too well from the past – Daryl Suckling. He had been charged with the murder of Jodie Larcombe, probably at Wyrama Station.

Wyrama Station is tucked away in the southwest corner of New South Wales, north of the town of Pooncarie. At the time, the sealed road lasted just 100 yards outside town before turning into the pot-holed, rocky road that had to be travelled on for 45 dusty minutes to arrive at Wyrama. On the banks of the Darling River, Wyrama Station is in a flat and desolate spot. In the summer temperatures regularly reach 40° to 50° centigrade and just as easily drop close to freezing at night. I had seen photographs of the homestead. With its wide verandahs and high ceilings, it was a classic example of early Australian architecture. Unfortunately, the property has since burned down. Levee banks protected the home and the surrounding shearers' quarters and machinery sheds from the occasional flood. The homestead's own graveyard was nearby. The explorers Burke and Wills would have passed close to this spot when they made their ill-fated journey to the Gulf of Carpentaria 140-odd years ago.

It was here on 9 March 1988, that police found what one of the officers described as a scene out of the movie *Silence of the Lambs*.

THE CORONER

The police had been called by the property's neighbours at Court Nareen homestead, about 40 kilometres away. The previous night they had been hosting dinner and had invited their neighbours from Wyrama. There was the 52-year-old caretaker of Wyrama, Daryl Suckling, and the woman he introduced as his niece, Sophie Carni.

The neighbours had no idea of Suckling's past. He was what you might call a consistent criminal. Since the age of 11 he had collected more than 130 convictions, including raping a minor and escaping from custody. In 1973 he deliberately swallowed razor blades while in Pentridge Prison so he would be moved to Royal Melbourne Hospital from which he escaped. I was later told that in 1977 a forensic psychiatrist had described him as 'a gross example of a personality disorder' adding there was 'little to offer such a case in terms of psychiatry'.

During the meal, Carni politely excused herself from the table on the pretext of going to the toilet and in another part of the house, she managed to tell someone her secret. She had been kidnapped by Suckling and was being held against her will at Wyrama. The dinner host detained Suckling and called Pooncarie police station. Its only police officer, Constable Nick Skomorrow, was on 24-hour call. He arrived at Court Nareen within the hour. The relieved 26-year-old Sophie Carni told Constable Skomorrow her story, a story that filled 20 pages of her statement and which I later heard in court.

She had got to know Suckling when he was in Melbourne's Pentridge Prison while her husband, Mark Carni, was on remand for theft. She felt sorry for Suckling because he seemed to have no visitors and after his release in 1983, invited him to move in with her and her husband in their Melbourne flat. Within a week, she realised it was a mistake because the two men were soon committing burglaries together. Eventually they were both caught and sent back to jail. This time Carni's feelings towards Suckling had changed; instead of being sympathetic she was angry and blamed him for her husband's return to crime. While she wanted nothing to do with him, every week she received a letter from Suckling in jail.

In August 1987, Suckling was released from jail and got the job as caretaker at Wyrama, mainly doing maintenance odd jobs and keeping the garden tidy. In December that year, when Mark Carni was back in jail for other burglary offences, Carni received a telephone call from Suckling.

SILENCE OF THE LAMBS

Around Christmas 1987 he contacted her again and said he had a present he wanted to give her. Carni told him she wanted nothing to do with him. After she hung up from the phone conversation, she walked to a friend's house. As she walked along the street she saw Suckling sitting in his car. He waved but she ignored him.

Three months later, Suckling called her again. Again he said he had a present for her and persuaded her to meet him the following Saturday. Sophie Carni told the police that Suckling had become a nuisance and she had naively thought that if she saw him he would leave her alone. On the morning of Saturday, 5 March 1988, Suckling rang Carni and said that as well as having a present for her he wanted to take her for a meal at a restaurant in the Dandenong area. That afternoon he pulled up at her house in a Toyota Landcruiser tabletop, the battered bush vehicle he had been given to use while working at Wyrama. Carni got in the vehicle with him but he drove not to a restaurant but to an area of deserted bushland near Dandenong known locally as the 'police paddocks'. It was more than just a well-known lover's lane, several murders mainly of a sexual nature had occurred there over the years and remain unsolved. Suckling asked Carni to close her eyes and hold out her right wrist. When she opened them, she saw he had given her a silver 'Citizen' brand watch. He asked her to close her eyes again for another surprise and this time she felt a knife pressed against her throat.

Suckling handcuffed her, taped her mouth and pulled her jeans and panties down to her ankles to prevent her running away. He wrapped a padlocked chain around her neck and told her that if she moved as he was driving, he would pull the chain and rip her head off.

As he drove them on the 1300 kilometre journey from Melbourne to Wyrama Station, he forced her to drink an alcoholic mixture, telling her he intended taking photographs of her naked. When they got to the homestead, Carni was held prisoner by means of chains and handcuffs. She told police she was repeatedly raped vaginally, orally and anally. She was drugged with alcohol and sedatives, including the 'date-rape' drug Rohypnol, as Suckling took pornographic photographs, instructing her on how to pose, telling her to smile and look as if she was enjoying it.

When the postman visited Wyrama, Suckling handcuffed Carni to a rail in the wardrobe so she wouldn't be seen. He told her that if she was seen, he would have to kill the postman and then kill her. In her statement she said that Suckling told her, 'If you scream I'm going to have to attack them and kill them and then kill you for witnessing their murder. I was going to cut you up and bury your separate parts in different places so if anybody found you they wouldn't know whose body it was ... I have a body buried down the road already.'

Carni told police she played along with Suckling until he began to trust her, removing her chains and even taking her to the neighbouring station on the night of 8 March. With the police called in by the neighbours, on 9 March, Suckling was interviewed and charged with five offences, including sexual assault. With Suckling locked up in the cells and his bail refused, police conducted the usual search of the crime scene at Wyrama Homestead. In the dusty, untidy house they found not only the chains, handcuffs and drugs mentioned by Carni but also a container of granules later identified as cyanide and a magazine containing an article on cyanide killings.

Police also found women's clothes, jewellery and personal items that did not belong to Sophie Carni. Wrapped in tissue paper in a garbage bag in Suckling's bedroom was a partial dental plate. There was a purple 'Cherry Lane' brand T-shirt dress, a silver twenty-first key pendant and several silver bracelets. Inside several photo sleeves were photographs of naked women in a variety of poses. In one packet of 31 photographs, 28 were of a studio model, the others showed a woman obviously distressed, lying naked across the front seat of Suckling's Toyota Landcruiser. The young woman's face was bloated from crying and her eyes red and tear-stained. Her fair hair was messy, lank and looked unwashed. Around her wrists were faint handcuff marks and she was obviously drugged. On her right wrist were silver bracelets and on her left wrist, a silver 'Citizen' watch. Hanging from the Landcruiser's sun visor in the photograph was a purple Cherry Lane T-shirt dress.

Sophie Carni had earlier handed to officers the silver 'Citizen' brand watch which Suckling had given her. One of the police officers spotted that the watch, the dress and the other items belonged to the distressed woman in the photographs. He had copies made of the pictures and distributed them to various police stations in an attempt to try and identify her.

It was prostitutes in Melbourne's red light district of St Kilda who recognised the woman as Jodie Marie Larcombe. This is where I came in. Jodie had not been seen since she was reported missing in late December 1987. Daryl Suckling was charged with her murder. Those distressing photographs of Jodie Larcombe were tendered to me in August 1989 as part of the evidence in the committal hearing of Suckling on the murder charge. Standing to my right in the dock at Glebe Court, he was a sunken-chested, diminutive and wizened man. Not an impressive-looking fellow. Unlike his neighbours, I would never have invited him home for dinner.

While Sophie Carni had been lucky, the prosecution case was that Jodie Larcombe had not been. They alleged that Suckling had picked up Jodie on the streets of St Kilda in the early hours of Boxing Day 1987, drugged her, photographed her, and taken her to Wyrama Station where he had killed her. It was chillingly similar to what Sophie Carni said had happened to her, which was why Carni's evidence was allowed to go before me in August 1989 when I was conducting the committal hearing to decide whether there was enough evidence to send him to trial for Jodie Larcombe's murder. It is what is called in law 'similar fact' evidence, evidence identical or almost identical to the case before the court. It is only allowed in exceptional cases and it is left up to the court to decide whether to accept the evidence. I felt this was one of those exceptional occasions. However, the prosecution didn't have a body, always a problem in a murder case. In November 1988 police, police divers and the local SES had spent two days searching the Darling River and the 17,000 acres around Wyrama Homestead. A gyrocopter was brought in to conduct an aerial search. They found no body, no signs of a grave. There was no witness to the murder, no confession from Suckling. All the evidence was circumstantial, so was it enough to send this man to trial?

What the police did have was more than 180 witnesses in their brief of evidence. In a committal hearing, defendants have the right to call any witnesses for cross-examination whose statements the prosecution intends to tender. They can also agree to the statements being simply tendered to the court. That does not mean they necessarily agree with everything in the statement, just that they do not want to challenge the evidence at that stage. The choice of witnesses they wish to call usually gives you some indication of what evidence they will be contesting. Most of these issues are sorted out before the start of the committal.

In this case, Suckling said through his solicitor, the colourful Leigh Johnson, that he intended to call every one of those 180-odd witnesses to attend Glebe Coroners Court. At the best of times, bringing in 180 witnesses, many of them from interstate, would have provided a logistical nightmare. This was also one of the worst times to fly people into Sydney; the committal was due to start bang in the middle of the national pilot's strike. My prosecutor, Bobby Redfern, and I were more than relieved that such a job of gathering witnesses was left to the police. Thankfully commonsense prevailed and Suckling settled for only six witnesses to be called.

It is the lot of a coroner that you will never get to know in life the people you come to know so much about in death. You can only piece together the information you are given by others and from this you hope to tell the dead person's story. It is a story you always find yourself hearing backwards, starting at the end.

Jodie Maree Larcombe had been working as a prostitute, her beat the streets of St Kilda. Born on 26 July 1966, she grew up in the Dandenong/Springvale area of Victoria where she lived with her family. Her parents, Ken and Dorothy, ran a trucking business. Jodie left school at 15 and worked at a series of jobs. She moved out of home when she was 16 to live with her boyfriend, a local drug dealer, triggering an involvement with drugs that was to increase until she became addicted to heroin. She got engaged at 17, broke up with her fiancé when she was 19 and turned to prostitution to feed her drug habit. Her first arrest came just a month after her twentieth birthday and her criminal record began on 15 October 1986 when she was convicted of seven counts of loitering for prostitution and use of drugs, mainly marijuana and amphetamines.

Jodie's last arrest was by St Kilda police for soliciting on 19 December 1987. She admitted to police in a statement that she was a prostitute and said she preferred to conduct her business in cars. She charged $50 for normal sex, $40 for oral sex and $60 for both. She had spent a total of three days in custody on two outstanding warrants and was released on 22 December.

There was evidence from her closest friend, also a prostitute, that when Jodie was last seen alive, she had been wearing a purple 'Cherry Lane' dress. In July 1987, her parents had given her a silver 'Citizen' watch as a twenty-first birthday present.

SILENCE OF THE LAMBS

Although Jodie had gone missing in Melbourne and there was no body, the case had been dealt with by NSW homicide detectives because all the evidence pointed to the murder having taken place across the Victorian border at Wyrama or in the near vicinity. It was on that basis that Suckling was charged in New South Wales and appeared before me and not a Victorian court.

As I said, you can usually get an idea of the way the defence is headed by the witnesses they ask to be called in the committal. In this case, there was Jodie's brother and sister, Darren and Tracy, and their mother, Dot. There was Constable Jack Nugter, the scientific officer from Broken Hill Crime scene unit who had handled the exhibits found at Wyrama Homestead, Constable Skomorrow, who had also found a lot of the exhibits, and Detective Senior Constable David Causer, who had taken over the Sophie Carni inquiry and charged Suckling with the attack on her. The final witness was Detective Senior Constable Mick McGann, the NSW homicide officer in charge of Jodie's case. The evidence of the rest of the 174 witnesses was in the police brief, tendered to the court. I read the statements sitting in my office.

It seemed to me that one of the main problems the prosecution had was to show that Jodie Larcombe was indeed dead. It would not look good convicting a man for murder if the victim later showed up alive. The police had to be sure themselves that Jodie was deceased. I believed there was ample evidence of that. Her fellow prostitutes said that she would not have left Melbourne voluntarily. They said she was not the type of person who could go off and start a new life somewhere. They described her, in their statements, as gullible, insecure, placid and sometimes stubborn.

Detectives had instigated inquiries with police forces in every Australian state and territory as well as New Zealand to see if there was any information about Jodie Larcombe. The inquiries related to details of what she might use during the normal course of her life, whether she held a driver's licence or owned a motor vehicle, whether she held a credit card, if she had lodged any amount with a rental board or enrolled in a methadone program or other similar clinic programs. The inquiries included checking with prisons, checking if Jodie was known by police intelligence, if she was listed with criminal record offices or through her fingerprints. There were inquiries as to whether she had been a patient in a hospital or mental asylum or if she had been reported as a missing person. The police had also checked with the Health Insurance Commission in case she had used Medicare; with the immigration department, with social security. They had ensured extensive media coverage, in papers, radio and on television. There was no trace that Jodie Larcombe continued to exist.

There was evidence that in May 1984, Jodie had five teeth extracted and a dental plate fitted. The dental plate found wrapped in tissue paper in Daryl Suckling's bedroom was identified as Jodie's. Her mother said that Jodie would never go anywhere without wearing it as she was embarrassed to be seen without it. To establish whether she had visited another dentist somewhere in Australia to obtain a replacement plate, 5000 pamphlets were circulated by police through the journal of the Australian Dental Association. The pamphlets showed details of her dental chart, a photograph of the dental plate and a photograph of Jodie. They also contained a short narrative with a request for information. Again there was nothing forthcoming.

The next step was to link Jodie with Daryl Suckling. There were the belongings police had found at Wyrama Homestead, which witnesses identified as belonging to Jodie. There was evidence putting Suckling in St Kilda around Christmas 1987 when Jodie had gone missing. At 1.16 a.m. on Boxing Day, he made a withdrawal of $40 from an ATM in Fitzroy Street, St Kilda. It was noted that Jodie had told the police she charged $40 for oral sex. Another important piece of evidence was a small notebook which police found in a box of letters belonging to Suckling. On one page was the date 27/12 and the word JODIE written in ink. The police document examination unit found that writing on the back of that piece of paper was done by Suckling while the word JODIE and the numerals *could* have been written by him.

The line of questioning of the six witnesses who Suckling had called to the witness box concentrated on the contact Jodie had with her family and the last time they had seen her. She had lived with her brother and sister in Melbourne until November 1987. Through the scientific officer and Constable Skomorrow, Suckling challenged the finding of the exhibits and what happened to them after that, the so-called chain of evidence. The chain of evidence follows each person who handled the exhibit and what they did with them and is important because it ensures the exhibits were not interfered with. It was Detective Causer who had received the Citizen watch from Sophie Carni. Detective McGann was called because he was in charge. One key witness neither the prosecution nor the defence could call was Sophie Carni herself. She had died two months earlier before the committal hearing started.

In August 1988 in Broken Hill Local Court, Carni had given evidence against Suckling and he had been committed for trial for abducting and sexually assaulting her. His trial on those charges was scheduled to start in November 1989. In June 1989, five months before the trial was due to start, she was found dead in her Fitzroy flat from an apparent drug overdose. There were no suspicious circumstances. What remained was the transcript of the evidence she had given in the committal hearing, including her cross-examination first by Suckling's lawyer and then later by Suckling himself after he sacked his lawyer for reasons unknown to me. I accepted that transcript as proof of the evidence that Sophie would have given before me had she been alive.

While the prosecution case against Suckling for Jodie Larcombe's murder was unusual because there was only circumstantial evidence, sometimes there is only one direction that the evidence can point in. This was one of those times. There was no other explanation for the evidence before me, including an explanation for Jodie Larcombe's dental plate ending up with Suckling. You don't just go and leave your dentures lying all over the place. On 24 August 1989, I had no hesitation in committing Daryl Suckling to stand trial for her murder. I remanded him in custody.

Three months later, in November, Suckling's trial for abducting and raping Sophie Carni began at the NSW District Court in Wollongong. There was, of course, no victim to point the finger at Suckling since Carni had died. There are provisions in the law for allowing the evidence that she had given in the committal hearing into the trial in such cases. This trial judge ruled against it. Without a victim and without her evidence, Suckling was acquitted of the rape and abduction at the direction of the judge. As Detective McGann later commented, the devil must have been looking after Daryl Suckling the day that Sophie Carnie overdosed.

While I moved on to other cases, the case against Suckling for murdering Jodie Larcombe meandered its way through the court system. It took me by surprise when nine months after committing Suckling for trial and remanding him in custody, he was out of jail in May 1990. Despite a long criminal record, his lack of ties in New South Wales and the fact that he faced a charge which carried with it a life sentence, the NSW Supreme Court granted him bail. He planned to live in Goulburn and he had to report twice weekly to the local police, not an onerous bail condition at all, considering the circumstances.

In October 1990, the NSW Director of Public Prosecutions 'no billed' the case; this means the charge is dropped but it is not an acquittal. It leaves police free to reinstate the charge if more evidence comes to light. I must say that I was bemused when I heard this had happened.

The DPP's reasoning was that because Sophie Carni was dead and Suckling had been acquitted of her rape and abduction at the judge's direction, the evidence of what happened to her could not be used against Suckling as 'similar fact' evidence in the trial. The DPP said in the absence of Jodie's body, the only evidence that linked her with Suckling established she had been with him sometime before she disappeared, that he took pornographic photographs of her and he had some of her personal belongings. The DPP said four Queens Counsel had examined the file and felt that on such evidence, Suckling had no case to answer.

I used to get frustrated about the whole system when they would 'no bill' a case when I thought there was sufficient evidence for a person to go to trial. It made you feel that unless the DPP was sure of getting a conviction, the office wouldn't give it a go. You could understand them dropping a case if the evidence was not strong but in the case of Daryl Suckling, I felt there was enough evidence against him. It was a case I felt should have been left to a jury to decide and not just to the DPP. I like to follow my cases to their conclusion. This one was close to my heart.

Jodie's parents were devastated that, as they saw it, their daughter's murderer was getting off scot-free. They sold their trucking business, moved into a caravan and devoted their time trying to find their daughter's body. They spent most of their time living near Pooncarie. Like many people in their position when they could get no satisfaction from the authorities, they turned to the media. As usual the media was more than happy to help right a perceived injustice and in this case I agreed with them. The case was mentioned in the NSW parliament and Jodie's parents did a lot of digging, no doubt with the help of the police involved in the case.

The police get frustrated when they feel they have a strong case and it never gets to trial. The full story, which I had not known at the time of the committal, emerged later through the media.

Not only did it look as if Daryl Suckling would never face trial for the murder of Jodie Larcombe nor for the abduction and rape of Sophie Carni, there were also another two victims who he would never face trial over – a third woman who had been abducted and raped and a fourth who suffered brain damage before he could be charged with her rape.

Before Jodie Larcombe and Sophie Carni, there had been Annette. In 1984, Suckling had been charged with the rape and abduction of Annette, then 22, who at the time was friendly with some of Suckling's relatives. Suckling was boarding with Annette in Victoria. One night, after she believed he had slipped a sleeping tablet into her coffee, he sexually assaulted her. She moved out, returning later to collect her belongings.

Annette would later tell Melbourne Magistrates Court during a three-day committal hearing how, when she returned to the house on 19 May 1984, Suckling told her to close her eyes as he had a present for her. Suckling put his arm around her neck in a headlock and put a knife to her throat. He told her if she struggled he would cut her throat. She said he took off all her clothes and tied her thumbs together with fuse wire, taped her mouth and tied her ankles together. He told her he was going to get her drunk so he could take pornographic photos of her and that he was going to have sex with her. Annette tried to escape but failed.

After hearing all the evidence and viewing the photographs, the magistrate committed Suckling to stand trial. However, the charges were later 'no billed' by the Victorian DPP who did not think Annette was a good witness. Suckling walked free.

Next was Christine. On 8 December 1987 Suckling left Wyrama Station for Melbourne, having told his neighbours he was going to visit a sick relative. Two days later, Christine, 17, and a friend were sitting on the steps of St Kilda Post Office when they were approached by Suckling who chatted to them for a while. A short time afterwards, Suckling drove up to Christine and asked for a certain address. Christine got in the Landcruiser to show him the way.

In a statement to police, Christine said Suckling then pulled out a knife. She was screaming as he drove along the street and he told her to be quiet or he would kill her. She said he parked in a quiet lane where he handcuffed her, stripped her and taped her mouth shut, as he did to Annette and Sophie Carni. He then undressed himself until he was wearing only a T-shirt and told her he was going to take her to another place where he would rape and kill her.

Christine, who is double-jointed, managed to twist up her arms and unlock the door of the Landcruiser. She leapt out while it was stopped at a set of traffic lights and alerted another motorist. The motorist followed Suckling's vehicle and noted the numberplate before taking Christine to St Kilda police station.

Suckling was questioned about the incident but allowed to leave the police station. Subsequently six warrants were taken out for his arrest but before he could be charged, Christine fell off a train, sustaining massive head injuries that affected her memory and meant she could not be considered a reliable witness. The warrants have since been withdrawn and Suckling, again, got off scot-free. It all sounds incredible when you see it written down but that's how it happened.

When Suckling was jailed again it was not for rape or for Jodie Larcombe's murder. In February 1991, he was arrested by the Australian Federal Police for social security fraud and later that year sentenced to a jail term. It was a twist that struck me as being similar to the gangster Al Capone when he was jailed for tax offences.

I later learned that one of the police officers, Detective McGann, who had been involved in investigating the cases of the four women had resigned from the force in disgust. He had moved on to the NCA, leaving his former partner, Detective Sergeant Peter Lennon, to continue on with investigations.

Sometimes families would ask me, 'What happens now?' when it seemed obvious that their loved one had been killed by someone but there was not enough evidence to charge that person. I would tell them that the case remained open and the police would revisit it from time to time. The police did not give up on Suckling.

On the morning of 3 June 1994, Daryl Suckling appeared before the magistrate at local court at Gosford on the NSW Central Coast charged once again with Jodie Larcombe's murder, with concealing a body and with interfering with a body. He had been arrested the night before at his home in Umina. The police had new evidence against him. It emerged that what had led to this second arrest had begun while Suckling had been in jail for social security fraud – for the police, at least, this cloud had a silver lining. A man had contacted a police station on the Central Coast and asked to speak to local detectives about a murder 'committed by a man called Daryl Suckling'. He told detectives he had been a cellmate of Suckling's in Goulburn Jail and Suckling had told him he had abducted and murdered a young woman several years earlier and that he had been involved in the abduction and rape of another young woman. The detectives contacted Detective Peter Lennon.

It was obvious to the police that as good as the informer's recall of the prison conversations was, it was going to need some form of corroboration before it could be used in a court. Encouraged by the police, the informer invited Suckling to move in with him when he was released from jail. Meanwhile, with the informer's knowledge, the police bugged his house and gave him a car, which was also fitted with a listening device. Suckling was a cunning criminal and it took a few months before he let his guard down and began to talk to the informer about Jodie Larcombe, gloating about how clever he had been and laughing at the police and Larcombe's parents, who he boasted knew he had done it but couldn't prove it. He said, 'Here I am, inoffensive, but I've gotten away with murder, they'll [meaning other criminals] never get away with murder.'

The conversation was chilling. He talked about murdering the informer's young girlfriend and putting her body in the same grave as Jodie Larcombe's so that in years to come, if the grave was discovered, no one would know who was in there because the DNA of the bodies would have become mixed. He said that before he had buried Jodie, he had cut off her nipples and genitalia, drying the nipples with salt and keeping them in his tobacco pouch. He had later dug up the body and cut it up, burying the parts separately.

The taped conversations were the basis for the police to re-arrest Suckling. In the end, they acted quickly. What made them move on that particular day was that Suckling had begun talking about drugging the informer's girlfriend, raping and killing her. He also became acquainted with another woman and her daughter, who knew the informer, and at one stage was heard on tape asking the woman if she wanted to become an

'MP', as he called missing persons. It was the same way he referred to Jodie Larcombe. Soon after, he moved out of the informer's house and it became difficult for police to keep track of him. Worried about the life of the informer's girlfriend and the other women, they arrested him.

Even Suckling's relatives now turned on him. One of them, who had previously given him an alibi for the time of Larcombe's disappearance, changed her story and said Suckling had told her that he had cut up a girl into three pieces and buried them on the road between Melbourne and Mildura. The relative said Suckling had told her he had spent the night with the girl and she had been taking drugs. When he woke up the next morning she was dead. The relative's son had seen Suckling carrying a bloodstained garden shovel into the backyard of their home in Melbourne.

The upshot of events was that Suckling finally stood trial for murdering Larcombe and was convicted. In September 1996, he was jailed for life, and in New South Wales that sentence means what it says. It used to be ridiculous when a murderer would get life and then get out in ten or 12 years.

It had been eight and a half years since Jodie Larcombe had disappeared and I could only guess at how her mother and father, who had sat through that first committal before me all those years before, were feeling. There was still something missing. I read in the papers the following day that Jodie's parents still hoped to find their daughter's body. After the trial they moved their caravan back to Pooncarie to keep looking. It also made them feel closer to Jodie.

Tragically, not long after, Mrs Larcombe committed suicide. Like most convicted criminals, Daryl Suckling had lodged an appeal against his conviction and sentence. A week after the appeal was heard in the NSW Court of Criminal Appeal, Mrs Larcombe shot herself in the bedroom of their caravan. Mrs Larcombe was 50 years old. You could say that she was Daryl Suckling's final victim.

Suckling lost his appeal and remains in jail. Jodie's body has never been found.

CHAPTER 7

In the Line of Duty

THE TROUBLE WITH talkback hosts is that while they never stop talking, they don't always know what they are talking about. I was driving home from Sydney Airport and had the radio turned to some program on 2UE when I heard my name mentioned. It seems I had upset the girlfriend of a gunman who had shot dead two police officers after the officers had been called to sort out a domestic dispute. I had just flown back into Sydney from Kempsey where I had finished the inquest into the police officers' deaths. On the radio, it seemed it was I who was the villain because I had been nasty enough to criticise the girl for not warning the police that her boyfriend may have been armed.

I didn't usually get upset about media comments to do with my work. It went with the job. And I had never entered into public debate about any of my decisions. But there's always a first time. I felt, in this case, all the facts should be aired not just the girlfriend's side of things. When I got home, I got straight on the phone to 2UE. They kept me hanging on the line for some time while they played some music, then the announcer finally came on.

'How do I know that you are who you say you are?' was his first line to me.

'Well, I can assure you that I am the State Coroner,' I answered and proceeded to tell him a few facts about the case. 'You are feeling sorry for the girlfriend but what about the police officers' families? What about the family of the gunman?' The radio announcer hadn't been in court. He hadn't heard all the aspects of the case.

Like I say, these guys sometimes talk about things they know nothing about. If the girlfriend had told the police about her boyfriend's guns, at the very least the officers would have been placed on guard against such an attack and the tragedy may never have happened.

When you see a person killed in the line of duty it is a terrible thing.

~~~

I was woken up early on the morning of 10 July 1995 by the duty operations inspector at NSW Police Headquarters to say two police constables had been shot and killed during the night at Crescent Head, a little seaside town near my old areas of Kempsey and Port Macquarie. I immediately got onto Inspector Steve Bills, the officer in charge of the police coronial unit attached to my office. He got moving, picked up one of the unit's police cars and collected me on the way to the freeway north. The five-hour drive from Sydney brought us to Crescent Head by 10 a.m.

It's a quiet place, 19 kilometres off the Pacific Highway and, as the saying goes, seemingly even further away from trouble. Famous for its surfing beaches, the town's population of about 1100 swells with tourists in the summer. Along with fishing, tourism is what makes the town its money. Crescent Head is the sort of place where people feel safe. It was part of the reason Constable Bob Spears and Constable Peter Addison had moved up to the area from Sydney earlier that year with their families. Peter Addison had been an undercover detective with the North West Region crime unit and Bob Spears had been attached to Liverpool detectives. They were both married, both aged 36 and both had children. Peter Addison's children were Robert, 10, and Jade, 15, and his police colleague's children were Scott, 20, Glen, 16, and Haley, 11.

Steve and I headed for Walker Street, Crescent Head, where the gunman John McGowan had lived. By the time we arrived, the area had been well secured, strung with crime scene tape and the bodies of the officers were on their way to the morgue at Glebe. It was now a well-recognised practice that whenever a homicide occurred anywhere in the state, the bodies were taken to Glebe or Westmead morgues for the post-mortems to be conducted by our forensic pathologists. Also on the way to Glebe was the body of McGowan, who had turned his gun on himself after shooting dead the two officers. Everything had remained frozen in time, exactly where it had been at around 1 a.m. when the shooting occurred. Parked at the edge of the driveway outside the red-roofed block where McGowan had a three-bedroom unit was the officers' white police four-wheel drive, its rear end to the house. In front of the police vehicle, in the middle of the road, was a pool of blood. Opposite was a parked car with five gunshots in it and beside it, the marks on the pavement that showed where Constable Spears had fallen and died. Along the side of the house behind the parked car was where the body of Constable Addison had been found. McGowan's body, with a shot to the head, had been eventually found next to a brick barbecue behind some low shrubs on his front lawn. There were marks on the ground where bullets were found. These marks, this evidence, were the meat and potatoes of a coroner's working life.

I was briefed as to what police believed had happened and shown around the crime scene and inside McGowan's house. I noticed he had a lot of military paraphernalia including books on Vietnam and World War II. These visits to the scenes of death were invaluable. I got a feel for the place, could picture what had happened when I later held the inquest and could question whether anything had been missed during the investigation.

An Investigation Team had been set up under the command of a senior investigator from outside the area where the two constables were stationed and the region's senior police were at the scene, some of whom I had got to know when I had been the local magistrate which was just a few months earlier. Detective Senior Sergeant Bob Williams from Port Macquarie, who I knew very well, had the unenviable task of heading the investigation into the shooting of two of his men and putting together the coronial brief for me. (Bob Williams, whose father had also been a police officer, went on to receive a Commissioner's Commendation for his work on this inquiry. Sadly he died in 2001, aged 56, from a heart attack.) I was more than satisfied that a proper investigation was being carried out so there was little more that I could do at Crescent Head. Steve Bills and I began the long drive back to Sydney.

By the time all the investigations had been completed into the deaths of Constables Spears and Addison and I was ready to begin the inquest, New South Wales was in the middle of the NSW Police Royal Commission and it seemed that no one had anything good to say about the police. Hidden cameras had recorded the worst examples of the corruption and this footage was shown on national television. Being in the court system you always had your suspicions about some police, but what surprised me was how ingrained the corruption had become in some police stations. This sort of corruption can never be condoned but what I did think was unfair was the way police officers were named in the Royal Commission on the word of criminals while the criminals were allowed to remain anonymous. It was the same for those police who were willing to give evidence against their former colleagues. Their names were suppressed while there was no such protection for the officers they named, most of whom were not allowed to defend themselves. Once an officer was named, he or she was marked for life, innocent or not. The fallout from the Royal Commission went beyond the discovery of corruption. The human element was forgotten in the inquiry. Many officers and their families suffered. Some of those accused even committed suicide.

It was against this background and with the public feeling towards the police at a new low that I flew up to Port Macquarie on Wednesday, 11 October 1995, back into my familiar courtroom in Kempsey to conduct the inquest into the shooting deaths of the two officers. Steve Bills and my court officer, Kay Dawson, accompanied me. Kay had been my officer while I had been Deputy State Coroner and one of the first things I did when I was appointed State Coroner was to request that she come and work with me. It was her job to keep the court proceedings going, swearing in witnesses and the like. She made sure everything ran like clockwork.

I had already read the brief which had been prepared by Detective Bob Williams and there were several things that disturbed me about the events of that night. There were several points at which things could have turned out differently, when the roller-coaster could have been slowed down and possibly stopped before it got out of control. Neither of the two constables were young hot-heads new to the force, both were experienced. I was keen to have WorkCover, the Commissioner of Police and the NSW Police Association represented at the inquest because I could see where the Police Service had let down the two officers. That night should not have ended like it did. Something had gone horribly wrong and it was my job to find out what.

As the evidence was called before me, it seemed to me the facts were quite clear.

IN THE LINE OF DUTY

On the night of Saturday, 8 July John McGowan, a 35-year-old electrician for Northpower, had been holding court in the bar at Crescent Head Country Club. He was in what witnesses described as a talkative, happy mood, but there were already threatening undertones. He became upset by a drinking mate who kept calling him a drunk and a loser. Earlier, McGowan had played a round of golf and began drinking at about 2.30 p.m., downing up to six schooners before leaving the club at about 5 p.m. He then bought a bottle of beer and a stubby of stout and drank them before returning to the club. According to some of those who knew him, he was a quiet bloke who liked fishing. Just one of the boys, you might say. To others, he was a Jekyll-and-Hyde character; calm one minute, exploding into violence the next.

Back at the club, he drank up to six bourbons, mixed with either orange or Coke, before moving to the town's only hotel for a final schooner. He had had what might be called a skinful by the time he left the hotel at about 11.30 p.m. His blood-alcohol level was .211, more than four times the legal limit for driving.

We called McGowan's former girlfriend, Debra, 24, into the witness box and she described how there had been times when he had become violent during their three-year relationship when he had been drinking. He would tell her at such times that he had been sent by the devil to kill her. He had actually made threats to kill her four or five times. Once she had gone to work with a black eye, courtesy of his fists. She had broken off their relationship but he had remained jealous, threatening men she dated and making it impossible for her to maintain other relationships. She said she tried to keep a friendship going with him. On that night in July McGowan believed she was pregnant to another man.

After his day of drinking, McGowan had telephoned Debra after midnight and threatened her again. On advice from the friends she was with, Debra called Port Macquarie police station and reported the threatening telephone call.

Constables Spears and Addison were out on duty in the 'wireless car' and took the call over the radio about the domestic dispute. They drove to the house of Debra's friends to speak to her and then travelled to McGowan's rented unit in Walker Street with the intention of arresting him. When they reversed their marked four-wheel drive into McGowan's driveway it was about 1 a.m. They had no idea what they were walking into.

As they approached the house, without their revolvers drawn, they were confronted by McGowan coming out of his carport. He was dressed in a military-style camouflage outfit, draped in hessian bags, wearing a balaclava and armed with a .223 Ruger assault rifle. Around his waist he had strapped a belt holding a Bowie knife in a pouch.

The constables retreated to the back of the police van, the furthest away they could get from McGowan. Neighbours were woken by the sound of the police officers calling out, 'Drop the gun, drop the gun.' McGowan's rifle had two magazines taped back to back for rapid-fire use. He fired at the officers, hitting Constable Spears in the head, killing him instantly.

As neighbours in Walker Street described what had happened, the emotion in the court was palpable. The widows of the two police constables had to leave the room. When he heard the shots, McGowan's next door neighbour, Ron Scott, who was the acting Patrol Commander at Kempsey police station, phoned the station. Senior Sergeant Scott didn't have his gun at home and stayed inside to protect his family.

Outside in the street, Constable Addison made a radio call to Port Macquarie station. 'Urgent. Person with a rifle. Urgent. Officer down.'

McGowan continued to shoot. Bullets sprayed into neighbouring houses and someone's pet dog was shot and killed. Constable Addison tried to return and help his partner, firing off his own gun as he ran across the road into one of the houses looking for a telephone – he had been in a radio blackspot. No telephone was available.

Neighbour Gregory Barnett watched from his window. He crawled along his verandah to see if he could help. He climbed over his back fence and went to the next road to stop anyone coming into Walker Street and walking into the crossfire. He was asked to describe the gunpower of McGowan's weapon compared with the officers' ancient Smith & Wesson revolvers. He responded with, 'John had a cannon and they had shanghais.'

Constable Addison showed what real mateship was about when he stayed to help his partner. He was frantically trying to reload his revolver with a 'speed strip' reloader, that allowed bullets to be reloaded two at a time, when the speed strip containing his live bullets fell to the ground.

Taking advantage of the situation John McGowan knelt down on one knee, carefully aimed and fired a shot hitting Addison in the left side of his chest.

Help was on its way and sirens filled the night air. The Tactical Response Group had been called in and fearing McGowan had fled, a search began of Crescent Head. His body was later found lying on his own lawn behind the brick barbecue. The last words neighbours had heard him saying were, 'I am sorry, I am sorry. I shot a policeman. Tell Mum and Dad I love them. Forgive me, God.'

What struck me was why McGowan's girlfriend never warned police that he had a gun. The two friends Debra was with that night gave evidence that after the two officers left, Debra had said to them that she should have told the police McGowan had a gun. Debra denied she had used those words or even that she knew her ex-boyfriend had a high-powered rifle. I preferred the evidence of her friends and said so. I was satisfied that had Debra told the police about the gun, then they would have been in a position to take a different approach in attempting to arrest McGowan instead of treating it as a normal domestic violence matter. I couldn't go so far as to say that Constables Spears and Addison would have been alive but at least they would have been better prepared to deal with him. Debra later saw this as harsh criticism of herself. So be it.

I needed to know more about McGowan and had called on Rod Milton, the forensic psychiatrist who had been so much help in piecing together a profile of Wade Frankum following the Strathfield Massacre, and of John Wayne Glover, the Granny Killer. Rod looked at the relationship between McGowan and Debra and at what had triggered his rage that night. He reported to the inquest that despite McGowan's threats, he believed it was doubtful anything of an adverse nature would have happened to Debra if she had broken off her relationship with McGowan completely. Dr Milton felt her attempt to maintain a platonic friendship with him after the end of their affair had backfired; instead of easing things it had a seriously provocative and frustrating effect on McGowan.

Why was McGowan armed and dressed like Rambo at one in the morning? I was not inclined to accept the scenario that he was on his way to carry out the threat he had made to Debra, mainly because more than an hour had passed from the time he made the telephone threat on her life to the arrival of the police. It would have seemed more likely that once the threat had been made, he would have armed himself and headed straight over to where she was staying. Nor did I accept the suggestion that he was lying in wait to ambush the officers. He would not have been sure that Debra had reported the threat to police guaranteeing their attendance at his home. She had never called in the police before or reported previous threats and assaults he had inflicted on her.

I found that McGowan was living out his fantasy of playing military games and Constables Spears and Addison were unfortunate to have come on the scene at the wrong time, just when McGowan was turning his fantasy into reality. He had been drinking, he had been using cannabis. I wondered what would have happened had Debra not called the police that night after the threat. Would McGowan have turned his emotional confusion and rage on other innocents? Perhaps he would have turned around and walked back into the house.

I was able to take all the evidence from the witnesses while at Kempsey and handed down my finding that the officers were killed by McGowan. I adjourned the question of recommendations to a later date at Glebe because I wanted to look at what could be learned from this tragedy.

A video was prepared for me and showed just how hamstrung Constables Spears and Addison were that night by their Smith & Wesson guns. The regulation revolvers had not changed since 1899 and the NSW Police Association had long been pushing for a .40 calibre Glock self-loading pistol. Not only was the Glock a semi-automatic but it held 15 rounds as opposed to the Smith & Wesson's six rounds. It was used by police in 42 countries and was noted for its safety features, accuracy, reliability and design. The demonstration on the video and my experience over the years convinced me that these old revolvers were just not good enough, particularly in a high-risk situation. It seemed to be that the preferable gun was a self-loader with a magazine, the very Glock pistol that the NSW Police Association had been calling on for years. I recommended that all police be issued with the new guns as a matter of urgency. As a result, police were finally issued with .40 calibre semi-automatic pistols with clip-on magazines and night-sights. Reloading time was cut from ten seconds to just two seconds.

Bullet-proof vests would probably not have saved the two officers because of where they were shot on their bodies; however, I recommended the acquisition of additional bullet-proof vests for police, also as a matter of urgency. Patrol vehicles with the potential to arrive first at a suspected crime scene should be equipped with sufficient bullet-proof vests for each officer. This was also done.

It had also concerned me that police could be caught in communication black spots with inadequate portable radios. I recommended capital works expenditure to try and eradicate these black spots throughout the state to enable police to remain in contact with their base in order to summon help when required. My final recommendation to the Commissioner of Police was for emphasis to be placed on adequate training for police officers in high-risk situations. As it turned out, the NSW Police Service was later prosecuted by WorkCover and fined $220,000 for breaches of the *Occupational Health and Safety Act* for failing to provide the constables with adequate radio equipment and tactical training for high-risk situations.

There was also the question of how McGowan came to have his gun. He had obtained it legally while he was a licensed shooter but had kept it after his licence expired. It was far too easy for a person to obtain a Class 1 shooter's licence and there seemed to be no checks on what happened when the licence ran out. I recommended that applicants for a licence must produce references of character and suitability from two or three referees and must demonstrate a genuine need for a gun. The Crescent Head case was one in a series of shootings, including the terrible massacre at Port Arthur, that brought home how easy it was to obtain guns. The whole system has now been tightened up.

The Crescent Head shootings had me seriously considering making recommendations as to the accessibility and ownership of firearms. Due to the intervention of the Port Arthur tragedy and the subsequent decisions of the federal and state governments on gun laws, this was not necessary. Gun ownership was (and still is) a hot topic. At the time, I found myself constantly having heated 'discussions' with my country relatives on the subject, particularly with my close mate the late John Rohr from Mudgee and my brother-in-law, Trevor Smith from Forbes. John was a member of the Mudgee pistol club (and best man at our wedding) and it was obvious we didn't see eye to eye about ownership and accessibility of firearms. It was a reflection of the debate that was going on in society about guns. Although I agreed there was a special case for farmers, there were many animated debates with John and Trevor and their friends. In the end we begged to differ on the subject.

There was one other important point that I wanted to make at the close of this inquest. In the light of what had come out in the Royal Commission, the public needed reminding that most police were not corrupt.

'I think it is timely for our society to be reminded that, despite the adverse publicity given recently about the alleged criminal activities of some police officers, the greater majority of members of the NSW Police Service are dedicated, conscientious, hard-working officers. Not enough credit is given to the excellent work carried out by members of the Police Service. Their efforts don't get recognised often enough. They are more often criticised and very often unjustifiably so.'

Crescent Head wasn't the first police shooting I had done. There was the death of Constable Alan McQueen.

The police officers were out on routine patrol on 24 April 1989 – McQueen, 26, and two colleagues, Constable Ross Judd of the anti-theft squad, and Probationary Constable Jason Donnelly, 20. They were driving in the Woollomooloo area of Sydney when they spotted a man behaving suspiciously. He was walking along Haig Avenue and it was obvious that he was paying more attention to the cars than someone who was just out for a stroll. While Constable Judd parked the patrol car, the other two officers approached the man. His name was John Porter.

They asked Porter if his car was parked nearby and if he had keys for it. When Porter had no satisfactory answers they told him they intended to search him. It was then things turned bad. Porter started to struggle, punching McQueen with his fist. As McQueen tried to handcuff Porter, Porter produced a .32 calibre pistol and fired off a shot, hitting Constable Donnelly in the left side, with the force of the bullet spinning him around. Porter turned the gun on McQueen, shooting him in the back at point-blank range. Porter later claimed he only had the gun because he was on his way to deliver it to someone. McQueen died 11 days later in hospital from chest wounds.

It was when police were looking for Porter three days later that eight SWOS officers burst into the home of one of his friends, David Gundy. Gundy was shot dead. All hell broke loose in the media over the notorious case. Porter hadn't been in the Gundy house at the time. He was arrested a month later in southern Queensland and extradited to Sydney, but not before the extradition was held up while someone had to go and collect his 'property'. Legally he was entitled to his 'property', in this case, a black felt hat. His extradition to New South Wales to face a charge of murdering a police officer was held up while someone went to get his hat. As I keep being reminded, the law can be a strange thing.

For Kevin Waller and I, the two high-profile cases raised a number of serious legal issues which had first to be dealt with before we could hear the cases. Kevin was going to conduct the inquest into David Gundy's shooting and I was going to hold the committal into John Porter's charges of murder, shooting with intent to murder, wounding and a number of other related charges. Porter and his lawyers sought to have the inquest into David Gundy's death put off until after his trial on the basis that material would come out that could prejudice the trial. Meanwhile the Royal Commission into Aboriginal Deaths in Custody wanted to investigate the shooting of David Gundy. In the end Porter's committal proceedings were held first, then the inquest into the Gundy shooting. I had no hesitation in sending John Porter to stand trial as the evidence against him was overwhelming.

He was not required to produce a defence at the committal hearing. When he faced trial in the NSW Supreme Court, he claimed the police had fired the first shot and he had only acted in self-defence. Unsurprisingly the jury rejected his story. In August 1990, Porter was jailed for life.

Soon after the end of the trial, the inquest into David Gundy's death began before a jury, a rare occurrence. A coroner can decide to have a jury or the parties involved can apply for a jury but the coroner has the final say, he doesn't have to give approval. In this case, Kevin discussed it with me. He felt there had been such a furore and it was such a high-profile case that he thought it better to let a jury decide whether the police had a case to answer over David Gundy's death. The jury returned with a verdict of accidental death. None of the officers involved in the raid on his house faced any criminal charges.

THE CORONER

When Alan McQueen died in hospital on 5 May 1989, he was the fifth NSW police officer to be killed on duty that year. Three of the other officers had died in traffic accidents and the fourth drowned when he tried to rescue a girl from the surf off Tallows Beach.

A year later I held an inquest into the strange death of Simon John 'Cyril' Edwards, a former police officer. His body had been found in the ocean off MacKenzies Bay near Sydney's Tamarama Beach on 31 October 1986. His wife believed he had been murdered but the police thought it was suicide, which might sound bizarre when you hear that his hands and feet were tied and he had been shot once in the head. As it turned out, suicide was not so unlikely once I heard all the circumstances.

Mr Edwards had been sacked from the police for neglect of duty after an underworld figure accused him of being involved in a car-stealing racket. He chose chicken farming as his new career but had been growing something much more profitable as a sideline. He had been due in court on 28 October 1986 to face charges relating to a $1 million marijuana plantation found on his property on the NSW Central Coast. The night before his court appearance, he told his wife he had documents and information implicating high-ranking police officers in criminal activities and said he was off to Sydney to meet two detectives who could 'fix' the charges against him. The meeting could be dangerous, he told her. He never returned home. His body was found three days later.

This may all sound as if it points to murder. However, shortly before his death, Mr Edwards had taken out a life insurance policy and made a new will. He faced the prospect of a lengthy jail sentence. On top of that, tests showed that even with his hands and feet tied he could still have shot himself in the head. In the end, I had to record an open verdict. If I accepted his death was suicide, then it was certainly an elaborate plan he had concocted to make it look like murder with the motivation that his wife would get the insurance payout. On the other hand, despite the strong evidence pointing towards suicide I wasn't sufficiently satisfied to the standards required by law to bring down a verdict of suicide. I was sure that there were those who, shall we say, would not have been disappointed by his death, having regard to the company he appeared to have been keeping after he left the police force. Yet there was no tangible evidence to implicate anyone in his murder.

Then in 1993 I conducted the inquest into the death of a weapons instructor, of all people. Constable First Class Juan Carl Hernandez, or 'Rocky' to his mates, was shot during an exercise at the old police academy at Redfern. He ordered one of the officers to fire at him but had forgotten that he had told the class to reload their hand guns just minutes earlier. The officer did as he was told, pointed the gun at the instructor and shot him once in the chest. Constable Hernandez, who had been a member of the State Protection Group, died four hours later in hospital. All the evidence was that he had lost track of what he had been up to on that day. One of the students in the training session told how she had watched it all happen with a feeling of disbelief. She wanted to stop what was happening but found herself frozen, unable to utter a word.

The Coroners Court called the commander of the weapons training unit as an expert witness and he said that Constable Hernandez had breached the fundamental rule of safety in the use of firearms – never point them at anyone unless you intend to use them. The commander felt that to stop this kind of mistake happening again, police officers should use replica pistols in certain training exercises. I agreed and recommended the proposal be adopted as soon as possible.

Back at Glebe, in July 1995 when I returned from the police shootings at Crescent Head, there were other bodies waiting for my attention. A young woman had died in Shoalhaven District Memorial Hospital bringing it under the coroner's jurisdiction because her death was not from natural causes. Kathryn Martin, 22, had gone to the hospital at Nowra, south of Sydney, complaining of abdominal pain, vomiting and diarrhoea, symptoms which were diagnosed provisionally as viral gastroenteritis. After being given some treatment, she was sent home and showed some improvement the next day. Early the following morning, about 36 hours after leaving the hospital, her husband found her dead on the bedroom floor.

The post-mortem examination revealed she had suffered a ruptured ectopic pregnancy and had died because it had not been treated. It was a very sad case and Mrs Martin's family understandably blamed the doctor and the hospital. A simple pregnancy test would have alerted the doctor to the possibility of an ectopic pregnancy and when I held the inquest into Mrs Martin's death, even the doctor said it had been an oversight not to have done so. Did that mean the doctor had been wrong? I felt not. There was a lot of medical evidence called about what should have happened; hindsight is a wonderful thing. We could all say what we should have done. All the medical experts commenting on the treatment were doing so with the benefit of that hindsight. It appeared that the symptoms of gastroenteritis masked any other symptoms of the ectopic pregnancy. It would have been proper for the doctor involved to have carried out a pregnancy test but he didn't and I felt he could not be criticised for not doing so.

Mrs Martin's husband and her family wanted me to recommend that pregnancy tests be conducted on all women of childbearing age who went to hospital complaining of abdominal pains. While I had great sympathy for the family, I did not feel it was a practical recommendation to make because of the strain on resources. I felt such a course of action should be a matter for the individual doctor and the hospital. It was one of the few cases when I could not satisfy the family.

I also had to look into the suicide of Carol Abrahams who had been Daryl Abrahams before a sex change operation.

Daryl Abrahams was a Canberra public servant, a divisional administration officer in the Industrial Relations Department. He had a wife and children but his wife, Clare, told me during the inquest into his death, that he had not been happy. His unhappiness had manifested itself in waves – maybe it would happen just once a year but during that time, she would see her husband change and realise he 'wasn't with them'. Unable to live as a man, Daryl decided to change his sex. He and Clare divorced, as was required before the surgery, although they remained friends. Daryl began living as a female, taking hormones and having elocution lessons to learn to speak like a woman.

In May 1994 he told his workmates that he was taking a holiday. He travelled to Rose Bay in Sydney, where his mother and father lived and where he had grown up, and had the surgery to change his sex. The evidence was that when he got back to work everyone seemed very supportive. Then things began to go wrong when Daryl, newly known as Carol, was forced to quit her job because of an eye condition, possibly caused by the hormones. The problem with her eyes led to her almost losing her sight. She lost weight, had trouble sleeping and felt lost. She felt that she had no one to turn to. Her depression was compounded by financial problems made worse because she had lost her job. Three months after the operation, she went home to her family where she told her father, Alfred, that she felt she had done the wrong thing; she had made a mistake changing sex. Carol left a four-page suicide note, caught a bus to Vaucluse, left her handbag and shoes at the cliff's edge and leapt to her death. Her body was never found.

Mr Alfred Abrahams said that no one had explained to Daryl the problems he might have faced after changing his sex. He said that 'nobody tells these people who make these enormous decisions just what they're getting into'.

Sex change operations were not all that common but it seemed to me that commonsense would dictate that both before and after making such a momentous choice, the transsexuals needed exceptionally strong support, with counselling and other therapy. Ms Abrahams had seen four specialist doctors and none of them had been derelict in their duty towards her. However, I was not impressed with the poor standard of health care available to transsexuals. I recommended either specific guidelines for health professionals dealing with transsexuals or legislation similar to that which existed in South Australia, which required that doctors and hospitals involved in such treatment should be accredited by the South Australian Health Commission. The case made the front page of *The Daily Telegraph* in Sydney – no doubt because of what the paper saw as its somewhat titillating nature. As far as I was concerned the more attention it got, the better. It was an important case. Just a couple of days later, sure enough, the NSW Attorney-General, Jeff Shaw, announced he would look at new regulations to cover sex change operations. Something good came of what was a very sad case.

There were some cases involving medical mishaps where I did decide to take the matter further. I referred one pharmacist to the NSW Pharmacy Board for disciplinary action after she got a prescription wrong. Mrs Elva Chan, 80, a grandmother of nine, had been suffering from chronic renal problems and visited a specialist. The specialist prescribed sodium bicarbonate to ease the workload of Mrs Chan's kidneys. The pharmacist misread the prescription and dispensed lithium carbonate, which has a side effect of increasing the toxicity of the kidneys. A week later, Mrs Chan was taken to hospital suffering lithium poisoning. She suffered a stroke and died within a month.

Dr Jo DuFlou had carried out the post-mortem and found Mrs Chan had suffered multiple organ failure. In old age one illness can cause a domino effect which leads to other problems. Dr DuFlou believed the lithium poisoning had been the trigger.

The prescription had clearly read $NaHCO_3$, the chemical compound for sodium bicarbonate. The pharmacist admitted she had misread it as $LiCO_3$, lithium carbonate. It was sheer carelessness.

In another case involving a pharmacist's mistake I decided to take no further action. It involved a man suffering terminal bone cancer, Ernest Gallagher, 75, who had been prescribed 2mg/ml of morphine to relieve his pain while he was in hospital. The pharmacist, who was on her first day at the hospital as relief staff, had misread the labelling and dispensed him five bottles of 20mg/ml morphine, ten times the prescribed strength. Mr Gallagher became violently ill and despite the dosage being corrected, he died the next day. The pharmacist said it had been very busy at the hospital and that she was only given a 20-minute orientation. I felt the pharmacist's mistake was the result of a moment of inattention. I did recommend greater care be taken at the hospital for the proper orientation for pharmacy relieving staff in the care and distribution of dangerous drugs.

It was as a result of coroners' recommendations, including one of my own, that pills are now packaged in childproof bottles and pills are not produced in colours that make them look like lollies. It became law that all lighters had to be childproof after the recommendations of the local coroner in Mudgee after a tragic case involving a child who burned to death.

Coroners can make a difference.

CHAPTER 8

'I've Lost It, Clive, I've Lost It.'

THIRTY MINUTES AFTER take off and Seaview Air flight CD111 was 320 kilometres out from Newcastle on its three-hour flight to Lord Howe Island on Sunday, 2 October 1994. The 12-year-old twin-engined Turbo Aero Commander, VH SVQ, not only had eight passengers on board with their luggage but also the luggage from another Seaview Air aircraft that was following it. With extra luggage making up the equivalent of an extra three adult passengers on board the plane was critically overloaded. At least one of the aircraft's engines was due for a serious overhaul.

Its young pilot, Paul Sheil, 25, was unlicensed, ill and most likely on antibiotics. He was a mad-keen aviator but inexperienced with this type of aircraft. His planned flight path was at double the altitude recommended for the type of plane. Would you have walked up those steps into the cabin as a passenger if you had known all that? Unfortunately the passengers had no way of knowing about these breaches.

At 12.38 p.m., Sheil started to experience problems and switched his radio frequency to a private line to talk to the other Seaview plane. Flown by chief pilot David Clive McIver and with Seaview owner John Green on board, the second aircraft was about 14 minutes away. Sheil's concerns were heard over the radio by a third Seaview Air pilot, Michael Bird, who was also heading for the island.

Sheil complained about ice covering his windscreen and building up on the propellers causing a serious vibration. His tone of voice demonstrated he was clearly worried, but he was given almost no advice on how to understand and solve the problems he was facing. Then the radio went dead.

A couple of minutes later it sparked back to life. Then at 12.50 p.m. came Paul Sheil's terrifying last call: 'I've lost it, Clive, I've lost it.' His radio died for the last time. Flight CD111 plummeted into the Pacific Ocean.

Green and McIver tried repeatedly to contact the young pilot. When there was no reply, they simply continued their flight to Lord Howe Island. They didn't raise the alarm, they didn't divert to look for the plane. Landing on the island, despite the lead plane not having arrived, Green went to his home.

At 1.50 p.m., search and rescue authorities became concerned about what had happened to flight CD111 and tried to ring Green at home. Another two calls followed over the next ten minutes but Green had still not arrived home. Eventually, at 2.09 p.m., Green called the authorities from his home to confirm the plane had gone missing. It was an hour and 19 minutes since Paul Sheil's frightened final call.

At the time of the Seaview crash I was working in Port Macquarie as a magistrate but I followed the search closely on the news. More than 20 aircraft and three ships, including HMAS *Sydney*, were combing 60,000 square kilometres of ocean. Under the control of the Civil Aviation Authority's search and rescue coordination centre, the aircraft flew north–south search patterns, using the movement of the sun to maximise their chances of seeing any survivors or wreckage.

It was the Bureau of Air Safety (BASI) who carried out investigations into plane crashes in tandem with the police. BASI's main concern was air safety and its priority to find out what caused the crash. The job of the police was to determine the identity of the deceased and other matters pertinent to the flight and the crash.

In Australia the tyranny of distance forces us to use planes like buses; often there is no alternative timewise. As a passenger you put your faith in a huge number of people when you get on board any plane. There's not just the pilot and the maintenance crews, there are the air traffic controllers when you are in airspace regulated by them, the airline's owners and the

'I'VE LOST IT, CLIVE, I'VE LOST IT.'

authorities that regulate the air industry, then known as the Civil Aviation Authority (CAA). You trust the planes are safe and the pilots know what they are doing. You trust the authorities are not just tough but ferociously dedicated to maintaining air safety. You trust these authorities to be open and honest in their dealings with the industry and to inform the public of air safety breaches. In America it is possible to track the maintenance records of planes using the Internet. It is not so in Australia. Over the years Australian coroners have found it difficult to obtain all relevant information relating to the cause of crashes they are investigating from BASI because the CAA and its replacement, the Civil Aviation Safety Authority (CASA), consider that certain information, although relevant to the coroner's investigation, should not be publicly disclosed. Coroners have been forced to use various means including the threat of Supreme Court action to overcome the objections and obtain the evidence they have sought. When I was the coroner at Westmead, threatening such action was the only way I had been able to get information from BASI about a helicopter crash I was looking into and a couple of country coroners had contacted me to voice similar problems.

When I heard about the Seaview Air crash I couldn't help but imagine the terror of those on board in their final few moments. Leeca and Anthony Atkinson (25 and 26 respectively) were heading to the World Heritage-listed island for their honeymoon. Well-known Hunter Valley winemaker Reg Drayton, 63, and his wife Pam, 58, were on their way for an idyllic break from the day to day of life. Stephen Lake, 50, his wife Carolyn, 45, and two of their children Judith, 18, and Benjamin, 13, on a school holiday trip made up the other passengers heading for the island paradise.

This was one scene of an accident where it was no good the coroner visiting. There was nothing to see. Only ten pieces of wreckage were ever found. No bodies were recovered.

When I had accepted the position as State Coroner in early 1995 I took over the Seaview investigation. Federal parliament had been pressured to set up an inquiry which was headed by retired NSW Chief District Court judge, James Staunton. The job of the inquiry had been to examine the relationship between CASA and Seaview Air, but not to answer the question of what actually caused the crash (CASA then had replaced the CAA). That was to be my task.

THE CORONER

It seemed ridiculous to have two inquiries, one under myself and one under Judge Staunton, so I had approached the NSW Attorney-General to ask whether Judge Staunton could be appointed a coroner and hold the inquest along with his inquiry. The *Coroners Act* made that proposal impossible; the judge was over 70 years of age and the act precluded a person being appointed a coroner at that age. Some years later when Judge Staunton was appointed to hold an inquiry into the fatal collapse at the Gretley mine in the Hunter Valley, the Attorney-General asked me if I had any objection to the act being amended to allow the judge to be appointed a coroner and hold the inquest at the same time. I welcomed the sense of this course of action.

Meanwhile I had decided, after conferring with Judge Staunton, the legal representatives of the families of the deceased passengers and pilot and other interested parties, that my inquest should await the conclusion of Judge Staunton's inquiry. That was on the basis that the evidence given before the judge would probably reduce the time and expense of an inquest. There was also the fact that as both inquiries were likely to be lengthy, there would be a clash regarding the availability of witnesses.

The Seaview inquest was formally opened to take brief evidence on each of the missing people to enable a ruling that death had occurred. This allowed the families to proceed to deal with the estates of their deceased relatives. The inquest was adjourned until Judge Staunton's inquiry was finished. From time to time, the judge would ring me to check on various points. When his report was released, I requested a copy of it from the federal government. It arrived on my desk, nearly 1000 pages of thorough and meticulous work. The inquiry had taken 18 months, amassed 17,000 pages of transcript, 900 exhibits and cost an estimated $20 million. I didn't have to read all of it. I wasn't concerned with all the details of the relationship between CASA and Seaview. My focus was the evidence that would try and explain what had caused the accident.

From Judge Staunton's report Seaview emerged as an unsafe and slipshod airline which regularly breached regulations. The airline overloaded its aircraft, carried unrestrained cargo and cheated on recording flying hours to avoid maintenance. It failed to record its pilots' flying hours and did not record aircraft defects. Judge Staunton said Seaview's owner, John Green, took advantage of aspiring young pilots hoping to fly for the major airlines and offered wages and conditions way below those provided for under the Pilots Award. Seaview management placed more emphasis on making money than safety considerations, operating it as an airline even though it was only licensed to be a charter operator.

The judge said the CAA had been too timid to take the strong action that was needed over the safety breaches. It had ignored warning after warning about Seaview. The negligence was compounded when CAA staff lied to cover up their own incompetence and the actions of Seaview management. Judge Staunton singled out four people who he said lacked diligence in their responsibilities relating to the safety of Seaview Air — two worked for the CAA, the other two for Seaview, including John Green.

With this report published it was now my turn. The report with its background information and technical data was going to be invaluable in helping me determine the cause of the crash. John Green did not agree. He wanted to ban me from taking the evidence from the Staunton inquiry. I got onto the NSW Crown Solicitor, who represented the office of the coroner in court actions, and off we went to the NSW Supreme Court. Mr Green claimed the evidence would be prejudicial against him at the inquest. He lost. Justice Brian Sully, who had been the prosecutor all those years ago in the drugs case at Paddington which led to my family having 24-hour police protection, dismissed Mr Green's case. He said the inquiry's findings could certainly be presented to the inquest because the NSW Coroner did not have the power to make a 'suggestion of guilt'.

Meanwhile, Mr Green had changed the name of his airline to KentiaLink Airlines, hoping, no doubt, to distance himself from the bad publicity. He might have done better not to challenge the evidence I was able to hear, then I could have got on with the inquest soon after the Staunton report was handed down. By the time the Supreme Court handed down its decision, it was 19 November 1997, more than a year after the Seaview report. Five days later I got on with the inquest and the Seaview name came back to haunt Mr Green. I had Philip Biggens, a barrister we called on sometimes, as counsel assisting me.

On the first day we called the man who had headed BASI's investigation into the crash, Ian McCallum. Mr McCallum, then acting director of safety for Ansett Australia, said he had not been able to pinpoint any evidence of a mechanical fault on the plane. He couldn't explain what had caused the crash, saying it appeared several things possibly contributed to it. These included the overloading of the plane, modifications to the plane, the health of the pilot Paul Sheil on that day, the adequacy of his training and his ability to cope with the conditions and control the aircraft when the ice built up. He said the young pilot should not have been flying the plane because of his health. Sheil's pilot's licence was invalid because the medical certificate he required to validate the licence had expired three weeks before the crash and he had failed to have a new medical examination. There was evidence before me that Sheil had been suffering from various health problems just before the crash, including an eye infection and a boil on his right arm, which had been bandaged from the wrist to the forearm. The day before the accident, passengers had reported seeing him using an oxygen mask in the cockpit, putting up a reflector shield in the plane and wearing dark sunglasses. However, Mr McCallum said he could not sheet home total responsibility for the crash to Sheil.

We also called Michael Bird, the pilot of the third Seaview plane heading for Lord Howe Island that day in October 1994. Flying about 70 to 80 nautical miles ahead of the doomed plane, he said Sheil had told him over the radio that his aircraft was picking up ice and he was going to drop from 21,000 feet to 16,000 feet to get rid of it. He said Sheil had told him he had a vibration but had not known whether it was ice on the propellers or ice on the airframe. Mr Bird said that after hearing his colleague's final words, 'I've lost it, Clive, I've lost it', his only option had been to continue to Lord Howe Island because he did not have enough fuel to turn back and look for the stricken plane. He said he had left the situation to his superiors, John Green and chief pilot Clive McIver, in the other Seaview plane following.

Clive McIver got his chance to tell his side of the story the next day. He said the problem of ice building up on the plane was one he had never experienced in 12 years of flying to Lord Howe. He heard Sheil say over the radio, 'I must have enough ice to start a cocktail party.' McIver said he did not offer assistance because he did not believe it had been asked for and that Sheil, although 'relatively inexperienced', was competent. Even when he heard those final chilling words as his young workmate told him he had 'lost it', McIver said he did not consider that it was a mayday call. He said he was waiting for further information, as he had no idea what had happened. In hindsight, he accepted he should have done more.

'I'VE LOST IT, CLIVE, I'VE LOST IT.'

I could not believe the inaction by McIver and Green. I did not accept that hindsight was any excuse. I could not think of any words which would be construed any closer to a cry for help than when Paul Sheil uttered, 'I've lost it, Clive, I've lost it.' For McIver to suggest it was not a mayday call was, in my opinion, completely unacceptable as being a reasonable reaction in the circumstances. There was no doubt that when he received that call McIver should have taken immediate action to help Sheil and all those on the other plane in whatever way he could. To say the least, the decision by him and his boss John Green to wait 79 minutes on Lord Howe Island to see if Sheil had landed before they alerted anyone was absolutely disgraceful and a gross dereliction of their duty, considering the positions they held at Seaview. I believed McIver and Green had behaved disgracefully and said as much when I handed down my findings at the end of that week. In the case of both men, I did not accept their glib explanations for their actions.

I could not find that the young pilot was medically unfit or inadequately trained but he was certainly to blame for allowing the plane to be overloaded by at least 260 kilograms, or the equivalent of three extra passengers. Had this led to the crash? I could not say.

I had to find that the cause of the crash was unclear and that while Green and McIver had been irresponsible in the way the airline was run there was no case for criminal charges. I recommended that black box recorders be installed on smaller aircraft to make it easier to work out the cause of any future crashes.

Unfortunately for the families of those who died, many of whom sat in court during the inquest to listen to the evidence, the exact cause of the disaster had been impossible for the experts to discover.

In a strange sequel to this, as I was writing this chapter, cousins of Doreen's, Kingsley and Helen Green, had a family get-together at Forbes, a Sunday barbecue where 160 people turned up. During the day I was introduced to a John Green. He was quite friendly and talkative, and as he was leaving that night he invited Doreen and I to his place if we were ever on Lord Howe Island. A couple of days later the penny dropped when Kingsley mentioned that the man was the owner of the airline that had crashed years earlier. I hadn't recognised him. When I'd seen him at the inquest, he had a beard. At the barbecue his beard was gone which added to my lack of recognition. He obviously remembered who I was and had moved on from the serve I had given him at the inquest. Small world.

THE CORONER

As a result of light aircraft crash cases and the outcomes, standards and requirements of civil aviation have improved. Fifteen months before the Seaview crash I had been at the scene of a fatal air crash myself. Seven people died in June 1993 when a Piper Navajo Chieftain belonging to Monarch Airlines crashed on approach to the Young aerodrome. When I was given the news, I collected Steve Bills and a couple of his investigating team and we jumped in the car and drove the four and a half hours to Young.

By the time we got there the police had set up a perimeter to keep non-essential people away from the scene of the crash; the bodies were still in position. We hadn't been there long when there was a huge fuss. A senior police officer said the bodies had to be removed but the forensic guys hadn't finished their work. The BASI investigators and some of the police forensic officers came to see me and asked me to intervene. As the coroner I was the one who had the final say.

When there is no one left alive it is up to the dead to tell their story as best they can. Where they had been sitting could help with their identification, where they had ended up could help with the cause of the crash. It was imperative the bodies were not moved before the investigators were ready. I overruled the senior police officer and the bodies stayed put until we were sure we had learned everything they could tell us. Seeing the results of plane crashes like that did nothing to help my own fear of flying.

When I had packed up and moved to Port Macquarie, Peter Gould was appointed deputy in my place and he took over the Monarch Airlines inquiry. The accident turned out to be the beginning of the end for the CAA and the catalyst for a major shake-up of air safety across Australia's aviation industry, specifically the operators using small passenger aircraft. As in everything which involves politics, that wasn't going to happen overnight and it wasn't going to happen without a lot of bureaucratic buck-passing.

The seven victims of the crash had all been known to John Sharp, who was then the federal opposition spokesman on transport. The accident happened in his electorate of Hume, just kilometres away from his family property at Young. He revealed in Federal Parliament that Monarch

'I'VE LOST IT, CLIVE, I'VE LOST IT.'

Airlines had had no valid insurance policy, leaving the families of the victims with no way to obtain compensation. Three months later he went further, using the protection of parliamentary privilege under which he could not be sued for defamation, to describe Monarch Airlines as a 'shonky operation' with a track record that should have set off alarm bells within the CAA. He told parliament that Monarch and other regional airlines regularly overloaded planes. One of those other regional airlines, he said, was Seaview.

In July 1994, BASI reported on its investigation into the Monarch crash at Young and said the airline's emphasis had been more on making money than on safety. BASI also turned on the CAA, saying they appeared to be biased towards promoting the viability of the operator rather than promoting safety. Meanwhile Seaview continued to fly and the CAA continued to oversee its operations.

In June 1996, Peter Gould handed down his findings into the Monarch crash. He blamed the disaster on the 'slipshod' management of Monarch Airlines by the general manager Richard Maclean. The plane's navigation equipment had been rendered inoperative when Mr Maclean ordered the removal of the plane's autopilot for repairs on 31 May 1993, 12 days before the crash. The parts needed to fix it cost $8.75 with another $700 in labour. Instead of grounding the plane pending the repair, he kept it flying without its navigational instruments.

Peter Gould ruled out pilot error as a cause of the crash finding the pilot, Wayne Gorham, had suffered from skill fatigue. He said the pilot would have been physically unable to attend to all the decisions and judgments required of him to land without the navigational instruments.

Peter Gould was also scathing about the CAA and the NSW Air Transport Council (ATC). He said the crash could have been prevented had they paid more attention to the law. He said the ATC had ample warning that Monarch was a disaster waiting to happen and they had done more than nothing – they had concealed a dangerous state of affairs, deceiving the public and its own minister. He said that rather than being the watchdogs of the industry, CAA management had bullied its safety inspectors and protected the airline industry from some constraints of safety regulations. He said there was no satisfactory explanation as to why the CAA had failed to ground Monarch and revoke its licence.

Before the Monarch inquest began, the CAA had been dismantled and replaced with the independent CASA. John Sharp, who had made a name for himself in parliament with his attacks on the standards of air safety from the opposition benches, had become the Minister for Transport due to a change of government.

⁂

Of course, it is not only the flying business where it takes a disaster to get things changed.

On Friday, 24 May 1996, a clear autumn day, the husband of Nene King, the editorial director of *Australian Women's Weekly*, died in a diving accident off Bondi. Pat Bowring, 45, was an experienced diver addicted to the sport. A former teenage swimming champion, he was fit and dived almost every weekend. He was also a gear junkie and loved to try out all the new equipment that came on the market. He made his living as an entertainment journalist and had dived all over the world.

On this day, he had been diving with two buddies on the wreck of the paddle steamer, *Koputai*, 2.8 nautical miles offshore. It was known as the Everest of dives because of its depth at 78 metres. Some idea of how deep it was is given by the fact that the limit for police divers is 50 metres.

Bowring was still descending when at about 2 p.m., in 20 metres of water, he signalled to his mates that he was having some trouble and returned to the surface, while they continued their descent. A strong current was running and there was a reasonable swell. The three men were using an anchored line, called a mermaid line, that they held onto during their descent and which helped them in recompression during the ascent. When he reached the surface, Bowring was seen a short distance from the stern of the dive boat and appeared to be having difficulty holding the mermaid line. Two people from the boat dived in to go to his aid; by the time they got to the spot, Bowring had vanished.

Two days later his black torn and tattered deep water 'dry suit' was pulled from the ocean about 200 metres from the spot where he had gone missing. The front zip was still done up but the back of the suit was ripped. Bowring's air tanks and other gear were never found. What remained of the suit was brought into Glebe where it was examined for

'I'VE LOST IT, CLIVE, I'VE LOST IT.'

teeth marks and human remains. It was thought Bowring had been taken by a shark.

So was it a shark attack, a heart attack or failure of his diving equipment? They weren't the only things I had to consider when I held the inquest into Pat Bowring's death in November 1996. There was also the bizarre claim that he had faked his own death. One witness had told police that on the afternoon Bowring disappeared, he had been swimming at Bondi and had seen a man appear out of the ocean. He later recognised him as Pat Bowring from a photograph in a newspaper. I believed it was obviously a case of mistaken identity and said so. If someone wanted to disappear there were easier ways to do it.

There was no doubt in my mind that Bowring was dead. We called the two men who had seen him from the dive boat to give evidence, lifeguard Richard Taylor and marine electrician David Apperley. Mr Taylor said that Bowring seemed to be having a problem and had appeared to be grabbing at part of his gear.

The only real clue to determining what had happened out there was the remains of the $1000 dry suit. Dr Christopher Lawrence, one of our forensic pathologists, helped us out there. He felt the damage to the suit was consistent with being caused by the teeth of a shark. There were no human remains found inside the suit, indicating that whatever had happened to Pat Bowring, he had not been able to put up a fight. He had died before his body was taken. He may well have had a heart attack, drowned and then been attacked. Or it was just as likely there had been something wrong with his diving equipment which had caused his death, and then his body was attacked by a shark.

To dive to the depths of the *Koputai* needs a special mix of gases. Bowring was part owner of Technical Diving International in Australia and an instructor in the use of 'trimix' gases, a combination of oxygen, helium and nitrogen, which enables diving past the normal deep air limits. Without being too technical, if he had breathed those gases on the surface, it would have killed him. Because his tanks were never found there was no way of knowing what amount or mix he had actually been breathing, or even whether he had jumped in without turning on his main tanks at all. I could be no more certain in my finding than to say that what had happened was an unfortunate accident.

I recommended stringent regulations to be put in place for recreational diving in New South Wales. I also recommended that a code of practice be set up for people involved in deep diving where gases other than compressed air is used.

His diving accident was not the first in the state by far and it was not the first involving deep diving. A couple of years earlier, Bowring had been a witness in the inquest into the death of one of his diving buddies. On 20 March 1994, he had been diving with Paul Cavanagh, a television executive, on the wreck of the *Coolooli* off Long Reef on Sydney's northern beaches. Witnesses had testified that Bowring said the dive had been part of the first trimix course to be run in Australia, statements Bowring denied under cross-examination. WorkCover banned trimix diving in 1991, a ban that had been lifted just 19 days before Cavanagh died after the NSW Crown Solicitor had given legal advice that WorkCover had been acting outside its authority when it ordered the ban.

No matter how experienced you are these kinds of accidents can happen and, like flying, when you make a mistake there's a good chance that you will die. Take Brad Smith and Richard Yarrow, both certified diving masters. In 1992 I had conducted the inquest into their deaths after their bodies were found entombed in the hull of the wreck of the HMAS *Himma* about three nautical miles off Narrabeen on Sydney's northern beaches. They had dived on the wreck at least four times before so they knew it well. It appeared that on this final time they made a fatal mistake.

Their bodies told us that Yarrow, 31, had died of hypoxia due to oxygen depletion in his scuba gear while Smith, 33, died of lack of oxygen. They were found inside the crew quarters on the wreck's lower level and the furthest away from the roof hatch, which was the only way into the cabin. It seemed they had become lost in the wreck. I had some police diving experts look into what might have caused two expert scuba divers to become disorientated. The verdict was that the men had not followed the basic procedure of tying a safety line to the outside of the compartment before entering. It was also standard procedure that only one of two divers enters a compartment at any time when diving on these kinds of

'I'VE LOST IT, CLIVE, I'VE LOST IT.'

wrecks. The men had probably entered the room at the same time, stirring up the years of silt on the floor, reducing visibility to zero. Without the safety line they couldn't find the exit and it was assumed they panicked and ran out of air in their search for a way out. The experts also believed the men had probably experienced narcosis, a drunk-like state accompanied by a feeling of euphoria, which impaired their judgment. Experienced divers like them would have recognised the dangers of entering the compartment without a safety line but no one could explain to me why Yarrow and Smith had done it. I concluded their deaths resulted from a moment of bad judgment, probably caused by narcosis. Like I said, a fatal error.

As I had been preparing my findings into Pat Bowring's death, downstairs in the morgue, the pathologists had just completed their inquiries into the cause of death of a 24-year-old man who died at a Bachelors & Spinsters Ball in the bush at my home town of Forbes on 7 September 1996.

B & S Balls were always fairly wild shows but the Forbes B & S Ball hadn't even started when Bryce O'Malley died. The ball was held in the village hall at Warroo, a little place about 35 kilometres west of Forbes. The police investigation had been hampered because most of the witnesses had been drinking and some of them were plain drunk. Many of them couldn't remember what had happened, others just hadn't been paying any attention. What was certain was that the young man died of severe head and chest injuries and all the evidence pointed to him having fallen from the back of a utility.

You live in the country, you're a young bloke – well, you have to drive a ute. Not just any ute. It has to have all the 'go-faster' toys – the bull bars, CD player and lots of lights for night shooting. And you have to be able to 'circle' and 'tailgate'. That's what was happening at Warroo Hall about two hours before the B & S Ball was due to start. Circle work involves driving cars in tight circles, often with the rear of the car sliding out. Tailgating involves a person hanging on to the tailgate or tow bar of a ute while it is doing circle work. I have heard it is great fun. I am no killjoy, but it's not the sort of thing you should be doing after consuming copious amounts of beer.

Several witnesses said they had seen Bryce O'Malley tailgating and riding in the back of utes while they were doing circle work. Then someone heard a group of people saying, 'Let's drag him out of the way before he gets hit' and saw three or four people pulling O'Malley from the area. The witness didn't think anything of it at the time, believing the young man had probably just passed out, but about 20 minutes later he noticed the man hadn't moved. When he rolled him over, he saw O'Malley's eyes were half open and his face had turned blue. An ambulance was called.

The police believed the accident happened about 7.30 p.m. and the ambulance was called about 7.50 p.m. When I returned to Forbes to hold the inquest, I made the point that I had no criticism of O'Malley's friends who had tried to help him. The reports from the pathologist pointed to the fact that his chances of survival had been pretty slim. It wasn't the first time I had been back in the Forbes courthouse. I had been there often as a relieving magistrate. Even when I was there for work, I stayed with my in-laws on their farm.

The police investigating O'Malley's death had a good idea. They had seen an ABC documentary called 'The Problem with Men, An Insight into Men's Health' which depicted the behaviour of men at a B & S Ball. The police also obtained a home video of cars doing circle work in the afternoon before the Forbes B & S Ball from a lady who had been visiting friends on a neighbouring property. I had the videos played in court and as someone who had never been to such a ball, I found them helpful.

Like I said, I'm no killjoy but one of the recommendations I felt I had to make was that circle work and tailgating needed to be banned from B & S Balls and all advertising prior to these balls should clearly state that. The car parking areas should be filled with cars or fenced so there was no space for these activities. It also made sense that some form of medical personnel or support, such as the NSW Ambulance Service or St John's Ambulance should be available at all these balls and that there be an increased liaison between ball organisers and the local police, including a greater police presence. I seem to remember that in my day, there were some balls which were similar to B & S Balls in that they were an excuse for people to carry on

'I'VE LOST IT, CLIVE, I'VE LOST IT.'

and drink a lot of alcohol, but I missed out on them. So did Doreen. Doreen's dad was very strict and she wasn't allowed to go. None of my mates went to them either, they just didn't interest us. Doreen and I went to a lot of balls, but they were a bit more sedate.

As we wound up 1996 with our traditional lunch around the bar table in Court One at Glebe, we had no idea what the next 12 months had in store for us.

Chapter 9

Snakebite

You wouldn't think an elderly church-going couple would have any enemies, but somebody wanted Anthony Perish, 91, and his 93-year-old wife Francis dead. They were shot dead in their home by a killer or killers who stole nothing and left behind no sign of a forced entry.

The couple had been dead for four years with their murders still unsolved, waiting for the police to complete their brief of evidence. Once this brief was done we could get started on an inquest to try and solve the mystery of what had happened to them. It was June 1997 and one of my old workmates, Dr Gus Oettle, was standing before me in the witness box explaining how they had died.

Their bodies had been found on the two single beds in the bedroom of their single-level house in Byron Road, a semi-rural isolated street at Leppington in Sydney's southwest on 14 June 1993, the Monday of the Queen's birthday long weekend. As the couple were the first two Yugoslav migrants to have moved to the area they were well known in Leppington. Anthony and Francis had built a successful market garden and poultry farm business and had won awards for their personal garden which they tended to every day.

Their bodies were discovered by their son, Albert, then 60, and his wife Thea. Strewn throughout the house was a trail of toilet paper soaked in kerosene. A crude timing mechanism made from a box of matches taped to candles and a notebook had been meant to start a blaze, wiping out any evidence, but it had not worked. As well as the smell of kerosene, the first paramedic on the scene had noticed a strong smell of gas. It appeared the killer or killers had also left on the gas fire, plugged in the electric water jug and switched on the electric hotplates on top of the stove to add to any fire. A pan containing fat was found on the stove top.

Mr and Mrs Perish each died from a single gunshot but no murder weapon had been found. Mrs Perish was shot in the side and Dr Oettle, who had performed the post-mortems on each of them, told me in court that it was as if she had been holding up her right arm with her elbow across her face in a shielding gesture. It appeared as if she had been shot from behind. Her husband, however, had been shot from the front, the bullet passing through the major vessel that supplied blood from his head and neck to his heart. It had then passed through his right lung and lodged in his chest wall. No defence wounds had been found on either of them, so they had not been able to fight back or perhaps they were taken by surprise. The evidence pointed to them having been shot on the patio; then their bodies moved and placed in the bedroom. A bloodstained jacket and other clothing were found in the laundry.

It would have been helpful to the investigation to have had the exact time of death but Dr Oettle could not be sure. He believed they had died a day, to a day and a half before they were found, which meant they could have been shot on the Sunday or Monday. The speed of decomposition depended on many things. Mrs Perish had been fully clothed which would have speeded up decomposition because her body temperature would have been preserved but on the other hand, it might have been cold at night and the windows may have been open. There was no evidence before me as to what the weather had been or to the state of the bedroom windows.

I had a number of neighbours called to give evidence to see if they had noticed anything suspicious or had heard gunshots, which would help pin down the time of death, but it appeared that gunshots were not an uncommon sound in that area. One of the neighbours told me that stray dogs were one of the targets for the locals who had guns. 'If my dog goes on someone's land, goes onto Perish's land, they have all full rights to shoot my dog. I mean, they don't want it damaging their paddock,' she said. Oh well, I thought, it takes all sorts.

It was difficult to be certain who heard gunshots and when. Added to the confusion was the fact that it was traditional to let off firecrackers over the holiday weekend. One neighbour, who normally gave the couple a lift to the 8 a.m. mass at church most Sundays, said she hadn't seen them all that Sunday. The signal that they wanted a lift was for them to leave their gate open. That Sunday morning it had been closed so she hadn't called in.

Another neighbour thought she had heard gunshots on the Monday night, but she said a family friend who arrived at her house around 8.30 a.m. on the Monday morning, had told her he thought he had heard automatic fire 'over the road' when he arrived. There was a lot of conflicting evidence and as I sat in my office at Glebe that lunchtime, during the inquest, I became frustrated. Who was the neighbour's 'family friend' and why wasn't he giving evidence to try and clear up what had been heard? There were other neighbours mentioned by some witnesses who said they had heard or seen something; where were they? This compounded the lack of evidence about whether the windows were open or shut and what the temperature was at the time of the murders. I was having concerns not only at the long time the police had taken to get the brief together but the level of thoroughness.

It confirmed that the police investigation was lacking when the next important witness was called. Detective Senior Constable Shirley Eyre was with the police crime scene unit's fingerprint section. In the Perish house she had fingerprinted everything she felt was suspicious, like the candles, matches and the tape used to stick them together, but found no prints. She had even tested the 11 cardboard inserts from the toilet rolls, which had been trailed throughout the house, but found no prints on them.

Had she tested the gas fire? Or the electric water jug? Or the switches on the stove? What about the pan of fat on the hotplates? Constable Eyre said no one had told her there was anything suspicious about these items and she hadn't tested them because they appeared to her to be only everyday items and she did not fingerprint everyday items. Had she been told how they fitted into the picture she said she would have certainly checked them for fingerprints. It was the same with the laundry; she had not been told that bloodstained clothing had been found there so she had not examined it. She could not be blamed.

There were so many loose ends, I felt I had no option but to call a halt to the inquest. To carry on in such a haphazard way was obviously going to get us nowhere. It was going to be a complete waste of everyone's time.

I called everyone back into court, including Albert Perish and his sister Elena. Members of the Perish family had written to me several times expressing their own doubts at the standard of the police investigation. A coroner gets many letters from family and friends of those who have died, some seeking to understand more fully why. I also received many anonymous letters saying I should reinvestigate this or that case. These were more often than not from people with an axe to grind against someone. In this case, I saw what the Perish family had meant. There were witnesses who could have perhaps shed light on the situation who had not even been spoken to. The results of certain tests had never been passed to Dr Oettle. The problems with the fingerprint evidence were obvious. The standard of investigation was inadequate and certainly not what should be expected in a murder inquiry. I formally directed that the murders be reinvestigated and told the police department to have it done by senior police officers not connected with the original inquiry. That was on 12 June. Someone pointed out to me that it was almost the anniversary of when their bodies had been discovered on 14 June.

Six years later, as I was writing this book, the inquest into the deaths of Anthony and Francis Perish had been reopened and was continuing. Two $100,000 rewards for information leading to a conviction remained unclaimed and no one has been charged over their murders. It was clear that the second police investigation, with the help of advances in forensic procedures, had been more thorough than the first. There were more than 20 suspects, or 'people of interest', some of them locals from the Leppington area. In the meantime Albert Perish, who had inherited his parents' poultry farm, had become increasingly convinced that someone had organised the crime to frame him. He had named his theories in seven statements to police, including a claim of involvement by a clandestine Bermuda-registered company connected with organised crime. The police had chased down every avenue of inquiry he raised. Carl Milovanovich, the current Deputy State Coroner, went on to bring down an open finding in the inquest because there was insufficient evidence for anyone to be charged.

It is very frustrating when you have your suspicions about a case but little else. It was like that from the day Caroline Byrne's death was reported to me on a cold June morning in 1995. Her body had been found on the rocks at the bottom of The Gap in Watsons Bay, a 30-metre cliff near Sydney Harbour Heads which is a well-known spot for people who want to kill themselves. The post-mortem had been carried out and I had the report and photographs in front of me. Her injuries were consistent with her having fallen but I never felt it was suicide, raising the possibilities that she either fell or was pushed. There was no direct evidence of who, if anyone, had pushed her but it just did not seem right to me.

Tall, blonde and with the kind of looks that turned heads, Caroline, 24, had been working as a model. She was the third of four children and had reportedly enjoyed a solid, stable and happy family life. At the age of 17 she was crowned Miss Spirit at the Campbelltown Fisher's Ghost Festival and she took up modelling while at Camden High School, appearing in swimsuits as a Page 3 girl in the *Daily Mirror*, which was then Sydney's afternoon tabloid newspaper. At Sydney University she got her bachelor of arts with a major in psychology. Her parents moved to what was then regarded as one of the top apartment buildings in the city, The Connaught, in Liverpool Street, overlooking Hyde Park. Caroline was said to be a poised, confident and all-round nice woman. In 1991, Caroline's mother, Andrea, who had been suffering from depression, killed herself with an overdose of drugs and alcohol. Nine months later, Caroline tried to commit suicide by lying in a bath of water and taking an overdose of pills.

The police officer who first investigated Caroline's death at the bottom of The Gap believed it all pointed to suicide. His report to me said that he believed she had been suffering from depression and could no longer cope. Although that was his opinion, it was only the start. All the circumstances surrounding her death had to be investigated and it became stranger as all the bits and pieces emerged.

Her father, Tony, began to write to me with his concerns. He never believed that his daughter had killed herself and, like the family of Mr and Mrs Perish, was not satisfied with the investigation. He raised several points. As in all such cases, I passed the material on to the officer in charge of the police investigation.

Caroline had been living with her boyfriend, Gordon Wood, then 33, in a unit they had bought together at trendy Potts Point. He was chauffeur and personal assistant to the famous stockbroker Rene Rivkin. The couple went to the so-called A-list places around Sydney – the expensive restaurants, the right nightclubs – the places where people went to be seen. There was evidence that the day she went missing, she had not gone to work but had been carrying out her own surveillance of Mr Wood, who been driving Mr Rivkin around. It was claimed she had seen something she was not meant to see.

Later, when my successor John Abernethy held the inquest into her death, two local restaurateurs identified Mr Wood in the crowded foyer at Glebe court as having been at The Gap on 7 June, the day Caroline had fallen or was pushed. Mr Wood had denied being there and denied pushing his girlfriend to her death. John Abernethy delivered an open finding but the police investigation is ongoing.

❦

While Caroline Byrne's death was being investigated by the police, another case which had caused me much concern was being played out in the courts. Jeffrey Gilham had pleaded guilty to the manslaughter of his brother, Christopher, and was placed on a five-year good behaviour bond. Behind this lay another tale.

Gilham had appeared before me back on Monday, 30 August 1993, charged with the murder of his brother on the previous Saturday. What was certain was that at about 4.30 a.m. on the Saturday, police and the fireys were called to the Gilham's family home, a riverfront property at Prince Edward Park Road, Woronora, in Sydney's southern suburbs. They found the body of the father, Stephen Gilham, 58, stabbed and charred in the bedroom and the body of the mother, Helen, 53, stabbed and burned in the lounge room. Christopher, 25, was found stabbed to death outside the house. Those were the facts. For the events that had led up to it we only had the word of the sole survivor, Jeffrey.

Jeffrey was then 23, a sixth year civil engineering student at Sydney's University of Technology and a keen sailor. As he stood before me at Glebe

Coroners Court, he appeared calm and composed, unlike the friends of his family who filled the public seats and were demonstrably distressed, crying as the case continued.

Jeffrey had spent the night in the police cells after being remanded in custody on the Sunday by a magistrate at Sydney's Central Local Court. The law is that the police must bring anyone charged before a court within 24 hours, which often made Sunday mornings at Central pretty busy if there had been a lot of arrests over the first half of the weekend. Jeffrey had been allowed to see a psychiatrist before appearing before me. The psychiatrist said he believed Jeffrey still did not fully comprehend the deaths of his family, speaking about them in the present tense as if their deaths had never occurred. The prognosis was that Jeffrey had been horrifically traumatised by what he had seen when he entered the house and would need medical help until he understood they were dead.

Jeffrey had told the police that he had been asleep in the boatshed at the back of the family home when he heard his mother's screams for help over the intercom. He had thrown on some clothes and rushed the 100 metres to the house where he found Christopher standing over their mother's body with a lighted match saying, 'I've killed Mum and Dad.' Their parents' bodies had been doused with petrol and as the fire spread, Jeffrey said he had picked up the same knife Christopher had used to kill their parents and chased him downstairs to the pool room. There, he stabbed his brother 17 times. Then he told a neighbour what had happened and the police were called.

Jeffrey Gilham had his solicitor, Chris Murphy, with him. Mr Murphy was as well known to me as he was to probably every magistrate and judge in New South Wales. He was a very busy criminal lawyer and he and I got on fine. He was a pretty good courtroom performer, so long as he kept on track. I think he would agree with this himself, that he would go off track and get over-emotional about things because he worked so hard for his clients. I had a lot of respect for him.

When it was his turn, Mr Murphy stood up at the bar table and said this was 'an enormously tragic' case. According to Mr Murphy, Mrs Gilham had mentioned to work friends that she had trouble controlling her elder son Christopher and had not known how to handle him.

As it was only at the initial stages of the investigation, I had no judgments to make and no decisions other than whether to grant Jeffrey bail. I had no hesitation in refusing him bail. I did, however, believe he should be placed in the psychiatric unit in jail and receive whatever treatment he needed. I made such a recommendation and adjourned the case.

That was the last I saw of Jeffrey Gilham because the next month I moved to Port Macquarie and the case passed to the new deputy, Peter Gould, who committed him to stand trial for Christopher Gilham's murder. When I learned in 1995 that he had pleaded guilty to the lesser charge of manslaughter, I wondered whether the deaths of three people had been solved too easily and too conveniently. Stephen Gilham's brother, Tony, believed it was too easy. Like Caroline Byrne's father, he believed there was a lot more to what had happened and he wanted the case reopened.

When I returned to Glebe as State Coroner I had the job of holding the inquest into the deaths of the three members of the Gilham family. I had all the reports before me, copies of all the statements and also the report of the decision of the NSW Supreme Court in Jeffrey Gilham's plea of guilty. That decision made it quite clear that the judge was satisfied Jeffrey Gilham had killed his brother because his brother had killed his parents. At that time the officer in charge of the investigation, my investigating team and myself were not all that happy with the decision. We believed there remained a doubt about what had happened. I'm not saying that Jeffrey Gilham killed all three members of his family but there was an uneasiness about his story. In the light of what the Supreme Court said, my hands were tied. I was in a bind and had to conclude after the brief inquest that Christopher Gilham was to blame for the deaths of his parents.

Tony Gilham continued his campaign to have the case reopened, enlisting the help of the Channel Nine program, *60 Minutes*. Mr Gilham and the program had approached Dr Gus Oettle for a second opinion. Gus sent me a copy of his report before the program went to air. He felt the evidence showed that Stephen, Helen and Christopher Gilham had all been murdered by the same person because the pattern of stab wounds on all three bodies was strikingly similar.

The power of the media can be great. The pressure led to the decision to hold a fresh inquest based on a couple of points: the murder weapon was found with no blood or fingerprints on it despite it being used to inflict 63 stab wounds, indicating it had been wiped clean; Jeffrey Gilham had only a small amount of blood near his fingernails and on his instep when he ran to the neighbour's house, which could lead to the conclusion that he had cleaned both himself and the knife.

When the fresh inquest was held in 2000, the evidence that emerged came as little surprise to me when I read it in the papers. By then I had retired but as always, I liked to see the cases I had been involved with through to their conclusion. This time the family of Stephen Gilham had hired a lawyer to ask questions on their behalf at the inquest, and they had pulled out one of the big guns. They had briefed the confident, highly-capable and formidable Ian Temby QC, who had been the inaugural head of the NSW Independent Commission Against Corruption (ICAC).

There was a psychiatrist, Dr John Shand, called at the inquest who said he had serious doubts about the genuineness and factual accuracy of Jeffrey Gilham's account to police about what happened on that night in August 1993. He labelled Gilham's answers to police when he made his record of interview as being inconsistent, inadequate and unintelligent. He did, however, concede that a number of emotions were possible and agreed that the accounts of the night that Gilham had given to three psychiatrists were remarkably similar. He said it was 'remarkable' that Gilham had shown so little emotion so soon after the tragic events.

Dr Oettle was called at the new inquest and said he believed the evidence showed Jeffrey Gilham was guilty of all three murders but a 'malfunctioning of the legal' system had allowed him to walk free on the good behaviour bond. It was strong stuff. A second forensic pathologist, a man I know and respect, Alan Cala, said if Christopher had been the one who stabbed his parents, then it was odd that he had no blood splatterings from them on his clothes. Christopher's feet should also have been bloodstained from walking in the bloodied area around his dead parents. As in most cases, the experts did not always agree.

Another expert, Professor Stephen Cordner, said that, in his opinion, spattered blood would not necessarily appear on the person wielding the knife. Professor Cordner, a colleague of Dr Oettle, did not share the views of Dr Oettle about the similarity of wounds to each of the three victims. The forensic pathologist who carried out the post-mortem examinations, the well-respected Dr Chris Lawrence, said while he believed the entry angle of the knife wounds on each of the Gilham family were generally the same, he did not believe that proved one person was responsible.

There was, of course, one person who knew exactly what happened. Jeffrey Gilham knew whether it was he or his brother who had killed their parents. Because his plea of guilty to manslaughter had been accepted by the Crown, Jeffrey had never had to tell his story in court, he had never been in the witness box and never been cross-examined on his version. On what turned out to be the last day of the inquest, it was his turn to face the questions. By this time, he was 30, a qualified civil engineer and had recently married.

One of the motives for the murders may have been the inheritance of $916,717.59 left by Mr and Mrs Gilham but when asked whether he had received the inheritance, Jeffrey Gilham declined to say. He also declined to answer whether he had washed his hands or showered after stabbing his brother, and also declined to say in which hand he was holding the knife when he stabbed his brother. When asked whether he was right-handed, he replied, 'Ah, I think I am ... yes I am.'

Finally he was asked by Mr Temby the question a lot of people wanted to know the answer to – whether he had killed his parents. Gilham refused to answer the question on the grounds it may incriminate him. Of course Gilham, like every other witness, had the right not to answer questions which might tend to incriminate them in any offence and by law, no adverse inference could be drawn from him exercising that right. The court adjourned for 50 minutes and when it reconvened, the question was put again to Gilham. This time he replied, and denied the murders.

The inquest had been conducted by Dr Elwyn Elms, who had retired as a magistrate but who was drafted in to do coronial work. He is a very smart man. After that final question, he terminated the inquest, as was his duty, because he believed there was sufficient evidence for a jury to convict a 'known person' for the killings. As I have said before, the law can be an ass and while it is usually obvious to even blind Freddy who the coroner means when he says this, the coroner is not able to state the name of the suspected person.

Two months later, the NSW Director of Public Prosecutions, Nicholas Cowdery QC, wrote to Tony Gilham to say they had decided not to proceed against Jeffrey Gilham. He said there was no reasonable prospect of a conviction; however, he said the decision could be reversed should new evidence come to light. A year later, Tony Gilham launched his own private prosecution against his nephew. By law such prosecutions are taken over by the DPP and again Mr Cowdery decided not to take it any further. That, whatever anyone may think, is where the matters rests as I write this.

At the same time as the inquiries proceeded into Caroline Byrne's death, officers with my unit were looking into a rare snakebite death.

I had been contacted by the ACT Chief Coroner, Ron Cahill, to take over the investigation into the death of Bill Edmonds. It had been front page news when on 28 December 1994, Dr Edmonds, 49, had been bitten by a tiger snake while on a picnic with his de facto, Dr Kate Blackmore. He died two days later in the intensive care unit at Woden Valley Hospital, in the Australian Capital Territory. As it was in the Australian Capital Territory, his death was reported to the Australian Federal Police and they referred it to Ron Cahill as a coronial matter. Dr Blackmore, who was not a medical doctor but an academic doctor like Dr Edmonds, had written to Mr Cahill with her concerns about the medical care given to Edmonds.

> 'During the last hours of life and in discussions with various professionals immediately after (Edmonds) death, I came to realise that there were grave and possibly fatal lapses in his care by medical and other health staff,' her letter said. 'I therefore beseech you to conduct a full coronial inquiry into the circumstances of his death so that this tragedy is never repeated.'

Mr Cahill had begun to look into the case but felt that as the events which led up to Edmonds' death happened largely in New South Wales it should be investigated in this state, so the case ended up on my desk.

I would often be invited to lecture nurses and other medical professionals and I used to talk to them about their duty of care to the patients and what their role was when looking after them. It was amazing to find out how little they knew about a coroner's work, what they should do in a coronial case or what the coroner in an inquest is looking for.

The nurses' professional body would have three conferences a year, two in the country and one in Sydney, and either myself or my deputy would attend. Other times they would come to Glebe where, I am afraid, the court staff would try to play one of their most popular tricks. They got me once while I was talking to the nurses in the main courtroom. My back was to the door which led out to the corridor to my office. Halfway through the lecture, the nurses started to giggle. The giggles became guffaws. I knew I wasn't that funny. It wasn't until later that I realised two of the staff, Jenny Prothero and Tony Astley, were playing out a sock puppet show from the door behind my back. It was a joke they played on everyone at the court at one time or another.

In those talks I would stress to the nurses that they had to protect themselves by noting down everything they were told to do, their observations and any drugs they gave. If they came before a court in a civil action or before me in an inquest, everything they did would be scrutinised and they could well find that what they said had happened would differ vastly from what their colleagues recalled had happened. I always impressed on the nurses that if they felt there was something not right with the medication, for example, they should get their supervisor to check and if they were still not happy, to go back to the doctor. I know nurses get a lot of satisfaction out of the work they do but being a nurse can be a thankless job in many ways. When anything goes wrong, they are in the firing line as are the doctors and the hospital. I would tell all the medical professionals that they could not be too careful in such litigious times.

I opened the inquest into the death of Edmonds in March 1996 in Cooma and lined up before me at the bar table was a veritable crowd of lawyers. There was one for Dr Blackmore, there was one for Dr Andrew West, who was the doctor who had first treated Edmonds, one for the NSW Health Service and Monaro Area Health Service and one for the NSW Nurses Association. I started by making it quite clear to them that this was an inquest and not a civil hearing to look at negligence. That was a matter for another jurisdiction. It was for me to look into the manner and cause of death and whether any criticism should be made of any person or any authority, and whether there were recommendations to be made to prevent anything like this happening again. Of course, it was stating the obvious but there were times when lawyers were involved that you could not say it enough.

I had flown down to Cooma with John Gibson to assist me, and one of the court officers, Dawn Stratford. Dawn accompanied me because my regular court officer, Kay Dawson, was unavailable. We had booked into one of the motels on the main road where we usually stayed when we needed to be in Cooma for inquests. I wanted to hold the inquest in the area where the incident had occurred and the doctors, nurses and ambulance paramedics who would be giving evidence were all local. I also thought we would get the inquest completed in Cooma. We had set it down for two days.

What had happened was that in December 1994, Edmonds and Dr Blackmore had driven down from their home in Sydney to spend Christmas on their property at Bungarby on the Snowy River. On 28 December they packed up a picnic and drove to an isolated cleared spot near the river. In the heat, Edmonds was wearing Dr Scholl-type slip-on sandals, shorts and a short-sleeved shirt. When he stepped out of their four-wheel drive he felt something grab his ankle. He told Dr Blackmore that he 'felt funny' before collapsing into a chair. He was grey and sweating. It was 11 a.m. Dr Blackmore later said that she had not initially thought of a snake because they had parked near a cleared area, under a tree where the only vegetation was twigs from the tree. She was a registered nurse who, at the time, taught nursing although she had not worked as a nurse for 20 years. She thought her partner may have had a heart attack.

She helped him into the car and they drove towards Cooma and the local hospital, at least an hour away. At 11.20 a.m., they arrived at the property of a neighbour and Dr Blackmore called out that Edmonds had been bitten by a snake and for the neighbour to call an ambulance. It was important to note that Dr Blackmore had said it was a snakebite and not a heart attack; this would become important later.

Dr Blackmore decided to keep going to Cooma so they would catch up with the ambulance coming the other way and save time. At 11.47 a.m., 33.5 kilometres south of Cooma, they met up with the ambulance.

One of the ambulance officers immediately recognised the couple; he had met them some years earlier when Edmonds had broken his leg on a Snowy River property. By this time, Edmonds was pale and complaining of headaches and nausea. The paramedics noticed puncture marks on his left ankle and put a compression bandage below his knee. It was in accordance with what I was told was 'protocol 52' which related to snake, spider and sea creature bites. It was also standard commonsense first aid for snakebites.

They immobilised Edmonds and headed for Cooma, with Dr Blackmore following in her car. It took 20 minutes to reach Cooma Hospital, a small hospital where the local GPs and specialists acted as casualty staff. The GP on call that day was Andrew West, who had been in the town for several years. I recall him as a serious-looking man. At 12.22 a.m., the ambulance arrived at the hospital and Edmonds was given oxygen and a second intravenous fluid drip. Dr West ordered pathology tests, including a venom detection test. The test entailed moving the compression bandage to take a swab of the bite area. Had Dr West looked at the bite he would have seen it was no ordinary bite but four or five bites, each injecting venom. While the tests were carried out Dr West returned to his practice, which was two to three minutes' drive from the hospital, asking to be called with the results.

The venom detection test results came through at 1.25 p.m. and revealed Edmonds had been bitten by either a tiger or a copperhead snake, both among the world's most dangerous snakes; the tiger snake being the fourth most dangerous, the copperhead coming in at number 11. Both can be treated by tiger snake antivenom. Dr West was told by the nurses that the hospital had one vial of tiger snake antivenom and one other vial of general antivenom that was able to treat any case of snakebite.

At 2 p.m. Dr West was called from the hospital with the results of other tests called coagulation studies, which reveal the ability of the blood to clot. These tests can show the seriousness of a snakebite. In Edmonds' case, they showed among other things that after five minutes, his blood had still not clotted. The normal time for blood to clot is about 32 seconds. Dr West said he would attend the hospital to administer the antivenom.

The nurses moved Edmonds to intensive care and at 2.15 p.m., rang Dr West to say they were ready. At 2.30 p.m., one ampoule of 3000 units of tiger snake antivenom was given. The nursing notes showed that Edmonds appeared to improve. He told the nurses he was feeling better, his headache and nausea were going and the nurses wrote that he was 'settled'. Unfortunately that did not last long.

By 4 p.m., the nurses saw that Edmonds was having difficulty swallowing and his eyes could not focus. The nursing supervisor asked if the hospital had any more tiger snake antivenom. Tiger snakes were commonly known to frequent the areas around Cooma and that very morning, the hospital had treated another suspected snakebite victim. Protocol, at the time, only provided for one vial of the specific antivenom to be held at Cooma because of the small size of the hospital. There was no more left in stock.

At 4.30 p.m. the nurses rang Dr West again and told him of Edmonds' worsening condition and of fresh coagulation studies which were still abnormal. Dr West returned to the hospital and decided to have Edmonds transferred to Woden Valley Hospital in Canberra. He first checked with the senior staff specialist and learned they had more antivenom. Dr West asked if he should administer the general snake antivenom left at Cooma but was told by Woden Valley Hospital not to waste time and to get the patient into an ambulance.

The ambulance arrived at Woden Valley Hospital at 7.10 p.m. and 30 minutes later, Edmonds was given another vial of tiger snake antivenom. Less than an hour later, he was given a third vial. His condition continued to deteriorate. Suddenly he complained of an inability to breathe and was put on a mechanical respirator. During the night he was given another three vials of antivenom. At 9.15 p.m. the next day, 29 December, he suffered a cardiac arrest and died. His muscles had broken down and his kidneys had failed.

Dr Blackmore put to me a list of criticisms of the treatment her partner had been given. She complained of the time it took the ambulance to get to the hospital, specifically that it slowed down to 60 kilometres on reaching Cooma. She complained about the time lapse in the administration of the antivenom at Cooma, the unavailability of a second vial and the medical treatment given by Dr West. She was also concerned about the time taken in making the decision to transfer Edmonds to Woden Valley. She said that concerns had been expressed to her by medical staff at Woden about the medical treatment given at Cooma, including that they believed her partner should have been given the antivenom within ten minutes of arrival at Cooma Hospital and then air evacuated to Woden Valley.

SNAKEBITE

John Gibson and I had considered who to consult to provide us with the expert knowledge we were going to need to determine if Edmonds had been given the correct treatment. We had decided on Dr John Raftos. He was director of emergency medicine at Sutherland Hospital in southern Sydney, an area with a lot of bushland, where they experienced many snakebite cases. He had treated several tiger snake victims. Kate Blackmore wanted the opinions of her own experts and had consulted Professor Malcolm Fisher, director of the intensive therapy unit at Sydney's Royal North Shore Hospital. She also wanted to call Professor Struan Sutherland. He was the foundation director and associate professor of the Australian Venom Research Unit in the Department of Pharmacology at the University of Melbourne. Professor Sutherland had divided his life between the study of snakes and spiders, snakebites and treatment and was the leading expert in the world in his field. I did not intend to call Professor Sutherland myself but I was happy for Blackmore to have him give evidence.

There was no way we were going to be finished within two days so I adjourned the inquest to Glebe and we flew back to Sydney. In May 1995 we reconvened at Glebe where I heard another day and a half of evidence in the city.

Professor Fisher, who was not called to give evidence but had given a statement, had said in the statement that he had asked himself, 'Do I consider a three-and-a-half hour delay between a bite and antivenom significant in the cause of death?' He had answered himself that it was 'one of three very significant factors, the other two are the delay in first aid application and the absence of an effective dose of antivenom'. The court's expert, Dr Raftos, had also said that the lack of emergency first aid in the application of a compression bandage was something that had to be taken into account.

Dr Blackmore had said in evidence that she believed Edmonds had suffered a heart attack yet she had told the neighbour it was a snakebite and she said in her police statement that at one stage she had thought it was a snakebite. Even if she only thought it might have been a snakebite, I would have thought that having had the nursing training that she had years earlier, perhaps she should have thought of doing something just in case. On the other hand, I could see how it was quite understandable that, in the suddenness of the situation and the urgency, she had not thought about applying a bandage. I had seen in many cases that in such a moment of panic people forget basic things.

After lunch on the second day, I handed down my findings. What I had to say was going to upset many people, not least Dr Blackmore. She was looking for me to criticise Dr West – certainly his actions were open to criticism – but there was also evidence that she may have been able to do more to help had she carried out standard first aid in case of a snakebite. 'If I am going to be critical in hindsight of Dr West, I would agree that there is some room for criticism of Dr Blackmore,' I began.

I said that I felt the ambulance officers did what they could and no criticism could be levelled at them. As far as the complaint that they had slowed down to 60 kilometres in Cooma, I noted that they had been passing a school area where children were playing and they had quite properly been observing the safety of others. I said the nurses had done everything they were obliged to do.

I turned to Dr West. I felt that up to 3 p.m., he had followed the proper protocol and done everything correctly. However, when the pathology swab was being taken, he should have looked at the bite and would have seen that it was much more serious than an ordinary bite. Had he done so, he would have given greater thought as to what treatment he gave to Edmonds and would have checked to see if there were more ampoules of antivenom or had Edmonds transferred directly to a bigger hospital. I noted that he did order the appropriate tests.

Dr West could have been fooled into thinking everything was alright because Edmonds had appeared fairly well when he arrived at the hospital. Evidence from the doctor and the nurses was that his condition had improved during the afternoon, although I noted that neither Dr Blackmore nor Professor Sutherland agreed with what the nurses said. But Professor Sutherland had admitted that his assumption was based on Dr Blackmore's statement and he had not looked at the rest of the record and the notes of the nurses.

There was no doubt that there should have been more ampoules of antivenom at Cooma Hospital; however, I did not feel it could be said with any certainty that the lack of a second ampoule at the hospital caused Bill Edmonds' death because this was no ordinary snakebite. Dr West had treated about 30 snakebites, including four in a period of 12 years at Cooma and one at Canberra, and he had found one ampoule to be sufficient every time. While I found that Dr West should have done more to ascertain the seriousness of the bite, I could not accept that he was culpable in his lack of care.

It was all very well for Professor Sutherland to be critical of Dr West but Professor Sutherland had never been in a situation of treating a snakebite patient; he was an academic. 'He does not have the experience of being in the forefront where you deal with patients daily and have to make clinical decisions based on symptoms,' I said from the bench. While I felt Dr West should have done more, any lack could not, even on the balance of probabilities, be said to have contributed to Edmonds' cause of death.

I recommended to the Commonwealth Minister for Health and the NSW Minister for Health that sufficient supplies of snakebite antivenom be retained in all hospitals in accordance with the recommendations of the Commonwealth Serum Laboratories and I know that has now been done. Cooma now holds more than one vial of tiger snake antivenom. Dr Blackmore did not agree with my findings.

Medical cases are never straightforward. There was one case of a man who died after being treated for some time by specialists. The specialists were not certain of the cause of death and declined to issue a medical certificate, which meant the case came to me and a post-mortem had to be carried out. The family was certain that their relative had died of the condition he was being treated for. Each family member was so certain that the treatment given was appropriate and the doctors so marvellous that when we went to the NSW Supreme Court to obtain an order allowing us to perform a post-mortem – as we had to do in the light of the protests of the family – the family's affidavits singing the praises of the specialists were tendered to the court. The court hearing had to be held as a matter of urgency so we could carry out the post-mortem and it was rushed on before one of the judges. The judge ordered a post-mortem, noting how distressing it was for the family.

The post-mortem revealed that the man had a cervical spine fracture which had not been diagnosed. Subsequent rough handling in the hospital had exacerbated it and led to paraplegia. In a second hospital, he was given morphine which had induced respiratory depression leading to death. I found that the man died of 'complications of a cervical spine fracture'. The family did an 180 degree turnaround. After initially saying they had no intention of taking action against the specialists, the family then sought a second post-mortem to gain more evidence against them. We wrote to the family to say the cause of death was now clear and all aspects had been fully investigated. What course of action they chose to take after that in terms of suing hospitals or doctors had nothing to do with the coroner.

There was a case I remember where it was impossible to carry out any post-mortem. A man had gone into a shop which sold farm chemicals and bought a chemical which was used on sheep. Unknown to the shopkeeper he was intending to use it to take his own life. The man wasted little time. He walked out of the shop and up the street and took a good swig from the container. He was rushed to Westmead Hospital where it was discovered, to the horror of staff in the casualty department, that the chemical reacted with water and moisture to give off toxic fumes. Part of the hospital had to be evacuated. The man, who was now dead, was then taken into the morgue which, in turn, had to be evacuated. His body was eventually placed in a 44-gallon drum which was sealed for everyone's safety.

In late May 1997, not long before I heard the Perish inquest, the nation watched as Bernie Whelan made a televised plea to the people who had sent him a note saying they had kidnapped his wife. The typewritten note was sent on 6 May, the day Kerry Whelan disappeared. It had demanded over a million dollars ransom to be paid by Friday, 16 May. Mr Whelan faced the media to ask the kidnappers to release his wife safely as a week had passed since the initial demand with no contact from whoever was responsible. The police believed she might be dead and were keeping me up to date as the inquiry progressed.

Not every missing person case is reported to the coroner. Only when the police were satisfied that a person was dead did they contact me. People can be missing for years without enough evidence to hold an inquest. I had one case of a man who had disappeared after embezzling money from a Sydney club. After several months, the police reported to me that they believed he was dead but his mother and father were sure he was alive. Every time I set down a date for an inquest we would get a report from interstate that he had been seen. Eventually I held the inquest but I was unable to make a finding. I could not be sure on the high balance of probabilities that he was dead. I say 'high' balance of probabilities because being just over 50 per cent sure would satisfy the balance of probabilities but it does not satisfy the law. I had to be satisfied not to the criminal level of beyond a reasonable doubt but on a high balance of probabilities.

In Kerry Whelan's case the police were soon certain that with no contact from her she was dead. On 6 May, she had left the Kurrajong home she shared with her husband and their three children, Sarah, then 15, Matthew, 13 and James, 11, for a 9.30 a.m. meeting in Parramatta. She parked her silver Land Rover Discovery in the underground car park at the Parramatta Parkroyal hotel. She was seen on the car park's security cameras walking up the ramp and out of the car park, her movements relaxed but hurried, as if she was late for an appointment. The cameras showed that she reached the road outside the hotel on Phillip Street at 9.37 a.m. It was the last time she was seen.

Mr Whelan, then 59, a millionaire businessman who ran Crown Equipment Pty Ltd, a forklift truck firm in Smithfield, had been expecting his wife at the business later that afternoon. They were due to fly to Adelaide that night for the opening of another branch. Aware of her plans he checked and discovered she had kept no appointments that day. He rushed to the Parkroyal car park where her car remained. The police were called and despite talking to more than 150 local shops and businesses, there was no trace of Kerry Whelan.

After the ransom note arrived the police went through the usual checks for a missing person but Mrs Whelan had not used the family bank accounts or credit cards since her disappearance. There had been no confirmed sightings of her. Although there was no body, the police notified my office and I had several conferences with the officers from the task force set up to look into the case, task force Bellaire, discussing where they should head with their investigation. They searched several areas of bushland south of Sydney looking for her body. As I write this, a man has been charged with Mrs Whelan's murder.

<hr />

We used to say that working at the Coroners Court heightened your awareness of what can go wrong. You would read a brief about a child that wandered out of an unlocked front gate and was run over and you would immediately ring home to your wife or husband or a brother who had children and ask them if the gate to the house was shut. The same applied to pool deaths. You would have a case notified to you about a child who drowned in a pool when the pool gate was unlocked and you would ring people you knew had a pool, warning them to make sure the gate was locked. Healthwise, it makes you aware daily of your own mortality. I had always been a smoker but had got down to about half a pack a day, sometimes only two or three cigarettes a day. I never really did a lot of exercise in these later years and at night I would still enjoy my glass of wine or a beer to unwind. I always thought I was healthy enough, and I remained proud of the fact that I never took my work home with me. Or so I thought.

CHAPTER 10

True Blue

THE TWO YOUNG police officers sitting in the public rows in front of me looked as if they had stepped straight out of a recruitment ad for the NSW Police. Senior Constable Anthony Dilorenzo and Constable Rodney Podesta were young, fresh-faced and fit. They were dressed in full police uniform, their blue shirts pressed with razor creases along their short sleeves, their handcuffs and guns hanging from their belts. They sat with straight backs, their faces expressionless as only a police officer's can be as, for four weeks, I examined what happened in 35 minutes on Bondi Beach seven months earlier and what led to them using their service firearms to shoot dead Roni Levi.

※※※

I was planning my usual Saturday morning, going up the street to do some shopping and then a bit of gardening, when I got the call on 28 June 1997 from the duty operations officer at police headquarters. The police had 'discharged their firearms' and a man had been shot dead at Bondi. I rang my deputy John Abernethy and told him I thought he should come with me. It was best if both of us went to the scene of a death because we would not be sure who would be eventually conducting the inquest. It meant both of us got first-hand experience. I picked him up at his home in Drummoyne and we were at Bondi Beach not long after 9 a.m., 90 minutes after the shooting and about 40 minutes after Roni Levi, a Frenchman who had been living in Sydney, had been pronounced dead at St Vincent's Hospital in Darlinghurst.

We arrived to find quite a crowd. As well as the onlookers, who always stand around to watch police operations, the media had begun arriving in force. The fact that a man had been shot dead by police was newsworthy in itself but the setting gave it even more resonance – it had happened on the country's most famous beach, arguably Australia's most famous location. Crime scene tape towards the high tide line cordoned off the area where the shooting had occurred and as John and I walked across the sand we were brought up to date with what had happened. The short version was that the police had reports that a man had been out in the streets of Bondi armed with a knife. Six officers caught up with him on the beach and two of them, Rodney Podesta and Anthony Dilorenzo, had shot him because they felt in danger. We were met on the sand by Detective Senior Sergeant Robert McDougall, the detective in charge.

Technically, the coroner was now in charge of the investigation. I approached this as I approached any other case, the added factor being that it involved a police shooting. Because of this, it was imperative that senior officers with no connection to Podesta or Dilorenzo or with their colleagues at Bondi police station should investigate it so there could be no criticism afterwards that the investigation was not thorough. Walking back up to the promenade, I gave an impromptu briefing to the media although I had to be cautious about what I said at such an early stage of the investigation. Although I had every faith in the police officers attached to the coroner's office it was our practice that, in cases which may involve allegations against the police, we engaged independent legal counsel, so there could be no criticism that the investigation and inquest was not even-handed. I told the media that we would be doing that in this case.

At Bondi police station, all six officers involved in the shooting had been ordered to stay away from each other and not talk about the shooting until their statements could be taken. It was not my job to speak to the two police who had pulled the triggers. John Abernethy and I were shown into the office of the Bondi commander, Chief Inspector Richard Baker, who gave us a briefing on what was being done and more information about the events leading up to the shooting. The homicide police had been called in to investigate it.

The next morning I picked up the Sunday papers to see, across the front page of *The Sunday Telegraph*, that amazing photograph, freezing in time the scene split seconds before Roni Levi was shot. Taken from behind the officers by a photographer, Jean Pierre Bratanoff-Firgoff, it showed a bedraggled Levi emerging from the surf, standing with his right foot in front of his left, his arms out from his sides with his brown jacket down his back, hanging off his elbows. Podesta and Dilorenzo are squatting slightly, each with two hands on his gun, arms towards Levi in a classic shooting stance. Behind Levi the waves were breaking on the beach, the long shadows cast by the early morning sun stretching out across the sand. It was the sort of photograph you kept looking at because it captured such drama. However, no matter how important photographs are, they are one-dimensional. This photograph could not tell us how far the officers were from Levi. Nor could it tell us what had happened before.

Nevertheless, it fuelled the saturation media coverage that was bound to accompany the shooting. Everyone had an opinion on whether the police should have shot him dead. Couldn't they have shot him in the leg or arm to disable him? Couldn't they have thrown sand in his face? Why didn't they use capsicum spray? Why couldn't six officers handle one lone man without having to kill him? I had been around the traps long enough to be able to put what I read or heard out of my mind. Publicity about a case never affected me. When it got to the inquest what I would be listening to was the evidence put before me.

Monday morning I was straight on the phone to the Crown Solicitor's office, my contact when I wanted independent counsel. They suggested David Cowan and we made an appointment for him to come and see me. He arrived with an instructing solicitor, also suggested through the Crown Solicitor's office. We got on well and it became their job to oversee the investigation, reporting back to me regularly.

A month later, Thredbo.

At 12.15 a.m. on Thursday 31 July I was woken by the telephone ringing. There had been a terrible landslide at Thredbo just 45 minutes earlier. Two ski lodges, Carinya and Bimbadeen, had been torn from their foundations in seconds when the hill gave way above them along the Alpine Way, the main road into the ski resort. It was not known how many people had been killed at this stage but it was feared as many as 50 to 100 could be trapped as it was the height of the ski season in the country's most popular ski resort. It was only because of the unseasonal lack of snow that the number of deaths turned out to be only 18.

I got John Abernethy and Steve Bills out of bed and we drove through the night. We were at Thredbo as daylight dawned on the scene of devastation. Among the twisted metal and concrete blocks we could see mattresses, furniture, clothing, skis and cars; the signs of daily life. The village was blocked off to all but essential personnel. The rescue services had begun arriving within ten minutes of the landslide and had continued throughout the night. Unfortunately there was little they could do as the area remained too dangerous for them, the wreckage of the buildings still moving down the slope and settling on top of each other. Voices had been heard from beneath the rubble for ten to 15 minutes after the landslide and locals had begun to scramble around in the debris with torches. They were stopped for their own safety when the police arrived. One police officer along with two ambulance officers took over, walking carefully across the debris in the chance they might have been able to find someone on or close to the surface. An ambulance officer had crawled into the area where they had heard male and female voices but could not see anyone. With the concrete slabs still moving and grating together beneath them, it was decided the site was too unstable even for them and they had also reluctantly moved away. When we got there, the rubble and debris was still settling and the loose dirt was hip deep. There was water running through the site. Surrounding lodges had been evacuated. Despite all the people standing around, there was an eerie quiet.

There had been a disaster plan put in place for such an emergency, the Snowy River DISPLAN (Disaster Plan), and it been executed seamlessly. Senior Constable Warren Denham from nearby Jindabyne had been alerted at 11.47 p.m. and less than an hour later had arrived in Thredbo where he took charge of the situation as the forward police commander. One of the other lodges, Christina Lodge, had been commandeered and established as the site control centre. Under the plan, Detective Chief Inspector Bob Cocksedge had been appointed to coordinate the investigation on my behalf. What had become obvious with first light was that, despite the muddy nature of the landslide, the landslide scarp was substantially dry, except in the top southwest corner where it appeared the slide had begun. In the middle of the wet area lay a fractured water main pipe.

We arrived around the same time as David Jordan, the senior engineering geologist with the Snowy Mountains Engineering Corporation. He was asked, along with engineer Graeme Bell, to assess the stability of the site. By 8 a.m. they reported back that it was safe enough for the search for victims within the remains of the buildings to begin. There were several large trees which needed to be moved to protect rescuers and the water seepage had to be stopped. First, the road had to be tested to see if it could take the weight of the digging equipment and trucks.

At 8.15 a.m., the Southern Mines Rescue team arrived and finally at 9 a.m., the recovery operation began. John, Steve and I walked around the site inspecting it from above, below and the sides. The hill where the two lodges had been looked as if it had been cleared for a ski run with everything swept away down the centre. As the rescuers worked, a row of people were placed along the Alpine Way to warn of any further movement. On three blasts of their whistles or the operation of an air horn, everyone had to get off the site immediately. Several times the site had to be evacuated when fresh movement was detected. At other times, work was stopped so trapped person locators could be used at various points. These locators, housed in what look like plastic suitcases, can detect noises, cries, knocking, tapping, scratches and other virtually inaudible sounds from earthquake or avalanche victims. As these devices were switched on total silence fell over the site. The terrible thing was that any sounds which had been coming from beneath the rubble soon after the landslide had stopped. No signs of life were being detected.

It was cold and the weather was limiting the time the rescuers could spend out there on the site. They were rotated every two to three hours. Never was there a truer phrase at times like this than 'thank God for the Salvos'. They were always there when they were needed, serving up limitless cups of tea and coffee, sandwiches and biscuits to keep everyone warm. We moved back to Christina Lodge for a major briefing session at 1 p.m.

Engineers, geologists, and emergency services personnel gathered with the senior police, Superintendent Charlie Sanderson, the Monaro local area commander who also served as the local emergency operations controller, and Commander Bruce Johnston, head of the South Eastern Police Region. It had become obvious that the rescue would be a prolonged operation and while speed was important, at no time could the safety of anyone trapped below the rubble or that of the rescuers be compromised. John, Steve and I knew there had been only one person in Carinya and 18 in Bimbadeen and their names had been collected. Many of Thredbo's senior managers were believed to be among the dead because Bimbadeen Lodge had been used as the official accommodation for Kosciuszko Thredbo Pty Ltd, the company that ran the village.

The first body was recovered at 8.50 p.m. that night. John Cameron, 46, the sole occupant of Carinya, was found in his bed. A post-mortem would reveal he had died of the effects of multiple injuries.

By that time, we had set off for home, arriving back at about 10 p.m. The next day I was kept up to date with any developments while in my office at Glebe. This was the worst natural disaster in Australian history and already blame was being thrown around. It was going to be a major inquiry. With the Bondi shooting and now Thredbo, I started to clear my desks, so to speak, and handed over the other cases including the inquiries into Kerry Whelan and Caroline Byrne to John Abernethy. Chief Inspector Cocksedge, who was usually crime manager at Wollongong area command south of Sydney, had already begun to piece together what had happened for the report he would prepare for me. It was his work in investigating a similar disaster, the Coledale mudslide, several years earlier that had prompted his appointment to the Thredbo inquiry. In 1988, Jennifer Hagan and her young son were killed after a railway embankment engulfed their house at Coledale, 55 kilometres south of Sydney. Inspector Cocksedge's inquiry led to charges of criminal negligence against four State Rail Authority employees, with their supervisor also charged with manslaughter. They were all subsequently acquitted but the Coledale accident had focused attention on corporate responsibility and who should be responsible when an authority gets it wrong.

Early Saturday, I was on my way back to Thredbo after being notified that a voice had been heard that morning at 5.37 a.m. from deep below the rubble. Doreen came with me for company as Steve Bills had not long got out of hospital after having heart bypass surgery and I felt I could not ask him to drive all that way again, and John Abernethy was unavailable. Doreen didn't want me to do the seven-hour drive by myself. She could see the strain and tension we had all been under dealing with such a big operation. Her brother Trevor and his wife Margaret were holidaying on the south coast and they met up with us at Queanbeyan, accompanying us to Thredbo. Doreen didn't want to go to the site, so Margaret kept her company in the village where they drank endless cups of coffee while waiting for me.

We first stopped at Jindabyne for a full briefing from the police. Their concern was that if anything went wrong, they might lose the man who was believed to be the sole survivor. They had identified him as ski instructor Stuart Diver, 27. He had been living in Bimbadeen Lodge with his wife Sally, also 27, who was the reservations manager at the Thredbo Alpine Hotel. The couple had been in bed when the landslide hit and Sally Diver had been pinned beneath the concrete that buried them. A post-mortem would show that she drowned. Stuart survived as he was trapped in a small pocket of air at the bottom of the lodge. Although he could hear the movement above him, his own cries for help had not been able to penetrate the mass of debris. The trapped person locator had been unable to detect him because of the massive concrete slab above him, the position of which had saved his life.

It took a day of delicate drilling and tunnelling from the time Diver was detected until he could be removed. For 11 hours a paramedic, Paul Featherstone, was in constant conversation with Diver, who had been floating in and out of consciousness since the landslide. Featherstone got as close as he could to Diver during those last hours to keep reassuring him. As the day went on and things continued to go well, you could feel the sense of excitement in the village.

The families of the victims had been streaming into Thredbo from around the country. Just before they were ready to pull Diver out, police brought the families to the edge of Bobuck Lane from where there was a clear view of the rescue site. The police had first got me out of the way because I had upset a lot of the families by refusing to allow them to identify their relatives either at the scene or at the nearest hospital, which was at Cooma. The NSW Premier Bob Carr had announced the bodies would be taken to Cooma but I had overruled him. They were going to the morgue at Glebe. International protocol states that in such cases the bodies must all go to a central spot where all the facilities to identify them properly are available. That was Glebe. I understood the distress this caused the relatives by doing this but it was paramount that identification be done in a thorough and proper manner, as had been done after the other major disasters including the Grafton and Kempsey bus crashes and the Newcastle earthquake. The NSW Institute of Forensic Medicine's senior grief counsellor, Jenny Cohen, was organising counsellors to be available at Glebe to support relatives after the formal identification. It was never going to be easy.

As Stuart Diver emerged from the rubble, it did seem like a miracle he had survived. He had been buried for 65 hours and 45 minutes and must have had tremendous capacity to have come through it. Everyone was abuzz.

I didn't want to drive home that night in case I was needed the next morning but I didn't want to stay at Thredbo either, so Doreen and I spent the night in a motel at Queanbeyan. That Sunday morning I rang the rescue headquarters and was told there was nothing else I could do at the time. As we headed home the police rang my mobile. They called to let me know that someone they had believed was missing in the landslide had been found and she was from Forbes. They knew that was my home town and thought I would know her. It was Susan Williams-Green, the daughter-in-law of Doreen's cousins Kingsley and Helen Green. I knew that there was a list of missing people but I had not known one of our relatives had been on it.

Susan and her husband Mark had been on a five-day skiing holiday and had been relaxing in their lodge on the Wednesday night when someone came to the door screaming about the landslide. Mark had raced outside to join the volunteers trying to find survivors in the wreckage and Susan had walked outside to Bobuck Lane where she stood looking at the devastation. When Mark got back to the lodge to find his wife gone, he searched for two hours without finding her. It was feared she had been carried away by the slide as it swept over Bobuck Lane. He found her two hours later at the nearby Black Bear Inn where she had been evacuated along with other skiers and locals. The couple decided to cut their holiday short and return home to Forbes but they were unaware that Susan was listed as missing so had not told the police she was safe. As soon as the police rang us, we contacted Helen to verify Susan was alright.

It was another four days, 7 August at 2 a.m., before the last body, that of Tony Weaver, 47, who headed the ski rescue patrol crew, was recovered. Those who had died included Sally Diver; ski instructors Mike, 46, and Mim, 41, Sodergren from the US; Wendy O'Donoghue, 41, marketing manager at Thredbo resort; property development manager Colin Warren; David Watson, a bistro supervisor; Steven Urosevic, 32, hotel manager; Mary Phillips, a ski instructor who also worked in a local restaurant; Oskar Luhn, a chair lift operator, and his friend, Aino Senbruns; Andrew McArthur, a resort employee; Stephen Moss, a catering manager; Dianne Ainsworth, 34, the head housekeeper for Thredbo Accommodation Service; Barry Decker, an accountant; Diane Hoffman, a photographer; Werner Jecklin, the manager of snow grooming; and John Cameron, 46, a builder from Five Dock in Sydney.

Post-mortems showed that most of the victims had died of asphyxia – Colin Warren, Steven Urosevic, Mary Phillips, Aino Senbruns, Werner Jecklin, Oskar Luhn, Dianne Ainsworth and Mike Sodergren. Mim Sodergren also suffered chest and pelvic injuries. Tony Weaver died of the effects of head and chest injuries; Wendy O'Donoghue, Barry Decker and David Watson died of the effects of multiple injuries; Stephen Moss suffered blunt force head trauma; Andrew McArthur died of chest injuries and asphyxia and Diane Hoffman died of the effects of chest and abdominal injuries. Sally Diver had drowned and John Cameron died of multiple injuries.

Of course, the work of a coroner does not come to a halt because of some high-profile cases. While I had cleared my desk of most of my cases, there were some that I had to complete, like the death of an 11-year-old schoolgirl on an amusement ride at a country show.

Shandy Lee Clare had been saving her pocket money for weeks to spend at the Rylstone-Kandos country show near Mudgee. The year before she had been unable to go on the Giant Octopus ride because she was under the height restrictions. This year she was tall enough. On 22 February 1997, she had spent most of the day on the ride. At 7.30 p.m., the arm of the ride carrying the car in which she was riding with friends broke away, throwing the car four metres to the ground. Her friends, aged 11 and 10, were seriously injured. Shandy died in Rylston Hospital.

We all love country shows, they bring a bit of excitement to town. But because the amusement rides are assembled and taken down so often, their owners have to take special care. In this case that care had been lacking.

I felt it appropriate to hold the inquest at Mudgee. The investigation showed there had been a crack in a metal bearing cap which had led to the steel arm of the ride snapping off. I felt it should have been detected in the routine checks by the owner of the Giant Octopus, who had supervised its assembly on the day, and also by the engineer who had certified the ride as safe only a month earlier. Loose nuts which had been vital to the operation of the machine were also detected during the inspection. It was obvious that the certification by the engineer had been highly deficient. The machine was poorly assembled and regular inspections and maintenance had not been carried out. On a public amusement ride, there was a high standard of care on the operators to ensure the safety of everyone using it and in my opinion, the evidence clearly showed that the lack of proper assembly, lack of proper inspections and completely incorrect certificates amounted to gross negligence.

I terminated the inquest and referred the papers to the DPP to consider criminal charges after finding there had been 'gross negligence on the part of two known persons'. I could not state who those 'persons' were; it was obvious that it was the owner of the ride and the engineer who had earlier checked it.

The ride could have been built as early as 1939 and the crack which led to the accident could have been present for as long as 15 years. To try and stop this being repeated on the hundreds of rides at other country shows, I recommended additional maintenance and registration criteria for rides manufactured before 1980. I also recommended all operators keep a log book of all inspections, maintenance and repairs and that WorkCover officers conduct random blitzes to make sure the operators complied. WorkCover should also have the power to revoke licences, even if the rides had been cleared as safe by an engineer.

Sitting in the back of Mudgee court listening to all this were Shandy's parents and I expressed my sincere condolences to them. It was an accident that could have been avoided.

In April 1997, Clinton Moller, a former police officer halfway through an eight-month sentence for refusing to give evidence to the police Royal Commission, had been found dead, hanging in his cell at Parklea Jail. Moller, 27, was also awaiting trial on charges of supplying ecstasy and amphetamines. The post-mortem found the cause of death was hanging and there were no other injuries to suggest he had been physically restrained but his family refused to accept it had been suicide.

Moller had fled overseas before he was due to give evidence before the police Royal Commission in January 1996 over claims he had been dealing in large quantities of drugs while stationed at, of all places, Bondi. Warrants had been immediately issued for his arrest and he was arrested eight months later and extradited to Australia where he was jailed for contempt of the Royal Commission. The former gym instructor and fitness fanatic was awaiting trial on drugs charges after his former fiancée told a committal hearing that he had begun selling amphetamines and ecstasy in 1993 because the police did not pay very well and he had wanted the same lifestyle he saw his friends enjoying. To say it is never easy for a police officer in jail is stating the obvious, and Clinton Moller found that out.

I was told when I conducted the inquest into his death that he had been spat at by other prisoners at Long Bay Jail and had urine thrown at him. He had lodged a request to be transferred to medium security Berima Jail, south of Sydney, home to most of the other ex-police officers jailed in the state, but the request had been turned down. The evidence before me was that on 11 April he was transferred to Parklea Jail, another maximum security centre. He had arrived with five cartons of personal belongings but was allowed to take just one into his cell. I was told that he chose the one containing his TV set. The prison officer who supervised his arrival said he had checked inside the box and it had appeared that there was only the TV and a blue towel.

The next morning Moller was found hanged with a skipping rope, which he must have smuggled into the cell somehow. As if that was not distressing enough for his family, when his mother had rung the jail that day as she drove to visit him, she was told she could not see him. When she protested, she was told, 'Sorry, Clinton Moller is deceased.'

I thought it was possible that he may not have intended to kill himself but had been making a cry for help to persuade the authorities to move him to another jail more to his liking. There was evidence that Moller had not shown suicidal tendencies and he had used a jumper to cushion the effect of the rope tied around his neck. I could not be sure he had committed suicide.

I was critical of the way his mother had been informed of his death and said so. I also strongly stated that, 'both police and corrective service officers should bear in mind that notifying families of a relative's death is a very traumatic occasion and should be done with great sensitivity and compassion'. This point should not have needed to be said.

In late November I was getting ready to begin the inquest into the Seaview air crash when Megan called me from Melbourne, where she was living.

'Dad, are you going to do Michael Hutchence?' she asked me. 'He was found hanged in his hotel room.'

'Who's Michael Hutchence?' I said.

Hutchence, 37, had been found dead, naked and hanging from his own belt from the door of his fifth-floor hotel room, Suite 524, at The Ritz-Carlton in Double Bay on Saturday, 22 November. His belt buckle had broken and his body was kneeling on the floor facing the door. His body had been taken to the morgue and a post-mortem was due to be carried out on the Monday. To those of us who worked at Glebe he really was another body, no more no less important than any other. To the world's media, he was much more than that. News had, of course, reached all over the world, which was why Megan was on the phone. She was disgusted that I didn't know Michael Hutchence had been the lead singer with INXS but I wasn't terribly up on popular music. The most famous singer I had met was Danny Kaye back in about 1959 when he attended a Fourth of July Ball to which Doreen and I were invited through an American company she worked for. Of course he (and us) were much younger then and he was more my style.

I would say that the death of Michael Hutchence, while not one of the most taxing, was certainly one of the most bizarre I have dealt with. This came about through the rumour that he had died during an act of auto-eroticism. I have no idea where this speculation came from except that much later someone told me that one of the English journalists based in Australia, reporting Hutchence's death for the tabloids back home, had been reading a murder mystery at the time about someone who had died during an act of auto-eroticism. Even more bizarre was that Hutchence's girlfriend, Paula Yates, was saying that she would rather their child, Heavenly Hiraani Tiger Lily, then just 16 months old, grow up believing her father had died trying to ejaculate during a strange sex act that went too far than that he had committed suicide.

We were waiting for Ms Yates at Glebe on Wednesday, 25 November, three days after Hutchence's death. We had been told she was arriving in Sydney that morning on a flight from London. By now I knew a lot more about who they both were.

Hutchence was the embodiment of sex, drugs and rock 'n' roll, the hedonistic lifestyle of a pop star enhanced by a string of famous and beautiful women. Born in Sydney, he had grown up between Sydney, Hong Kong and Los Angeles and had a brother and step-sister. Yates, although talented in her own right as a television interviewer, was more famous for being married to Sir Bob Geldof of The Boomtown Rats and Live Aid fame. They had three daughters, Fifi Trixibelle, Peaches and Pixie. In 1994, Yates left Sir Bob for Hutchence and it was the beginning of a child custody battle which had meant Yates was unable to bring her daughters to Australia to live here with Hutchence. Hutchence had arrived back in Sydney on 18 November to get ready for an INXS tour of Australia, leaving Paula at home in London where she was waiting for a judge to decide whether she could leave the country with the girls. It was being opposed by her ex-husband.

I was willing to take some time that day to see Paula Yates because I had been told she wanted to talk to me. Glebe court was under seige from the media all morning. Yates arrived early, driven straight from the airport. She was let into the underground car park beneath the Institute of Forensic Medicine to give her some privacy from the press. She was met and taken to the viewing room where Hutchence's body was laid so she could say her goodbyes. She left the building by 9 a.m., without speaking to any of my staff.

Since his death, and fuelled by the speculation about any auto-eroticism links, the office had been inundated with calls from reporters. That afternoon I released a short statement.

'Post-mortem examinations have determined the cause of the death of Michael Hutchence was hanging. However, a coroner's investigation is still to determine whether the death was suicide. Routine toxicology tests are being carried out and the results will not be known for some weeks.'

That Christmas I was more than ready for our annual break in Forbes. While we were usually always busy at the Coroners Court, most years we had some quieter times. In 1997 there had been no chance for any of us at Glebe to catch our breath. It was one of my busiest years as a coroner. Doreen had started to notice that after three years as State Coroner being on call 24 hours a day, seven days a week, I was showing signs of being tired and a bit crankier than normal.

In the third week of January I was back at my desk. I had received the results of Michael Hutchence's blood tests and they showed the presence of alcohol, cocaine, Prozac and other prescription drugs. To my way of thinking, on the test of a high balance of probabilities, it was suicide and I could see nothing would be gained by having an open inquest. The only people who would have gained would have been the media. It would have been a circus. Normally with a suicide, there would be no inquest and that would be the end of it; because of the notoriety of this case, I felt the only way to stop all the rumours was to publish my reasons for my decision. I had spoken with his parents, his father Kel Hutchence and mother Patricia Glassop, and they were satisfied with the conclusion I had come to that their son had committed suicide. They were also relieved that his death was not going to be further sensationalised over days of evidence given at an inquest. That can put families under a lot of strain and it was a factor I always took into account.

On Friday, 6 February, we called the media to Glebe and I handed down my reasons, making sure that any reporters who wanted a copy of my findings could have one. I said Hutchence had intentionally hanged himself between 9.45 a.m. and 11.50 a.m. and that no one else was involved in his death. I made a point of discounting the rumours that his death was connected to an act of auto-eroticism. There was no forensic or other evidence to substantiate this suggestion. I ran through the series of events which indicated Hutchence had been in a severely depressed state.

He was first prescribed Prozac in December 1995 by Dr J Borham, in London, to treat a pre-existing depressive problem. Doctors recommend that Prozac, a common anti-depressant, not be mixed with alcohol because the combination can lead to further depression.

On 17 October 1997, Hutchence visited a London psychiatrist, Mark Collins, because he was experiencing minor depression. Dr Collins said that he detected no hint of suicidal thinking on his patient's part. On 1 November, Hutchence saw Dr Borham for the final time to receive another prescription of Prozac.

I was able to piece together his last hours through statements we had obtained from his family and friends. When Hutchence flew into Sydney on 18 November the long-running custody battle between Ms Yates and Geldof over their three daughters was weighing heavily on his mind. He wanted her and her daughters to join him but the trip needed the approval of Geldof. On the night before his death, Hutchence had dinner with his father at an Indian restaurant at Edgecliff, a suburb not far from the hotel he was staying at in Double Bay. There was evidence that he had been in good spirits while appearing very worried about the outcome of the custody case. He had driven back to the Ritz-Carlton where he waited in the bar for his former girlfriend, the actress Kym Wilson, and her partner Andrew Rayment. At 11 p.m., all three went up to his room.

Wilson made a statement to police in which she said that Hutchence's mood was 'elevated' but he was worried because during the morning he expected to hear the news from London about the custody of the three girls. He had asked Wilson and Rayment to stay with him for support in case the outcome of the custody hearing was unfavourable. She said they spent the night drinking champagne, vodka, beer and cocktails until they left at about 5 a.m.

Paula Yates said in her statement that she had rung Hutchence about 5.30 a.m., Sydney time, on 22 November to tell him that the custody matter had not been finalised and had been adjourned to 17 December. She said he sounded desperate and told her he was going to beg Bob Geldof to let the children accompany her to Australia.

Bob Geldof said he received two calls from Hutchence. The first time he told Hutchence to call back. The second call was received by Geldof not long after that, about 5.30 a.m. Sydney time, when Geldof said Hutchence became hectoring, abusive and threatening. He said Hutchence had begged him to let the children come to Australia but had not sounded depressed. In the ensuing argument, Hutchence became so upset that his swearing awakened a woman in the next hotel room.

At 9.38 a.m., he called his manager, Martha Troupe, in New York and left a voicemail message: 'Martha, Michael here, I've fucking had enough.' Martha Troupe rang the Ritz-Carlton back immediately but the phone in Suite 524 rang out. At 9.50 a.m., Hutchence rang her again and the call was recorded on her answering machine. Hutchence sounded 'slow and deep' as if he was affected by something. Troupe then called John Martin, the tour manager for INXS, who told her he had received a note from Hutchence saying he was not going to rehearsals that day.

Hutchence's final call was to a former girlfriend, Michelle Bennett. Hutchence had called her earlier and left a message, where he sounded drunk, on her answering machine. He rang again at 9.54 a.m. and began to cry. According to Ms Bennett, he sounded very upset. She was concerned for his welfare and told him she would come immediately. When she arrived at the hotel she was unable to rouse him by knocking on his door and ringing him. She wrote a note and left it at reception. Hotel staff found his body at about 11.50 a.m.

I said that I was satisfied Michael Hutchence had taken his own life.

'I am satisfied that the deceased was in a severe depressed state due to a number of factors including the relationship with Paula Yates and the pressure of the ongoing dispute with Sir Robert Geldof, combined with the effects of the substances he had injested at that time.'

The postscript to this was that in October 1998, Ms Yates lost custody of her three daughters to Geldof. Less than 12 months later, in September 2000, she was found dead of a heroin overdose in her West London flat. The local coroner later found that it was an accidental overdose and not part of any suicide bid. Divorce and the strains of the resultant arguments over children don't spare anyone, however rich and famous.

❦

Three days after handing down my findings into Michael Hutchence's death, I was back in Court One to start the inquest into the shooting of Roni Levi. David Cowan and I had had extensive discussions about how to conduct the hearing. Neither of us felt we could or should shortcut any of the evidence, as sometimes happened in simpler cases with the agreement of everyone involved. With about 100 witnesses to be called, we had set the hearing down for at least six weeks. The reason for so many witnesses was that we had to explore Levi's erratic behaviour not just at the moment of the shooting but also the factors behind it. We would also examine the legitimacy of the subsequent police conduct. Did the officers fear for their own safety and the safety of the community during the stand-off? In essence, had the officers been acting in the execution of their duty when they pulled the triggers?

The bar table was, not surprisingly, crowded with lawyers. Appearing for Podesta and Dilorenzo were Ken Madden, a former policeman, and a popular and capable solicitor, and barrister 'Jock' Dailly, who also did a lot of police work. The NSW Police Service was represented by Greg Willis. Levi's family, who had flown in from Paris, had briefed Ken Horler QC and Michael Marx, while Melinda Dundas, who had been married to Levi, was represented by the team from Newcastle Legal Centre, solicitor John Boersig, lawyer and academic Ray Watterson and barrister Robert Cavanagh, a tall, imposing man with rather wild hair. He had appeared before me in other cases and he was like a dog with a bone, he would never let go.

There was argument from the start. Dundas and Levi's family took umbrage at Dilorenzo and Podesta wearing their guns in court. They were not the guns used to shoot Levi, those guns were exhibits in the inquest. The family asked the police to be directed not to wear them. The lawyers and myself had discussions in chambers. The lawyers for Podesta and

Dilorenzo said the two men had received death threats and needed them for protection. In the end we came to a compromise and the guns were handed to court officials before the two men entered the courtroom each day.

Roni Levi, 33, was a freelance photographer who had been living in Australia since December 1993. He was brought up in Paris with his three brothers. He had married Melinda Dundas but their relationship had ended a few years earlier, although they remained great friends. In February 1997, Levi moved to Bondi where he shared a flat with Warren Brunner.

When David Cowan rose, he began painting a word picture of Levi as a polite, mild-mannered person interested in art, painting and photography. He was a vegetarian who neither drank nor smoked. It was a description no one disagreed with. However, in the weeks before his death, he had changed. He had been depressed and anxious, seeing a psychiatrist and appearing muddled and babbling to his friends. He told a friend he felt he was losing his mind.

Mr Cowan said a forensic psychiatrist concluded that Levi underwent an acute psychotic episode on the morning he died but the nature of that episode was in doubt. We examined what led up to it.

On the night of Friday, 27 June, Levi had been dining at the home of friends who were also entertaining two visiting French doctors. They found Levi incoherent. He had difficulty speaking and was confused. They suggested he go to hospital to be looked at immediately. Levi agreed and they arrived at St Vincent's Hospital's emergency department about 9.30 p.m.

There was a statement from the doctor, Elizabeth Meagher, who said that Levi was cooperative but confused. She said he had told her he had felt like that for about three days but she said he had not appeared depressed or worried about it. At one stage Levi asked her, 'Do you think thoughts can come down the telephone line from one person to another?' She replied that she did not think so and asked Levi whether he thought it possible. 'Oh no,' he said. 'No, no. Of course not.' She did not think his condition was serious enough to warrant an urgent assessment by a psychiatrist and as Levi gave every indication that he was willing to stay overnight, she felt he should be examined by the appropriate specialist the next morning. A full medical examination was carried out to exclude organic or physical causes for his apparent condition. A CAT scan to check for brain tumours was to be carried out the next morning.

During the night Levi wandered around the hospital and spoke to several members of staff about hearing voices. In the opinion of medical staff he did not require scheduling under the *Mental Health Act* at the time. He was a voluntary patient. At 4.30 a.m. – that lonely time of the morning again – it was discovered he was missing. An hour later, the hospital rang Levi's flatmate, Mr Brunner, to notify him that Levi had left the hospital. For whatever reason, his flatmate did not hear the telephone.

Mr Brunner was woken by a banging on the bedroom window at about 6 a.m. He opened the door; Levi walked straight past him into his own bedroom and then back out of the flat. His behaviour was described as manic. Thirty minutes later Levi was back banging on the door of the flat. This time he went to the kitchen and emerged holding a black-handled Wiltshire Staysharp kitchen knife.

'What are you doing?' Mr Brunner asked him and Levi replied, 'It's not for you.' Mr Brunner tried to reason with him and persuade him to leave the knife behind. Levi headed off down the street with his flatmate after him.

At 6.56 a.m., Mr Brunner raced into Bondi police station, which was on Wairoa Avenue not far from the flat, and told police that Levi had just threatened him with a knife, saying he had 'just snapped' and was running around the streets with the knife. Four minutes later, Brunner was back at the flat accompanied by two officers, Senior Constable John Lewis Jones, who had been about to finish work after his night shift, and Anthony Dilorenzo, who was just starting for the day. The officers, their guns drawn, burst into the flat hoping to find Levi.

At the same time, Constables Christopher Goodman and Geoffrey Smith, who were based at Paddington police station, heard the messages over the radio and were in a marked police car on their way to Bondi to help in the hunt. Rodney Podesta, who had just arrived for the start of his day shift at Bondi police station, was in a paddy wagon heading towards the beach.

At the beach, a dishevelled Roni Levi was walking out of the surf fully dressed, the knife in his hand. He ran across Campbell Parade, the boulevard that runs along the back of the beach, as Podesta drove up to him and asked him to stop. Levi ran back across the road to the beach. The car with Dilorenzo and Jones arrived and all three officers ran after Levi onto the sand as a growing crowd of spectators watched the drama. Dilorenzo and Jones both shouted, 'Stop. Police.'

Dilorenzo was gaining on Levi, hoping to tackle him before the surf but Levi stopped and turned around to face the police, about a metre from the water. He brandished his knife at the police before heading out into the surf until the waves were past his waist, waving the knife and making strange noises. At one stage, he turned the knife on himself, pretending to stab himself in the stomach.

By 7.08 a.m., the two officers from Paddington, Goodman and Smith, had arrived. Neither Podesta, Dilorenzo or Jones had their batons with them. All three had their guns out and trained on Levi's stomach as they trailed him on the beach. They tried to calm Levi and coax him out of the water. A police boat had left Sydney Harbour to help out and a negotiator was on the way. On the promenade, Brunner was watching.

At 7.21 a.m., Levi finally waded out of the waves. The officers pleaded with him to drop his knife. Senior Constable Grant Seddon had arrived and joined his colleagues on the sand. Levi was becoming more agitated. He flicked the knife from hand to hand. Jones dropped his gun on the sand and walked towards Levi in a conciliatory move. Levi marched at him, gesturing with the knife. Goodman said later that 'you could feel' Levi's frustration. There was evidence Levi had lost his glasses and would not have been able to see clearly.

Things began to heat up even more. Levi started moving up the beach, Jones and Seddon on his right, Goodman and Smith on his left. He was moving towards Dilorenzo and Podesta. Seddon used his baton to try and knock the knife out of Levi's hand but Levi anticipated his moves. As Levi advanced again towards Dilorenzo and Podesta, Dilorenzo would later say he saw 'my wife and my kid flash through my eyes'. Podesta fired first. Then Dilorenzo fired twice. Podesta fired the fourth shot. Levi, hit three times in the chest, lay face down on the sand. When the paramedics carried Levi on a stretcher up the sand, Podesta broke down and started to sob. When interviewed later, both Podesta and Dilorenzo said they believed Levi wanted to die, in other words, he wanted to commit what was called 'suicide by cop'.

On that first day of the inquest, Ms Dundas went into the witness box. She told me that she found police claims that Levi had lunged at them with a knife utterly incomprehensible and she had never seen him become violent. She said violence was completely out of character for him. She said she had asked police why they had not shot him in the leg instead of killing him but had not received a reply.

David Cowan and I had also discussed the order in which the witnesses would be called. On day three it was the turn of the police officer in charge of the investigation, Acting Inspector Robert McDougall. As he was in the witness box, I was already formulating some of the recommendations I would make at the end of the inquest. The shooting of Roni Levi was one of the most serious events involving police that I had encountered. It was to be expected that the NSW Police Service would make available to the officer in charge of the investigation all necessary resources to properly investigate the incident. Notwithstanding the best endeavours of Inspector McDougall, he was unable to secure the immediate assistance of investigators from a region other than the one encompassing Bondi and was obliged to use officers attached to Bondi police station to take statements from witnesses. It was not until the Monday that this situation was rectified. The lack of immediately available outside resources resulted in four of the six police officers not being interviewed. They were directed to make their own statements. Podesta and Dilorenzo were the only two interviewed in the appropriate way.

Inspector McDougall was cross-examined at length by lawyers for Levi's family. He admitted that Podesta and Dilorenzo did not undergo blood tests to detect the use of drugs or alcohol. Barrister Robert Cavanagh suggested it would have been 'in fairness' to the officers and to the community had they been tested. Inspector McDougall replied that he would have asked the officers to undergo the tests if he had had any suspicions whatsoever that the officers had been using drugs or alcohol.

The next two weeks were taken up mainly with eyewitness accounts, including the photographer who had taken the picture moments before the shooting. As with all eyewitnesses, their accounts differed. Levi was threatening the police with the knife; he lunged at them. Alternately Levi was moving pretty slowly; he did not lunge or charge at police. While the witnesses' beliefs in what they had seen differed, the evidence of all the eyewitnesses was crucial in this case. This brought us to Friday, 27 February.

That night as we all made our way home, three police officers from Glebe police station were preparing to finish their shifts and getting ready to play touch football with some Aboriginal kids at Wentworth Park, not far from where they worked. After the game, Constables Peter Forsyth and Brian Neville and Probationary Constable Jason Semple, had a few beers at a nearby hotel and were walking home. At about 11.30 p.m. near the community centre at inner-city Ultimo at the top of William Henry Street, they were approached by three young men and a girl and offered drugs. The officers produced their police badges and told the youths they were under arrest. Suddenly one of the youths pulled a knife and lunged at Forsyth and Semple. Forsyth, 28, who was just 100 metres from his home, where his wife and two children were waiting, was fatally stabbed, suffering a wound to the heart. He was pronounced dead at 12.15 a.m. on the Saturday. Again my phone rang in the middle of the night. I joined the then Police Commissioner Peter Ryan at the scene. We were told by the investigating officers what they believed had happened. Forsyth's death in such circumstances affected me deeply.

The impact of a police officer being stabbed to death in the middle of an inquest into the death of a man armed with a knife who had been shot dead by police was not lost on myself or the media. While the media could play Peter Forsyth's death for all it was worth, whether it gave Podesta and Dilorenzo a bit of good publicity in the court of public opinion, it did not help their case in the court in front of me. I could not be concerned about public opinion or media hype.

That following Wednesday, 4 March, David Cowan and I had a special briefing from the then head of police internal affairs, Assistant Commissioner Mal Brammer. It was an update to a meeting we had held back in October, four months after the Bondi shooting, when I had first been told about undercover investigations into Podesta and Dilorenzo. The investigation into Dilorenzo had begun during the days of the NSW Police Royal Commission, long before the shooting, because of concerns over the company he was keeping. Along with Podesta, he was a regular at the notorious Liberty Lunch restaurant on Bondi's Campbell Parade that then had a reputation as a place where cocaine and ecstasy could be easily obtained. Dilorenzo's brother, Mark, had just been released from jail where he served a sentence for supplying heroin. Four weeks before the Bondi shooting, the Bondi police station commander had ordered all his officers to stay clear of the Liberty Lunch. Podesta was then put under surveillance in May 1997 when he had continued to visit Liberty Lunch.

At this new meeting with Mal Brammer, my concern was whether there was any evidence that the two officers may have been drinking or involved with drugs the night before the shooting. I was assured that there was no such evidence. The behaviour of Podesta and Dilorenzo and their drug taking was later examined by the Police Integrity Commission. The commissioner, Judge Paul Urquhart, found no evidence that the two officers were using drink or drugs when they killed Levi.

This March meeting was in my office and, like the October meeting, it was in confidence. It was seen in some quarters afterwards to have been held in secret to keep the information away from the inquest. There was nothing sinister about the meeting and nothing sinister about the decision not to include any of the evidence about Podesta and Dilorenzo's attendance at Liberty Lunch. The fact was that there was nothing about drug dealing to go before the inquest because there was no evidence it had influenced the shooting. Full stop.

While the other four officers on Bondi Beach gave evidence before me, Podesta and Dilorenzo chose not to on the grounds they might incriminate themselves. Their records of interview were tendered to me on Thursday, 5 March. They both said they had fired to avoid being stabbed. The evidence had finished, only submissions remained. At the close of proceedings that day, I called all the lawyers into my office.

Under section 19 of the *Coroners Act 1980*, if at any time during the course of an inquest evidence was given which established a *prima facie* case against a known person for an indictable offence, then the inquest had to be halted.

I said to the lawyers, 'Look, this is what my opinion is. I am leaning towards halting the inquest because I believe there is a *prima facie* case against Podesta and Dilorenzo.' It had not been an easy decision for me to make. I had thought long and hard about it in the previous few days. In some cases you might change your mind three or four times. You would hear some evidence and think the case was heading one way, then a day later you would hear something else which made you change direction. What swayed me in the Bondi case were the eyewitness accounts. There were a number of witnesses who said the police had no alternative but to shoot – but there were almost equally as many who said the police did not have to shoot. I took the view that it would be open to a jury to believe those witnesses and therefore I had no alternative but to refer the matter to the DPP. It was a difficult decision because I could understand both sides but I was constrained by the law. By law I was not entitled to take into account what defence a person might put up. I had to have regard only to the evidence which favoured a prosecution. I did not agree with the law but I couldn't change it. It has since been updated.

I let the lawyers know what I was thinking because the next stage of the inquest was to be submissions and if I went ahead with my course of action, I would not need to hear from them all. I did, however, want to give Jock Dailly the chance to address me on behalf of Podesta and Dilorenzo. So the next day, I listened as Mr Dailly said the actions of his clients after the shooting were hardly those of men who wanted to kill. Both were severely depressed as a result, he said. Meanwhile Ken Horler for the Levi family, described all six of the police officers on the beach as uniformed cowboys out of control.

That Friday afternoon, as I took my seat on the bench, I indicated I had something to say. I began with the issues raised in regard to St Vincent's Hospital and its treatment of Levi. I could not be overly critical of the hospital staff in their assessment of Levi; he had agreed to stay the night. The hospital's accident and emergency department would have been a very busy place on a Friday night and Saturday morning and the hospital's practice when dealing with patients who appeared to have a psychiatric problem was to contact the Inner City Mental Health Service Crisis Team and have one of the team nurses make an assessment. I said I did not accept that patients should be triaged over the telephone. Someone from the crisis team should have attended the hospital. If Levi had been an involuntary patient, when it was discovered he was missing, the police would have been notified and greater efforts made by the staff to try and find him. I said that I had recommendations in regard to this which I would hand down the following week.

Then I moved on to the police investigation. What gave me cause for concern was that despite the best efforts of Inspector McDougall, investigators from another region were not made available until the Monday, the day after the shooting. This resulted in the four officers being told to make their own statements. There was no evidence that the fact they were not interviewed at the time adversely affected the investigation but it was not the best practice. I made the point that there was also no evidence of a cover up by police officers. I was perfectly satisfied there had been a full investigation. However, there were also recommendations I wished to make about police procedures.

I turned to section 19 of the *Coroners Act 1980*. From the bench, I could feel the tension running through the courtroom. I said I had listened carefully to the submissions put by Jock Dailly on behalf of Podesta and Dilorenzo and noted he had highlighted evidence which was in their favour. I said I could not ignore the body of evidence to the contrary.

> 'In my opinion the evidence establishes a *prima facie* case against known persons with regard to the death of Roni Levi. Accordingly I am required to terminate the inquest and refer the matter to the Director of Public Prosecutions.'

Podesta and Dilorenzo were facing possible manslaughter or murder charges. I pushed back my chair, rose and left the bench through the door behind me as all hell broke loose. Adding to the furore was that Peter Forsyth's funeral had been held the day before, flags at government buildings and police stations had flown at half mast and hundreds of people had gathered in Sydney's Hyde Park to listen in silence to the service inside St Mary's Cathedral. The timing was all wrong but there was nothing I could do about that.

※

This was the hardest case I had presided over in 25 years; it pushed my objectivity to the limit. I was always noted for being pretty strong on the side of the police because I believed, and still do, that they do a good job. When they do the wrong thing, they have to accept the consequences.

New South Wales Police Association deputy president Mark Burgess faced the media on the steps of the courthouse and got himself some publicity by saying that I had 'clearly got it absolutely wrong'. He followed with:

'This week we witnessed the funeral of Peter Forsyth, an officer stabbed to death in the line of duty and rightly hailed a hero. Today we witness the finding of a coroner that Constable Dilorenzo and Constable Podesta, both police officers who managed to prevent themselves, colleagues and members of the public from possibly being stabbed to death, potentially face serious criminal charges. Do our police need to die to receive support?'

※

I didn't mind criticism, I had been a magistrate and a coroner for long enough to accept people would not agree with me. What upset me was that I had no option, the law as it stood at the time gave me no leeway. Once I saw there was a *prima facie* case for an indictable offence, I could not take into account any defence. I presumed Burgess would have known that. There was also the point that although I had terminated the inquest, I still had to make recommendations and had adjourned the hearing until the next Wednesday. Proceedings were not closed so I decided to refer Burgess' comments to the Attorney-General for possible contempt of court proceedings. I did not like pursuing that sort of line but he was not doing anybody any good with the way he was going on. The Attorney-General decided not to lay any charges but it did keep Burgess quiet.

Burgess was not the only one who felt I had done the wrong thing. I was up the street shopping when a man, a total stranger, tapped me on the shoulder. I turned around and he said, 'You bastard.' On the Monday at the pre-school where Doreen worked, one of the parents said, 'I'm disgusted with your husband.' We went to a church service and a friend said, 'I didn't think you would be game enough to show your face here today.' The priest came and quietly took me to the back of the church.

The Daily Telegraph ran a front-page story accompanied by photographs of Podesta and Dilorenzo carrying the headline, 'True Blue'. Talkback radio was full of my decision and that only fuelled people's emotions. I received many condemning letters, most of them anonymous, including one from the mother of a police officer. People continued to approach me in the street. It was not what they said but the way they said it; there was some real spite there. It angered me that Doreen copped it as well. It was no longer about my job, it had become personal and it interfered with our lives. While I still had a lot of support from friends, there were even some of them who thought I was wrong. In the end, Doreen and I just stopped going out because if we went out, we got abused. At least I was a public figure and could cope with what was happening, Doreen couldn't. She had never had training to deal with this. She decided she was going to get away and went off to Alaska to stay with John and his family for some weeks until everything blew over.

Meanwhile I handed down my recommendations. In the wake of the Bondi shooting, I recommended better and updated training for police when dealing with mentally ill people. I also recommended mandatory alcohol and drug testing of police as soon as possible after such incidents, to protect the community and to protect the police from unfounded allegations. It had been submitted to me that in the case of deaths as the result of police shootings, the investigation should be carried out by seconded interstate police officers but I felt that would create practical problems. I was more in favour of the current system of the matter being investigated by senior police officers from outside the region where the incident occurred and that it be monitored by an officer of at least the rank of assistant commissioner or chief superintendent. I also said that an officer of the rank of assistant commissioner or above attend the scene of all police shootings involving death and that all necessary resources be made available immediately to the officer in charge of the investigation, as happened in Victoria.

Among my other recommendations were two directed to the Minister for Health – that a psychiatric triage be carried out not indirectly but in person by a doctor with psychiatric training or a psychiatric nurse; and that all hospital policies should include a protocol to deal with all patient abscondments including notifying family and, in appropriate cases, the police.

THE CORONER

In June 2001, Judge Urquhart handed down his findings in the Police Integrity Commission (PIC) into Podesta and Dilorenzo. By then, Podesta had quit the police and Dilorenzo had been sacked. The PIC inquiry found that Podesta had used cocaine and ecstasy before he joined the police, while he was an officer and also before and after the shooting of Roni Levi. It also found he had an improper relationship with Dilorenzo's brother, who had admitted to using cocaine after his release from jail. The PIC concluded Dilorenzo himself had used cocaine and had an improper relationship with drug dealers. Back in March 1998, no one but a select few had known of the investigation into the officers and it had nothing to do with what happened on Bondi Beach.

⁂

The outcome of Peter Forsyth's death was that several days after the fatal stabbing, a father contacted police to tell them his children had been involved. His 14-year-old twins, a boy and girl, were put on probation for two years for concealing a serious offence. A 16-year-old girl who was also at the scene received 12 months' probation. The drug dealer who stabbed Forsyth, Murray Hearne, 20, was jailed for 27 years and ordered to serve a minimum of 20 years.

⁂

In the aftermath of the Bondi shooting inquest, I was having trouble sleeping and Doreen noticed that I seemed to be on edge a lot. I was also withdrawn, I wouldn't talk about what was bothering me. To me, however, it was work as usual.

Chapter 11

'Thank God We Got the Coroner Out Alive'

I HAD ASKED THE Attorney-General's Department to do some hunting around and this is what they had come up with – an old, somewhat dingy courtroom beside the old Sydney Hospital behind the Hyde Park Barracks on Macquarie Street in central Sydney. In its previous life it had been the NSW Land and Environment Court. I needed a special courtroom in which to hold the inquest into the people who died in the Thredbo landslide. It had to be large enough to house 50-odd lawyers and all the back-up personnel and documents they would bring. It also had to be available for a long time and fitted out with the latest technology so we could have instantaneous transcripts of the proceedings flash up on the lawyers' computer screens. Power, video, audio and data cabling had to be installed and rows of computers set up on the bar tables.

⁂

The inquest was going to be a marathon, so all the other cases going through Glebe were being handled by John Abernethy. There were the two young women aged 16 and 20 who drowned, their bodies found fully clothed 50 metres from the cliffs at the Kiama Blowhole, south of Sydney in April 1997. It was suspected that the girls, who were cousins, had made a suicide pact to die at the blowhole – the same spot where in 1992 seven of their relatives and close friends including three young children had been washed to their deaths by the huge swell that had brought them to the blowhole to watch the show.

There was the death of Peter Dalamangas, 23, at Star City Casino after a brawl with bouncers in the early hours of Saturday, 31 January 1998. His brother, James, 27, himself a licensed security guard, ended facing court on the Sunday charged with assault. In court, the police alleged the brothers were with friends who were told to leave the casino at 6 a.m. on the Saturday as they had been offensive to staff. The group refused and became violent. Peter died after being restrained by security staff using a sleeper hold around his neck.

His body was brought to the morgue where forensic pathologist Alan Cala carried out the post-mortem. He found Peter Dalamangas died from the combined effects of neck and chest compression and pre-existing coronary heart disease. He had suffered from severe narrowing of the coronary artery, which could have been caused by steroid abuse, and for someone who had such critical narrowing of the artery, the pressure of the restraint might have led to the onset of an abnormal heart rhythm. Dalamangas was a rugby league player who worked out regularly at the gym. He was also the suspect in the murder of a 30-year-old bouncer who was shot five times in the face, neck and chest as he sat in his car outside a friend's house in Campsie in late 1997.

We made sure his family received the details of the post-mortem report but they did not accept the findings. They were adamant their son had been murdered and nothing less than murder charges against the security guards would satisfy them, despite three security staff being charged with assault. Peter's brother James launched a $250 million civil action against the casino.

Some of the family members, including the father and brother James, wanted to see me so I invited them to Glebe and took them through the post-mortem findings and listened to their concerns. The brawl was captured on the casino's security video, which we had received as part of our investigation, and I was happy for them to look at the tape. We set up Court

'THANK GOD WE GOT THE CORONER OUT ALIVE'

One at Glebe with the TV screen and video but the family became so irate and unruly that I had to tell them that unless they behaved themselves, we would not be able to show the tape.

They set up continuous correspondence with my office. I would get a letter on a Monday morning demanding that we investigate this and that. The next morning I would get a letter from their solicitor making the same points. The day after that would see the arrival of a letter from the Attorney-General forwarding me copies of the two previous letters he had also received copies of. It went beyond being persistent and became harassment of the court staff. The morgue staff had it even worse. The abusive behaviour by James Dalamangas led us to install a special glass security screen at the front of the morgue office. At one stage there was consideration given to taking out an Apprehended Violence Order (AVO) against James after he abused one of the morgue staff at a local sandwich shop.

The Dalamangas family decided to fly out a forensic pathologist from Cyprus to do their own post-mortem and sought an order to exhume the body. In June, Dalamangas' body was returned to the morgue at Glebe. I arranged for the state forensic pathologist from Western Australia to fly over and carry out a second post-mortem along with the family's doctor so we could not be accused of not being independent. The family had claimed the initial post-mortem had missed several crucial things, including fractured ribs.

After the 12-hour autopsy, the family's forensic pathologist, Marios Matsakis, said he had found two small bruises on Dalamangas' neck that he said had been missed in the initial examination. Dr Matsakis' conclusion was that Dalamangas had been strangled. Neither he nor the Perth pathologist found any evidence of fractured ribs. Nevertheless, I had the ribs excised from the body because in my opinion, they could be vital in any court case that might be brought. At this point John Abernethy took over the investigation.

When I began the Thredbo inquest in August 1998 it became a full-time job. I used to call into my office at Glebe, two or three times a week, early in the morning on my way into the city courtroom so I could keep up to date with paperwork. John Abernethy looked after most of the P79A forms. While the Thredbo inquiry was one of the more interesting cases I heard, it was not one of the most enjoyable because it was very technical. I tried to make it as smooth as possible by asking the former Supreme Court judge Terry Cole QC to convene a meeting, without lawyers, of all the engineering experts before the inquiry began. As with most experts they were unable to agree between themselves on some things. The time of the consultations was deliberately limited to a couple of weeks. Terry Cole sat with the 25 experts listening to everything they had to say and then sorted out what the issues were. The main issue was, of course, what had caused thousands of tonnes of soil to shear away from the slope and slide down the mountainside. Terry Cole's report reduced the debate about what had possibly triggered the landslide to an increase in the groundwater pressure in the slope above Carinya Lodge in the material placed there during the construction or upgrading of the Alpine Way. The source of the influx of groundwater could not be agreed upon. The potential sources were either from the construction of a retaining wall, which allowed additional groundwater infiltration, or the failure of a leaking joint in a water pipe. With the help of Terry Cole's report, we were able to cut down the number of experts we needed to call at the inquest.

I had asked the Crown Solicitor's office for counsel to assist me and the Attorney-General rang to say Ruth McColl SC would do it. She is a highly experienced and respected barrister and I found her very thorough and able to memorise massive amounts of material. She is now a NSW Supreme Court judge. She was ably assisted by Jeremy Gormley, who has gone on to become a Senior Counsel. Aware of how technical it would be, they called in two other barristers to deal with specific parts of the evidence. The Crown Solicitor's office provided Karin Harrison to instruct them and she kept everything and everyone organised. She always had anything you needed on tap. It was a huge undertaking.

We decided the best way to handle all the evidence was to divide the inquest into three sections: eyewitness accounts, and the rescue operation; expert evidence dealing with numerous issues relating to the construction of Thredbo village; and the decisions of the various authorities since then.

Thredbo had been identified as a suitable location for an alpine resort back in the early 1950s, before there was even a road into the area. When

'THANK GOD WE GOT THE CORONER OUT ALIVE'

the Alpine Way was built during the construction of the Snowy Mountains Scheme to connect Cooma with Khancoban, the developers saw their opportunity. Thredbo was established by a syndicate that floated as a public company, Kosciuszko Thredbo Limited, and controlled the village from 1956 until about December 1961. Since then, several companies had managed Thredbo, some with very similar names. At the time of the landslide, the head lease over the village was held by Kosciuszko Thredbo Pty Limited. Kosciuszko National Park was managed by the Kosciuszko State Park Trust until late 1967 when the National Parks and Wildlife Service was created.

The Alpine Way was built by the Snowy Mountains Hydro-Electric Authority (SMHEA) in the early 1950s and upgraded in 1958–1959. The SMHEA maintained the road until 1968 when it came under the management of the National Parks and Wildlife Service. The Alpine Way was, however, never intended to be a public highway, it was only meant to be a short-term construction road. Thredbo had developed along the Alpine Way, so there was a great deal of history relating to the area which could have been relevant to the cause of the landslide and therefore the deaths. It all had to be investigated. Ruth McColl and Jeremy Gormley also felt that we had to go right back to the beginnings of the village to get a true picture.

A firm of geotechnical engineers, Pells Sullivan Meynink Pty Ltd (PSM) had been retained by the NSW Police, in consultation with my office, to prepare an independent report on the cause of the landslide. Their report concluded that it was triggered by a leak from the underground water pipeline. This water main was built in mid-1984, about two metres from the shoulder of the Alpine Way using AC pipes with 'supertite' joints, despite the fact that the slope in which it was constructed was subject to both vertical and horizontal movement. 'Supertite' joints were never designed to resist such pull forces.

With the slope along the Alpine Way being only marginally stable, its continued stability depended on it being kept well drained. The water main was designed and built by Kosciuszko Thredbo Pty Ltd (the company which held the Thredbo lease from 1961 to 1987). Approval for its route was given by the Department of Main Roads and its construction approved by the National Parks and Wildlife Service. At the time, all three authorities knew that the control of groundwater was critical to the stability of the road. The

THE CORONER

water main jeopardised that stability by introducing a potential source of leaking water.

The engineer with Kosciuszko Thredbo considered the building of the water main as 'minor work' and a 'fairly simple job'. The company subsequently made a submission to the inquest that it had not known of the marginal stability of the road shoulder. They seemed to have forgotten that only a few years earlier, development had been blocked because of a geotechnical report on the instability of the Alpine Way in that very spot. In 1978, Thredbo had been cut off for several weeks after the road collapsed. I found the company's submission remarkable.

While there was the Pells Sullivan Meynink Pty Ltd report and the outcome of Terry Cole's report, I was conscious that courts had to administer justice in public, a principle that applied as much to an inquest as any other hearing. If I had stuck only to those reports, then there would be no public airing of the controversy between the experts, something I felt was necessary. So it was decided that some experts had to be called to give evidence and be cross-examined.

The majority of requests from the media was for details of when Stuart Diver was going to be giving evidence. They were going to be disappointed, as I decided not to call him. He had been through enough and nothing would be gained by putting him on public display. He had already told his story publicly, on Channel 7, after engaging the celebrity agent Harry M. Miller to sell it for him. We already had Stuart Diver's statement and that would be tendered to the court.

In many respects, the inquest into the Thredbo tragedy had no precedent. It was the worst natural disaster in Australian history and it was a natural disaster which affected an essentially urban community set in the middle of a national park.

On the first day of the inquest, Monday, 10 August, the dingy old courtroom was packed, although I was told that the families of only three of those who had died were there. That was not surprising given that they came from all over the country and some from overseas. Ms McColl and I had decided that the way to begin such a massive inquiry was to set the scene. She told the court that the landslide covered an area which varied in width from 13 metres to 35 metres and was 90 metres long. It extended from the edge of the Alpine Way to almost the foot of the valley slope on the southern edge of the Thredbo River. It involved the movement of approximately 1300 cubic metres of earth which hurtled down the hill at 30 kilometres per hour, sweeping away Carinya Lodge and carrying it into Bimbadeen Lodge. It was a velocity class 6 or 7 landslide, the magnitude of which could be expected to result in the total destruction of buildings and loss of life. And the primary trigger of the landslide? Ms McColl opened the inquest on the basis that the most probable cause was the leaking pipeline. She said the PSM report had concluded that the primary trigger was the leaking underground water pipeline that ran beneath the edge of the Alpine Way above Carinya and Bimbadeen Lodges and that it had been probably leaking for about two months, the water saturating the soil base which eventually collapsed. There was criticism by some parties of the fact that Ms McColl opened the inquest on the basis that the most probable cause was the one identified by the geotechnical report, but this criticism was misconceived. Tim Sullivan, of PSM, who prepared the report had access to all the statements prepared by the police, including those of the other experts. He had also made it clear he was prepared to modify his opinion on the basis of further evidence.

Ruth McColl went on to outline what expert evidence would be called. She said that from the time the Alpine Way was built, it had been prone to landslides. Geotechnical excavations showed that the Carinya site, in particular, was unstable and had been the location of a previous landslide, which had probably occurred before the Alpine Way was built. By the 1960s, there was evidence that engineers had labelled the area unbuildable. There were terms like geological slip or geological fault on the plan in relation to the site. Over the years, this advice was overlooked or ignored. The lodge was built in 1969.

The first witness we called had seen the whole landslide happen. Manos Ellard, 22, a hospitality worker living in Thredbo, had just finished dinner and was standing on the balcony of a friend's home that looked out directly across the valley. He said his attention was captured by a loud cracking noise and he turned and stared. 'There was just a dark patch of soil that moved,' he said.

He said he watched Carinya Lodge just drop, then the momentum carried it down the hill. In just four to five seconds both lodges had been obliterated and it was all over.

THE CORONER

Another witness brought it home how people's lives can change in seconds. Tony Burke had been drinking with a close friend of his, Colin Warren. They had walked back to Bimbadeen Lodge and stood outside the front of the lodge having a cigarette. At about 11.45 p.m., Mr Burke shook his friend's hand and headed towards his home. He had only walked a distance of about 500 metres when the landslide swept through, killing Mr Warren.

As the inquest continued, there was anger from some of the residents that they had not been allowed to rescue friends they could hear were still alive beneath the rubble. A ski instructor, Martin Thomas, said he was climbing up the landslide site about 20 minutes after the collapse and heard a male voice speaking in an American accent. He said he believed it was Mike Sodergren. He said he heard Mr Sodergren call out, 'Help me, I don't want to die.' A voice he believed was Mim Sodergren's called out, 'Hello.' But because the area was deemed unsafe, Mr Thomas was moved away by police. It was obviously distressing for those people at the scene to hear the voices of their workmates and friends. An ambulance officer, Ron Carey, said he had heard three voices begging for help. 'Every one of them sounded sick, as though they were dying,' said Mr Carey, who was stationed at Jindabyne.

He said that in the dark and with no equipment and the danger of an unstable slope, it would have been suicide to go in and rescue them. He said he was worried the rescue authorities had made the wrong decision but when the light of dawn showed the true state of the situation, he knew they had done the right thing.

The main argument was always going to be who was to blame for the landslide. Soon after the tragedy, the operators of Thredbo had placed a newspaper advertisement saying the landslide 'occurred due to the failure of the road embankment associated with the presence of deep fill at that particular section of the Alpine Way'. It was in their interests to reassure occupants of the other lodges that the problem was isolated. They were not correct. There had been landslides along the 1.3 kilometre section of the Alpine Way leading into the village from the time the road was built. It was never meant for the amount of tourist traffic using it. The embankment that collapsed onto Carinya and Bimbadeen Lodges was only marginally stable due to the method used to build the road, with inadequate base

'THANK GOD WE GOT THE CORONER OUT ALIVE'

construction along steep mountain slopes and inadequate drainage. The recorded landslides were in 1955, 1958–59, 1964, 1965, May and June 1968, 1973, 1974, 1978 and 1989.

The 1964 landslide was of particular concern. A 15.24 metre length of the outer segment of the fill on the Alpine Way had suddenly given way next to the Winterhaus Lodge in the village. It narrowly avoided hitting the building. Remarkably, although it was dangerous and so close to the village, there was no record of it in the documents of the Kosciuszko State Park Trust, which had looked after the area. There was evidence given to the inquest that there were large sections of the Alpine Way where the road could collapse at any moment, posing a significant danger to the lodges built below the level of the road.

The advertisement placed by the operators of Thredbo village a year before the inquest began was not of as much concern to me as what happened three months into the inquest. Kosciuszko Thredbo Pty Ltd issued a press release giving details of an opinion by an academic expert on the cause of the landslide. The press release stated that the expert drew some different conclusions from those of the experts retained by the court. The academic expert had concluded that in his opinion, the landslide had been caused by the building of a retaining wall along the Alpine Way near the landslide site four months earlier. This was one of the theses looked at by Terry Cole in his 'scrumdown' with the experts. The theory was that the wall had resulted in additional infiltration of water, increasing groundwater pressure. A surprising feature of the building of the wall was that no geotechnical study had been done to assess its impact on groundwater and stability. The National Parks and Wildlife Service had retained the services of a geotechnical engineer to advise on the stability of the Alpine Way, yet assumed it was safe to conduct major work like this along there without obtaining specific advice. The outcome of the expert 'scrumdown' was that the area of leakage which sparked the landslide was 20 metres away from the retaining wall and that the wall was not the problem.

To me, the move by Kosciuszko Thredbo Pty Ltd could be interpreted as a blatant attempt by them to put pressure on the court to alter the course of the inquest and I said so. I also consulted with Ms McColl on whether they could be prosecuted for contempt of court. The report from this academic expert was to be tendered to the court and would be freely available to everyone. No one was hiding anything and everything would be looked at. Kosciuszko Thredbo Pty Ltd could not go around making statements like they had. We decided we would not ask the Attorney-General to bring contempt of court proceedings, but the threat kept the company quiet.

There was also a challenge taken to the NSW Supreme Court by the families of some of the victims who wanted to force a geologist who inspected the site to give evidence. I had called David Warren-Gash, the NSW government geologist who had between 1991 and 1996 conducted several geotechnical studies of the Alpine Way. He had installed inclinometers on the road above Carinya and Bimbadeen Lodges and prepared several reports on areas of instability. In court, he refused to be cross-examined on this research on the grounds that his answers might tend to incriminate him. I ruled that he did not have to answer the questions. The families wanted him to be forced to answer, and Ms McColl was against me on this. She had questions she wanted to ask him as well. But under the terms of the *Coroners Act*, I did not have the power to order a witness to answer in these circumstances when they had said their answers might incriminate them. The families wanted the Supreme Court to find that a coroner had the power to compel a witness to testify if that person claimed immunity. The court upheld my view.

Towards the end of this hectic year, by Christmas of 1998, I had to admit to myself that I was not feeling too good. I had been getting out of breath walking up stairs. In early 1999, I finally gave up smoking. Like most smokers, I had 'given up' a few times before – for a few months or a couple of days. This time was different. I decided to use nicotine patches, starting with the strong ones and cutting them in half as the weeks went on. It turned out not to be as difficult as I thought and I managed to give up. It seemed to make no difference. I continued to get out of breath and started to get a sore chest. One week in early July 1999, my sister rang to say that my brother-in-law in Nyngan had suffered a heart attack and was being brought to the Royal Prince Alfred Hospital in Sydney. Doreen saw it as a wake-up call and said she thought I should go and get myself checked out. When I went to see my local doctor that Friday afternoon after work, he

'THANK GOD WE GOT THE CORONER OUT ALIVE'

shared her concern and booked me in to see a cardiologist on the Tuesday. On the Monday, I went in to work as usual and told everyone I would be taking the next day off. It was rare for me to have a day off, so the staff were surprised.

The cardiologist gave me an ECG and said it looked great. He had me climb on the stationary bike to perform a stress test and said, 'We've got problems.' He said it showed I had some blockages around my heart and I needed an angiogram. He rang Concord Hospital who said they could fit me in on the Thursday. He wouldn't let me go back to work on the Wednesday.

The news from the specialist on the Thursday was bad. Then said I had four blockages, two of them major and that I needed heart bypass surgery immediately. Doreen and I were both stunned. I contacted my manager at the court, Graham O'Rourke, and told him it would be three or four months before I was back. The Thredbo inquest had to be put on hold, but there was nothing I could do.

The specialist said he could do the operation on Saturday morning at St Vincent's Private Hospital. They kept me in Concord on the Thursday night and the next morning I was transferred by ambulance to St Vincent's. Doreen rode with me in the ambulance. When we pulled up at St Vincent's, the male nurse in the ambulance with us said, 'Thank God we got the coroner out of Concord alive.' It made us laugh but I think he may only have been half joking.

At St Vincent's, the surgeon, Philip Spratt, came in to explain the operation to me. He seemed to think that like Quincy in the TV series, I was a doctor. I told him I had studied law, not medicine. There was a video which showed what happened during heart bypass surgery and the surgeon asked if I wanted to see that. No, I said, I just wanted to see a priest. Doreen thought I was serious – I'm still not sure myself whether it was a joke. As someone who dealt with death every day, people have wondered what it was like for me to suddenly stare my own mortality in the face. I can tell you that I didn't have time to think about it. It all happened so suddenly.

When I came around in the recovery ward after the long operation, I could see Doreen and Megan looking at me strangely and then looking at each other. They looked at my bandages and realised they had forgotten to tell the surgeon that I was left-handed. He had taken the artery out of my left hand to replace one in my heart. It meant that I couldn't use my left hand easily. It took me a long time to get the strength back in it, and I had to learn to write again.

I must have driven the nurses in the recovery ward mad. I was asking them what drugs they were giving me, had they checked my charts, had they recorded on my charts everything they did? I was so used to giving lectures to nurses about writing everything down and protecting themselves! I can't even remember doing it, as drugged as I was. A few days after surgery, there was a bit of concern when they couldn't get my pulse rate down. My heart was racing. What they did was stop my heart and put the 'paddles' on me to start it again. It worked and just over a week after going into hospital, I was home again with orders to watch my diet and to not over-extend myself.

It had taken me by surprise to learn I was stressed. I suppose you have stress but never think about it. It had exacerbated the problem but what caused it in the first place was cholesterol. I had one main artery 80 per cent blocked and the other 70 per cent blocked. The surgeon said that what had helped me was the advice of a chemist friend, years earlier, who had told me to take aspirin every day to thin the blood. I didn't take one every day but I had been taking them regularly.

As part of getting fit again, I had to go to the heart rehabilitation section at Westmead Hospital, next to the Coroners Court. Three times a week I would do exercises on a walking frame and various other machines. It was during the rehabilitation I decided that it was time to give my job away. I had always thought I would retire when I was 60 but 60 had come and gone and I was feeling pretty good and enjoying my work as State Coroner so I'd kept going. I was now 62. Doreen and I decided to sell up in Sydney and return to Forbes. The time was right.

※

I got back to work in November and we got the Thredbo inquest up and running again but I made an appointment to see the Attorney-General, Jeff Shaw. I asked if I could retire as State Coroner but wanted to stay on to finish the Thredbo inquest. My final day as NSW State Coroner was to be 28 January 2000. I had chosen the date simply because by then I would have finished hearing all the evidence in the Thredbo inquest. I hadn't realised that if I had waited another week, I would have completed five years as State Coroner. By coincidence it was also exactly 27 years and a day since I had become a magistrate. My deputy John Abernethy moved into my office as the new State Coroner and I remained as a coroner for the time it took me to finish off the inquest.

By the end of June 2000 I had completed the Thredbo report, bang on the time I had imposed on myself. I felt it was long enough for the families to wait. I was going to hand down the findings at Glebe, because we had given up the lease on the old Land and Environment Court and because it was more appropriate. We also knew that as well as an army of media, there was going to be a lot of people in court to hear the decision. We set up speakers in the foyer of the court for those who could not fit into the courtroom but we didn't want the families of those who had died to be stuck outside so the court made sure enough seats were reserved for them.

As I walked from the door onto the bench of Court One on Thursday, 29 June, I was conscious it was my last act as a coroner. I am not someone who gets emotional about his work, as you might have gathered so far, and what I felt was pleased that the inquest had been finished. This was not a time for me to be making leaving speeches. It was a time for the families of the victims to discover what had happened.

The report ran to 206 pages and everyone who wanted a copy got one. We also posted the report on the Internet. It was not enough just to hand down the report, I wanted people to hear for themselves what decisions I had come to so I had decided to read a summary of my findings and my recommendations.

It was clear to me that the landslide on 30 July 1997 that had killed 18 people should have been foreseen. Foreseeability was, however, a concept relevant to any civil action, not to the identification of a cause in the coronial context. While foreseeability could play no part in my decision as to what caused the landslide, failure to respond appropriately to events was something I could take into account.

Even though the landslide was triggered by the leaking water main that should never have been buried in the unstable ground, it was caused by decades of failings by state government agencies and the developers of the village. There was a failure of any government authority responsible for the care, control and management of Kosciuszko National Park and the maintenance of the Alpine Way to take any steps to ensure that the village was rendered safe from exposure to such a marginally unstable environment.

I said:

'My examination of the history of the road has left me with no choice but to come to the conclusion that the propensity of the Alpine Way to landsliding which could lead to destruction of lodges and serious injury to persons within them was known to these authorities throughout the relevant period. Despite this, no specific recommendation was ever made by those directly responsible for the road that would have led to the reconstruction of the road above the village ... I have been unable to resolve satisfactorily in my mind how this occurred.'

※

There was a haphazard approach to stability in the village. Looking at the site upon which Carinya Lodge was built, stability and geotechnical problems there were recognised and understood before any development of the village in that area. At some time, probably in the late 1960s, that knowledge was lost, ignored or forgotten. It was a matter of grave concern to me that a representative of the Roads and Traffic Authority (RTA), the successor of the Department of Main Roads (DMR), inspected the Alpine Way for six years or so from 1991 until 1996 and never recommended that the road above the village be rebuilt. In addition, while the RTA had developed a system of assessing the stability of roads and slopes into which they were going to be built, they never used it to assess the Alpine Way. I said I hoped they had learned from this harsh lesson.

I felt it necessary to mention the rescuers because there had been criticisms of the rescue operation made by lawyers on behalf of the families. I said that I had found the rescue was carried out expeditiously and diligently in the light of the extremely dangerous conditions which existed in the aftermath of the landslide. I commended the exceptional services of all those involved in the rescue.

It had been submitted to me by counsel representing the families that those involved over the years with the Alpine Way had demonstrated,

'THANK GOD WE GOT THE CORONER OUT ALIVE'

through their arguments to the inquest, that they were 'throwing responsibility around like the proverbial hot potato, no one wanting to catch it and no one wanting to end up with it'. While I privately agreed with this it was not my job to decide issues of responsibility, as I have said, that was the job of the civil courts. It was my job to direct recommendations to those responsible for the Alpine Way and the dangerous conditions which had emerged at the inquest. Nor was it my job to get angry, because once you lose control you cannot make a proper decision. Deep down, I was most concerned at what had happened.

Because it was the National Parks and Wildlife Service (NPWS) and its predecessor, the Kosciuszko State Park Trust, which had been responsible for the care, control and management of the national park and Thredbo village, it was inevitable that my concerns were principally addressed to that organisation. I had seen and heard enough during the inquiry to be concerned about the capacity of the NPWS to properly assess the stability of roads built on hillsides. I felt they operated in isolation from the development of good building practices involving hillsides. I recommended an independent committee be appointed to assess the ability and appropriateness of the NPWS to retain responsibility for urban communities and road maintenance within the parks.

Another recommendation was that the RTA examine its system of assessing slope stability in the light of the lessons I hoped the authority had learned from the landslide and that the Alpine Way and other park roads which suffered the same poor condition be monitored regularly by geotechnical experts in order to detect any instability. I said the Building Code of Australia and any local code dealing with planning, development and building approval procedures should be amended to take into account proper hillside building practices and geotechnical considerations.

Finally, I turned to the rescue operation. While the rescue services performed an excellent rescue in all the circumstances, the local emergency plans had not recognised the potential hazard of landslide in the alpine area. I recommended that this be remedied.

I finished up by thanking everyone who had worked with me on the inquiry.

When I walked off the bench for the last time, it was not to champagne and canapés. I had a brief interview with the ABC and then had to head to Channel Nine's studios in Willoughby where I had promised Mike Munro, then the host of *A Current Affair*, an interview when I retired. On the way I had to stop at a chemist because the pain in my stomach was so severe. That weekend, 12 months exactly since my heart surgery, I was back in hospital, this time having my gall bladder removed.

I had already been farewelled at what we called a 'bench ceremony'. I had been to plenty myself before it was my turn. On the Friday morning we all trooped up to the ceremonial court at the Downing Centre Local Court complex. On the bench was the Chief Magistrate, Patricia Staunton, the two Deputy Chief Magistrates, Charles Gilmore and Graham Henson, and other magistrates. The court was full of friends and colleagues including Ruth McColl who had become president of the NSW Bar Association, which was gratifying, and my family was there. My son John, his wife Ineca and my grandchildren Caitlin and Greta, had come from Alaska for the occasion joining Doreen, Megan and friends and relatives who had made the trip from Forbes.

There were all the usual speeches and everyone said complimentary things – Patricia Staunton, Jeff Shaw and the president of the NSW Law Society, John North. When it came to my turn to speak, I was feeling a bit overwhelmed by some of the comments about my work but I wanted to say that I had thoroughly enjoyed my career and had never thought about pursuing anything different. I had had the extreme good fortune to work with some tremendous people. I truly believed the old adage – that your court was only as good as the people who worked there. My court office staff were outstanding – I thanked them all for their help and assistance. I said that the main concern as a coroner was for the families, that families had to be satisfied that the matter had been fully investigated and that the conclusions reached were the only conclusions in the circumstances.

I also thanked Doreen and my family. I referred to the Roni Levi case, without naming it, saying there had been occasions when there had been a lot of backlash against my family over decisions I had made and they had stood by me and given me the support I needed. The bench ceremony was adjourned so we could stand around and have tea, as one does at these things.

'THANK GOD WE GOT THE CORONER OUT ALIVE'

The court staff had arranged a party at Wentworth Park, the dog track at Glebe. We'd had a few parties there in the big hall. At about 5 p.m. we all met up and heard more speeches but this bash was the informal leaving do! People I had worked with over the years turned up including solicitors, police, members of the fire brigade and funeral directors. I was humbled that so many people were there.

◈◈◈

It was a great celebration and an appropriate finale to 47 years in the court system. I'd seen and done a lot during my career and was satisfied. The time was right and leaving it all behind seemed like the right thing to do.